Narrative Care

Narrative Care: Biopolitics and the Novel

Arne De Boever

BLOOMSBURY
NEW YORK • LONDON • NEW DELHI • SYDNEY

Bloomsbury Academic
An imprint of Bloomsbury Publishing Inc

1385 Broadway
New York
NY 10018
USA

50 Bedford Square
London
WC1B 3DP
UK

www.bloomsbury.com

Bloomsbury is a registered trade mark of Bloomsbury Publishing Plc

First published 2013
This paperback edition first published 2014

Library of Congress Cataloging-in-Publication Data
De Boever, Arne.
Narrative care: biopolitics and the novel/Arne De Boever.
p. cm.
Includes bibliographical references and index.
ISBN 978-1-4411-4999-2 (hardcover: alk. paper) 1. Fiction–21st century–History and criticism. 2. Ethics in literature.
3. Biopolitics. I. Title.
PN3504.D39 2012
809.3'051–dc23
2012035938

ISBN: HB: 978-1-4411-4999-2
PB: 978-1-6289-2524-1
ePDF: 978-1-4411-4472-0
ePUB: 978-1-4411-2877-5

Typeset by Fakenham Prepress Solutions, Fakenham, Norfolk NR21 8NN
Printed and bound in the United States of America

To Olivia and Ada

Contents

Acknowledgments

I began thinking about *Narrative Care* during the last year of my graduate studies. I finished the manuscript four years later, shortly after the publication of my first book *States of Exception in the Contemporary Novel.* The problematic of *Narrative Care* is closely related to that of *States of Exception* and the book's cover image is meant to suggest this: it echoes the cover of the other book, putting the problematic of the novel's relation to the state of exception in a new perspective.

Narrative Care could not have come about without *States of Exception* and I am grateful for the early criticism I received from my dissertation advisors at Columbia University—Bruce Robbins, Stathis Gourgouris, and Patricia Dailey—on some of the ideas that are circulated here. An early version of chapter one was presented at the international conference "Matters of State" held in Leuven (Belgium) in April 2009, and I want to thank my fellow panelists, in particular Alex Houen and Pieter Vermeulen, for their feedback on the chapter. For some time Pieter and I were planning to edit a special journal issue on biopolitics and the novel, but those plans never materialized. I would nevertheless like to thank those who intended to contribute an article to this issue, in particular Gregg Lambert and J. Paul Narkunas.

Much of the research for this project was completed at the California Institute of the Arts, where I benefited from conversations with my colleagues Maggie Nelson, Martín Plot, Janet Sarbanes, James Wiltgen, and Nancy Wood. I am grateful to the students in my courses "What is Biopolitics?" and "Take Care of Yourself" for their questions and comments. "Take Care of Yourself" was part of an interdisciplinary course cluster on bioart and I want to thank Michael Bryant, Tom Leeser, Robert Mitchell, Timothy Morton, Anne-Marie Oliver, and Phil Ross for sharing their ideas with me in this context. Thanks also to Frédéric Neyrat and Frédéric Worms for accepting my invitations to come speak at CalArts, and for furthering my thoughts on care, biopolitics, and the aesthetics of existence. Warren Neidich—artist and theorist of the brain—generously gave me permission to reproduce his work on the book cover. My most important debt is to two contemporary philosophers whose brilliant writing and personal generosity have driven this project forward: Catherine Malabou and Bernard Stiegler.

I could not have completed the research for this book without the support I received from the School of Critical Studies' and the California Institute of the Arts' faculty development funds. My graduate student Austin Walker worked as a research assistant on this project during the Spring of 2011 and expertly uncovered many of the references I came to rely on during the final revision of the manuscript.

Excerpts from Chapters One and Two have appeared in the academic journals *theory@buffalo* and *Occasion* and are included here in a revised form.

Introduction: Towards a Pharmacology of the Novel

The more he stares at the words take care of, *the more inscrutable they seem.*[1]

—J. M. Coetzee, *Slow Man*

What readings of contemporary literary fiction all too often lack is any theoretical discussion of the novel form as such.[2]

—Timothy Bewes, "The Novel as an Absence"

The Moment of Narrative Care

In the Spring of 2008, I went to see the French artist Sophie Calle's work *Prenez-soin de vous* (*Take Care of Yourself*) in Paris. Originally mounted in the French pavilion of the 2007 biennale in Venice, the work was being shown again in the reading room of the old Bibliothèque nationale de France in the Rue Richelieu. The idea behind the work was simple: after Calle received a break-up letter (from writer Grégoire Bouillier) that ended with the sentence "Take care of yourself," she started pondering what the sentence might mean. And so she decided to ask over one hundred women to interpret the letter according to their professional activity and to send the results of that process back to her. The reading room of the library was packed with the responses that Calle received.

One of the things that puzzled me as I was engaging with both Calle's work and the space in which it was being shown, was the question that would come to inform (in a heavily revised form) the project of this book. What might be the relation between Calle's project on care and the library? The question was triggered by curator Daniel Buren, who stated in an introductory text accompanying the exhibition that there was no place more appropriate for Calle's work to be shown than the old library. Why? I was not particularly interested in the question of the archive that had already been addressed in numerous publications. Although Buren's concerns may have been aesthetic and practical rather than philosophical, literary critical, or political, his remark ultimately put me on the track of an investigation of what I am calling *narrative care*: of the relation between the contemporary novel, the history of the novel as a genre, and care.

Calle's work is one of the many texts and films that are discussed in Frédéric Worms' book *Le moment du soin* (The Moment of Care).[3] Worms partly arrives at his interest in care through the topic that was at the center of my first book: the state of exception.[4] Worms suggests that in a time of emergencies, crises, and exceptions, care rises to the surface not simply as an ethical concern about how one is supposed to go on living but also as a political one, given politics' relation with exception and catastrophe.[5] One can think of New Orleans' devastation *not* by Hurricane Katrina (as Spike Lee insists)[6] *but* by the breaking of the levees; or of the states of exception that Naomi Klein discusses in *The Shock Doctrine*, a classic work of political economy for the twentieth and twenty-first centuries.[7] Indeed, the post-9/11 era of crises—political, economic, and now social; not to mention the climate crisis and the food crisis—has accomplished something like a *political turn* in the humanities and the social sciences, one that has become paired to what is sometimes described as an interdisciplinary *vitalist turn*.[8]

The latter refers to a renewed interest in the notion of life that is closely related to the study of emergencies, crises, and exceptions. Giorgio Agamben has written about bare life, a notion he adopts from Walter Benjamin to refer to the inhuman kind of life in between human and animal life produced in a state of exception.[9] In response to Agamben, and to Agamben's overly biological conception of the life that is produced in the state of exception, Eric Santner has proposed the notion of creaturely life to do justice to the psychic dimension of life in a state of exception. Trauma, for example, can be understood as a psychic state of exception in which one is reduced to creaturely life.[10] In a book of essays in which she reflects on the September 11 terror attacks, Judith Butler has put forward the notion of precarious life as part of a plea for the recognition of the increased interdependency of peoples and nations.[11] And these three examples hardly cover the full spectrum. As one of my colleagues remarked while he was going through the program for the 2010 Modern Languages Association convention in Los Angeles, it seemed every other discussion panel on the list was about the notion of life.

To do justice to the full scope of these developments, these references need to be considered in relation to other disciplines, including the sciences. Part of the reason why the notions of bare life, creaturely life, and precarious life have found such fertile ground in critical theory is also because of a related turn to life in the sciences. Although Agamben, Santner, and Butler do not engage with these developments (in some of her recent public presentations, French philosopher Catherine Malabou has taken Agamben to task for this), it is worth noticing that while these philosophers' work on life was being produced, the scientific understanding of life was also changing, leading to vigorous ethical and political debates. Some of the work in critical theory that crosses into the life-sciences emerges from an interest that is shared by Agamben, Santner, and Butler, namely Michel Foucault's work on biopolitics. Thus, Foucault-scholar Nikolas Rose, for example, published a book titled *The Politics of Life Itself*, in which the question of life is expanded—in the best Foucauldian tradition—beyond merely philosophical concerns into the fields of biomedicine, bioethics, and questions of biopower and biopolitics (for example, the notion of "biological citizenship").[12] Melinda Cooper's *Life as Surplus* has also done much to tie together, in the neoliberal era, developments in biotechnology and contemporary capitalism, thus fleshing out some of the fascinating but vicious connections between life, economy, and terror from the 1970s to the present.[13]

In all of these works, it is only in Worms' *Le moment du soin* and Santner's *On Creaturely Life* that literature plays a role.[14] Although literature takes up an important place in Foucault's *oeuvre*, especially in his early and late works, it remains curiously absent from his lecture courses on biopolitics. *And yet, life, care, and the state of exception take up a prominent place in contemporary fiction, and arguably in the history of the novel at large.* In *Narrative Care*, I propose to have a closer look at the intricate relations between the novel, biopolitics, and care.

Given my title, I should reference from the get-go the large body of work that it calls to mind, and that is associated with narrative medicine programs such as the one run by Rita Charon and Maura Spiegel at Columbia University. I am thinking of books such as *Narrative in Health Care* (which includes a foreword by Charon), the co-authored *Narrative Means to Therapeutic Ends*, and Gary Kenyon's fascinating *Storying Later Life*, on narration and aging (my own interests in this particular issue have ranged towards Andy Clark's work on cyborgs and the importance of external memory-support systems not just for Alzheimer patients but to enable all of us to function in society).[15] In this field, there is also a plethora of work on the brain, including Catherine Malabou's *What Should We Do With Our Brain?*, which I discuss in Chapter Two.[16] However, with the exception of Malabou's book, none of these works will be explicitly addressed in the present study, which ultimately confronts something quite different (as this Introduction will show).

A Pharmacological Theory of Care

Put succinctly, this book is a study of "care" in four contemporary novels: J. M. Coetzee's *Slow Man*, Kazuo Ishiguro's *Never Let Me Go*, Paul Auster's *The Book of Illusions*, and Tom McCarthy's *Remainder*. In the introduction and the conclusion, W. G. Sebald's writings and Pedro Almodóvar's films are also taken into consideration. I am interested in how these novels and films talk about care. Specifically, this study addresses the literary-political questions that the novels raise through their representations of care.

My selection of texts—too narrow for some and too wide for others, as early readers of the manuscript reported back to me—is centered around Anglophone novels and includes one Australian, one American (US), and two English novels. By opting for such a "wider" range of texts—I did not limit myself, for example, to US novels—, I wanted to reflect one basic feature of my topic, namely that care is an issue that cuts across contemporary fiction today. Indeed, care has not only been at the forefront of US political debates (I began this project as a project about care in the US novel). It was also a central concern in the French presidential elections (care or *soin* was and remains a key campaign issue for the socialists) and much of my theoretical framework will derive from French thinkers reflecting on the topic. Judging from the economic and social reforms that are being implemented in response to the economic crisis in the US as well as in most European countries, it may very well be that care is turning into the key issue of the twenty-first century.

One other reason why I opted for such a "wider" range of texts is because *Narrative Care* develops, through close-readings of particular novels, a theory about the relation of the novel as a genre to biopolitics and care. For such an unfashionable project ("Biopolitics and the theory of the novel?," as someone asked me once after a conference presentation—"Good luck!"), any selection—no matter how wide—is bound to appear too narrow. It is not just that *Narrative Care* is limited to Anglophone novels, as I have already said; it is also that the novels I have chosen largely deal with biopolitics and care in modern Western (neoliberal) democracies.[17] How can this possibly "settle" the investigation of the novel's relation to biopolitics and care (if this were my aim)? Should not "the rest of the world" have received some more attention? How does, for example, the postcolonial novel fit into the theoretical framework I develop? How do biopolitics and care circulate in colonial discourses? And along similar lines: while it is true that my selection of materials includes artwork by Sophie Calle and a film by Pedro Almodóvar, should not the book have discussed some explicitly feminist or queer novels? Forget about "settling" the issue—how about simply broadening the perspective?

While I appreciate, of course, the representative point that these questions are also making—it remains an important one—I have selected the four novels precisely because of how they deal with what I consider to be the two most important biopolitical issues: sexuality and race. Although sexuality is certainly more prominent in this book than race, attentive readers will see both of these concerns return in all of the chapters, from my initial investigation of Paul Rayment's relation to his Croatian nurse Marijana in Coetzee's *Slow Man* to the intricate relations of erotic love and friendship between Benigno, Alicia, Marco, and Lydia in Almodóvar's *Talk to Her*. It is, ultimately, through the questions that these works raise rather than through the difference that their authors represent that I aim to fracture the inevitable limit of any selection of texts, so as to venture beyond the highly particular accounts they present into other realms. As I see it, the only satisfactory way out of the representative problems that any attempt to theorize "the" novel's relation to biopolitics and care inevitably poses, is to abandon such a project altogether—in other words, to abandon the project of theorizing about the form of the novel in criticism of the contemporary novel. I have chosen another path in the hope that the problematic I open up may be helpful to others, working on other novels.

Here are some of those larger questions, then, that I will be interested in: what do we mean when we say "Take care" or "Take care of yourself"? How can our criticism of political interventions in the biological lives of the citizen be reconciled to our defense of the welfare state? Does our defense of the welfare state risk to make us stop caring about politics? In short, given that we seem to be in need of care in the post-9/11 era of crises, what is the kind of care that we want? Or have we truly arrived in a time, as Jean Baudrillard suggests in one of his last texts, in which "you must fight against everything that wants to help you"?[18] Surely, that imperative must also be applied to Baudrillard himself, and to that very sentence?

It is from his perspective—through a defense of care that acknowledges the potentially poisonous dimension of care as well—that I develop what I call, after the French philosopher Bernard Stiegler, *a pharmacological theory of care*. The notion of the pharmakon has risen to attention again in French theory. Isabelle Stengers discusses the pharmakon in her *Au temps des catastrophes: Résister à la barbarie qui vient* (In the Time of Catastrophes: Resisting the Coming Barbarism),[19] a book that situates itself within an epoch of crisis to explore how one might resist what Stengers calls a coming barbarism (she refers, for example, to some ethical and political questions surrounding GM foods that are also addressed in Vandana Shiva's work).[20] Stengers introduces the notion of the pharmakon into her book when she suggests that to blindly follow the call for resistance is not the solution either. Indeed, in the case of GM foods for example, she criticizes—like her colleague Dominique Lecourt[21]—the biocatastrophists who simply ignore scientific data and continue resisting GM foods from a quasi-theological attachment to a sacred creation. But neither is she with what Lecourt calls the "technoprophets."[22] Instead, she considers the pharmacological dimension of resistance in a time of crisis: *both* its potentially curative *and* its potentially poisonous effects.

The most extensive contemporary reflection on the pharmakon and pharmacology comes from Stengers' interlocutor Bernard Stiegler, who addresses the problematic of the pharmakon in the last four chapters of a book titled *Taking Care of Youth and the Generations*.[23] In this book, which builds on his previous work on technics, Stiegler updates the question of care into the high tech era. Thanks to the translations of Stephen Barker, the gist of Stiegler's philosophy is beginning to become known in the English-speaking world. Human beings are by nature prosthetic beings, as Stiegler shows. They are beings by default who, in order to individuate, need to project themselves into technical extensions. These extensions, he argues—and the argument goes back to both Plato and Jacques Derrida's discussion of Plato—are *pharmacological*: curative, on the one hand, but also poisonous (one can think, for example, of the Attention Deficit Disorder affecting so many American and European children today). They operate like a drug (a pharmakon) and thus they demand a therapeutic or practice of care. That is, in a nutshell, the argument that Stiegler develops towards the end of his book on care. The question of pharmacology moves to the foreground of the book that he published a few years later: *Ce qui fait que le vie vaut la peine d'être vécue: De la pharmacologie* (What Makes Life Worth Living: On Pharmacology).[24] There, he continues his analysis of care from an explicitly political perspective (this is one of the ways in which his work differs from Worms').[25] In neither Stiegler nor Stengers's books, which are both works of philosophy, does literature receive any consideration. Literature, however, could certainly be considered as one of those pharmacological extensions that Stiegler talks about.[26] For a discussion of literature in this context, however, we must turn to "the most literary of all philosophers," Derrida (and to the other competitor for this title: Plato).

The issue of the pharmakon is, of course, not new. Derrida put it on the map in 1968, when he published two articles in the French journal *Tel Quel* that together make up "Plato's Pharmacy." As often in Derrida's work, the central point of the text arises through a problem of translation: in his reading of Plato's *Phaedrus*, Derrida notes that the word Plato uses for "drug" means both "medicine and/or poison."[27] The insight complicates matters for Plato's translator and critic: for if the word truly means both these things at the same time, it becomes impossible to decide whether the word *pharmakon* in Plato's text refers to a cure or to a poison. Instead, both these meanings are always simultaneously present, destabilizing or deconstructing a unified or coherent meaning of the text. The point matters greatly within Plato's discussion of both life and memory's relation to the *technè* of writing, the art of writing. For whereas the accepted reading of the *Phaedrus* casts writing in a predominantly negative light—as a pharmakon, that is, a poison that is linked to death—Derrida's deconstructive reading also draws out writing's potentially curative dimension. Plato considers this much more explicitly in another dialogue that Derrida comments on, the *Republic.* While the *Republic* includes Plato's famous indictment of writing and painting as nefarious for both politics and philosophy, Plato also notes that the drug of storytelling might at times be useful to govern the ideal city he envisions. Statesmen (and stateswomen; women too could rise to this position in Plato's *Republic*) are in this sense like doctors: with the proper training, they can learn how to administer the drug of storytelling so that it becomes beneficial rather than destructive.[28] Storytelling is, then, characteristically pharmacological: it can cut both ways, depending on how it is administered.

Such a "positive" view on storytelling has, of course, been criticized because of its close connection with ideology. But I do not think this criticism should keep one from considering a more radical interpretation of the therapeutic dimension of storytelling that the *Republic* alludes to. Not storytelling as blindly complicit with the governance of our biological and psychic lives, but storytelling's contribution to what could be called a critical aesthetics of existence: a practice that would resist, precisely, the governance in which storytelling *also* participates.

These are some of the insights that inform *Narrative Care*'s reflection on the politics of the novel as a genre. I develop them in what follows through close-readings of the four novels I have mentioned, and in the context of the theoretical concerns I have outlined above. As the subtitle of the book suggests, biopolitics plays a central role in the discussion. Given my reliance on Derrida in the previous paragraphs, this might appear strange: in his last works, Derrida reveals himself to be very critical of biopolitics. Although he indicates in a short paragraph in *Rogues* that he will take up the notion of biopolitics "another time,"[29] that other time never arrived in the writings published during his lifetime and one needs to turn to his posthumously published seminars for a more extensive engagement with the matter.

Indeed, the first volume of *The Beast and the Sovereign* includes three sessions—eleven, twelve, and thirteen—where the problematic of biopolitics is addressed.[30] However, there too Derrida is very dismissive of biopolitics and he appears to take on the topic only to expose in it the most cutting deconstruction. A few things nevertheless deserve to be noticed. First, in Derrida, the investigation of biopolitics develops out of an engagement with literature: the central text for his seminar is Jean de la Fontaine's fable "The Wolf and the Lamb." Secondly, in the eleventh session of the seminar, Derrida starts out with a reflection on curiosity, a term that he traces back to the Latin word *cura*, translated by *soin* or "care."[31] Care thus hovers in the background of his engagement with biopolitics, and one can only imagine what a seminar by Derrida on care might have yielded.

As I have indicated in two short texts on Derrida's seminars published on the website documenting the translation of the seminars,[32] my particular interest lies in the fact that Derrida's discussion of biopolitics at the end of the first volume of *The Beast and the Sovereign* develops, in the second volume of the seminar, into a reflection on the novel. As such, this is rare in Derrida's work. Although he talks about novelists and novels, he never developed an extended close-reading of a novel, let alone a theory of the novel. And yet, in the second volume of *The Beast and the Sovereign*, he comes very close to this. The novel in question is "this book that is often taken to be the first novel in English,"[33] Daniel Defoe's *Robinson Crusoe* (to which I will turn in Chapter One). The theory—which is never fully worked out—would bring together the question of writing and life/death that was central to "Plato's Pharmacy" with an investigation of Martin Heidegger's reflections on "things."

How does the novel, that pharmakon, relate to life/death? The question seems especially relevant in the case of a novel (which is not, strictly speaking, an autobiography or a biography) whose full title is *The Life and Strange, Surprising Adventures of Robinson Crusoe of York, Mariner*. Does the novel keep the life that it narrates alive? Can it be a "living repetition of the living,"[34] to quote from "Plato's Pharmacy"? Or does the novel bury within its pages any life that it tries to represent? Can there be a living work of art? Is every work, in this sense, a biography or autobiography?[35]

In "Plato's Pharmacy," Derrida inflects these questions with psychoanalysis (the role of the father) and religion/theology (the role of god). But I would like to push things further by linking them to biopolitics, on the one hand, and literary theory, on the other. This means that I will be asking two questions: first, *what power is being wielded when the novelist is creating her or his characters?* Here, I look at the related question of *the peculiar nature of the character-life*. My second question will be: *what is the place of care within this novelistic power-exercise?* That will involve considering *the novel as a form of life-writing, a kind of aesthetic care of the self and of others* that I characterize as *a form of bioart*. In "Plato's Pharmacy," Derrida already notes that the word Plato uses for painting is *zoographia*, "life-drawing" or "life-writing."[36] My aim is to consider the novel as a form of "zoographein," or life-writing. What kinds of readings might this open up? What might such readings tell us about care and contemporary politics?[37]

Although my use of the term "biopolitics" is thus very much informed by Foucault, for whom biopolitics referred (as I explain in Chapter One) to the ways in which governments increasingly intervened in the biological life of populations, I also mobilize it here in different ways, developing different interpretations that lie (in my view) occluded in Foucault's thought and that ultimately connect with Foucault's late work on the care of the self.[38] Chapters One and Two, on *Slow Man* and *Never Let Me Go*, remain relatively close to Foucault's teaching on biopolitics. In Chapters Three and Four, on *The Book of Illusions* and *Remainder*, I take some more liberties with the notion, without (I hope) stretching it to the point where it no longer means anything. My aim in these last two chapters, as will become clear, is in part to consider aspects of postmodernism and memory/trauma studies from a biopolitical perspective.

A Biopolitical History of the Novel

Although my investigation is focused on contemporary novels, *Narrative Care* also has an explicit historical dimension. Following the suggestion of the four novels, the book observes that historically, the rise of the novel coincides with the rise of what Foucault calls governmentality and biopower.[39] This raises the question of whether there might be a relation between governmentality and biopower and the novel. While much has been said about Foucault and literature and about literature's relation to disciplinary power, the connection between literature and biopolitics remains relatively unexplored.[40] And yet, the four novels I consider invite us to pursue it. This means, in part, to let go of a narrow concept of biopolitics in order to consider its more literary articulation.

Like many others, Edward Said—one of the twentieth century's most important theorists of the novel—has noted in the posthumously published *On Late Style*, that "[i]n Western literature, the form of the novel is coincidental with the emergence of the bourgeoisie in the late seventeenth century."[41] "[T]his is why," he continues, "for its first century, the novel is all about birth, possible orphanhood, the discovery of roots, and the creation of a new world, a career, and society. *Robinson Crusoe. Tom Jones. Tristram Shandy.*"[42] Said goes on to note—and indeed, his entire project in *Late Style* is informed by this—that the novel's second great problematic "is about the continuity that occurs after birth, the exfoliation from a beginning: in the time from birth to youth, reproductive generation, maturity."[43] Recalling a phrase by François Jacob, he notes that the novel thus explores something like "*la logique du vivant*,"[44] the logic of the living.[45]

Said, of course, will be interested in the "exceptions, examples of deviation from the overall assumed pattern of human life"—and indeed, I think there is a politics to his position. It is when he references Gillian Beer's work on *Middlemarch*, which shows that the novel "was powerfully influenced by what she calls Darwin's plots for the patterns of generation,"[46] that a possible biopolitical dimension comes to supplement Said's remarks. This is especially clear when these references occur in a chapter that discusses how "all of us, by virtue of the simple fact of being conscious, are involved in constantly thinking about and making something of our lives."[47] He skips—perhaps assumes?—the novel's complicity with biopolitics, and instead moves directly towards his discussion of artistic lateness, of a late style "that involves a nonharmonious, nonserene tension, and above all, a sort of deliberately unproductive productiveness going *against* …."[48] Indeed, it is something like this that I encounter in this study of the novel and biopolitics as well. I read it, however, as the novel's resistance against its biopolitical origins.[49]

My first chapter revolves around J. M. Coetzee's novel *Slow Man*, which tells the story of a man called Paul Rayment who loses a leg in a bike accident. Paul, who is modeled after Saint Paul, stubbornly wants to remain independent afterwards and take care of himself. *Slow Man* is about his rage against the welfare state and its caring administrations. However, through the caring skills of his nurse Marijana, Paul recovers the notion of caritas from the Christian concept of pastoral care. Although the welfare state is historically linked to pastoral care, caritas has gone lost in modern times, and it takes Paul a leg to rediscover it.

However, the love that such caritas brings into play is not easily managed. When Paul's caritas turns into eros, the caring relation with his nurse is disturbed. It is at this point that the novelist Elizabeth Costello—a character from one of Coetzee's other novels—enters upon the scene and that the novel develops its reflection on care into a meta-fictional investigation about care's relation to novel-writing. This reflection is developed *historically* in the novel and in Coetzee's *oeuvre* as a whole through references to Daniel Defoe's *Robinson Crusoe*. Coetzee suggests that the rise of the novel is complicit with the rise of governmental biopolitics. It is in this light that the *politics* of novel-writing needs to be reconsidered.

If the novel could already be characterized in *Slow Man* as "a biologico-literary experiment," Kazuo Ishiguro takes this even further in *Never Let Me Go*. Ishiguro's novel is narrated by Kathy, a being who was cloned to donate her organs to regular human beings in need of a transplant. The novel—which largely takes place at Hailsham, a boarding school for clones—confronts the pressing questions about life, death, humanism, education, and agency that haunt the clones during their short life-span. When Hailsham is compared at one point in the novel to a concentration camp, Coetzee's suggestions about the novel's relation to governmentality and biopolitics are taken to a new level: *Never Let Me Go* develops them into a theory of the "novel as a camp." Indeed, "Hailsham" could very well be compared to a novel/camp, given the emphatically scripted nature of its students' lives (the novel's rewriting of Mary Shelley's *Frankenstein* becomes particularly meaningful in this context). In such a reading, characters could (like the clones in Ishiguro's book) be compared to what Giorgio Agamben in his study of the concentration camp has called "bare life," an inhuman kind of life between human and animal life: pure biopolitical substance.

As in the previous chapter, I substantiate my claim about the novel's relation to biopolitics and the camp through a discussion of Ian Watt's classic theory of the novel, *The Rise of the Novel: Studies in Defoe, Richardson, and Fielding*.[50] Watt's descriptions of the novel's mentality resonate uncannily with Foucault's descriptions of governmentality and biopolitics. I suggest that it is from the single reference to the camps in Watt's study that the history and practice of novel-writing need to be reconsidered. The chapter closes with a critique of both Kathy's acceptance of her situation, and another clone called Tommy's unarticulated rage against it, so as to develop, from the perspective of the critical reader, a pharmacological position that combines both.

In Chapter Three, I turn towards another contemporary practitioner of life-writing, Paul Auster. Auster, whose work has (with the exception of his novel *Leviathan*) rarely been read in a political light,[51] has been obsessed with life-writing throughout his *oeuvre* and *The Book of Illusions* develops this obsession in its full creative and theoretical force. It tells two life-stories: that of Hector Mann, a Jewish Argentinian-American filmmaker from the silent era, who disappears out of his California home one morning in 1929 never to be seen again; and that of David Zimmer, a Hampton College comparative literature professor who writes a book about Mann's films after losing his wife and kids in a plane crash. Mann reads the book and invites Zimmer to his ranch in New Mexico, where he has gone on to make films. However, because of a death he caused in the past, he practices his art on the condition that no one will see it and that the work will be destroyed after his death. It is an "act of breathtaking nihilism" that Zimmer, who is in a nihilist phase himself, admires.

But a number of pressing questions remain. Why did Hector invite Zimmer to the ranch? And why did he ask Alma Grund, the daughter of his cameraman, to write his biography? Are these late-life decisions to be condemned as weaknesses, indicative of Hector's incapacity to ultimately go through with his grand project of destruction? Or might they be related to the hidden history of the twentieth century that the novel also tells, through the important dates in Hector's life? It is difficult not to have the Second World War and the Holocaust in mind when, at the very end of the book, all of Hector's life is burning. Through a close-reading of one of Hector's films, *The Inner Life of Martin Frost*, the chapter uncovers Auster's concern with life-writing and the power-relation of novelists to characters, a concern that takes on biopolitical significance when it is considered in light of the history of the Holocaust that lies occluded in the book.

Chapter Three continues the historical reflection on the rise of the novel as a genre that I began in Chapters 1 and 2 through a discussion of a sadistic scene in Auster's novel and a reflection on sadism's place in both the history of the novel and the history of biopolitics. Although this already includes a brief discussion of the work of Alain Robbe-Grillet, that reference only reaches full swing in my fourth chapter, on Tom McCarthy's *Remainder*.

In *Remainder*, McCarthy, whose admiration for Robbe-Grillet is hardly a secret, manages to combine the interruption that is characteristic of all of the above texts—Hector Mann's project of destruction; Tommy's anger; Costello's entry into Paul Rayment's life—*with* the practice of novel-writing. In a harrowing scene that Zadie Smith describes as the novel suffering a nervous breakdown, McCarthy interrupts his narrative in order to draw attention to the power-practice of writing. This break occurs in the context of a narrative of care. After suffering an unspeakable accident, McCarthy's narrator has to reconstruct himself from scratch. The reconstruction is successful but leaves him with some doubts about his authenticity, his capacity to naturally experience the real. With the help of a large settlement he receives in compensation for his accident—£8.5 million—the narrator begins to pursue this real through what he calls re-enactments: exacting re-enactments of déjà vus, memories, or everyday scenes that he experiences.[52] The re-enactments are a form of therapy—they function as a drug or pharmakon, and as such their curative effect also turns out to be poisonous. The narrator becomes addicted to them, and in order to keep getting his kicks the re-enactments need to become more and more elaborate. The novel closes with a scene, possibly inspired by Jean Baudrillard's description of a fake bank heist, that perhaps unsurprisingly completes in death: for in order to experience life through a work of art, the work of art must collapse, and life can only enter into it as death.

This appears to be the biopolitical lesson that these four novels pass on, and that I will also uncover in Walter Benjamin's reflections on modernity (at this point, we have clearly moved away from a narrow, Foucauldian definition of biopolitics). Art will never be able to become a living repetition of the living. Instead, life always remains removed from it, different from it, situated at a distance from the literary law. As Giorgio Agamben has argued, it is precisely this distance that biopolitics attempts to overcome. Striving for a perfect coincision between life and law, it makes public function and private life completely coincide, thus turning life into a work of art, and killing it. The novels show, however, that the answer to such a situation is not a blind rage against the work of art, or against the potentially curative dimension of biopolitics. Instead, they explore other aesthetics of existence that would manage to combine both the distance of life—captured, for example, by Tommy's anger—and, say, the institutions of the welfare state. It is here—that is, in what I characterize in my third chapter, following Bernard Stiegler's reflections on this issue, as the difference between "nuclear" and "pharmacological" criticism—that the politics of narrative care becomes most explicit, as a politics beyond both blind obedience and blind resistance. That is, I argue, what it means to narrate, and also to care. That is why the two are related. This position is further developed in my conclusion, where I turn to Pedro Almodóvar's film *Talk to Her* as a pharmacological narrative of care that mobilizes many of the concerns raised above. Almodóvar's film also enables me to return to and further some questions about sexuality that are raised throughout the book.

By then, I will have moved from a biopolitical theory of the novel to a theory of the novel informed by Foucault's work on the care of the self. As I stated above, my aim is ultimately to present the novel as a work of bioart that is traversed by both biopolitical concerns and by concerns with the care for the self and the care for others. Although the novel might be complicit with biopower, it is also—and for this very reason—a site where experimentation with care takes place. Indeed, because of the governmentality it incorporates, the novel could be read as a site where care's imagination exists in a perpetual struggle with the novel's biopolitical origins. It might be for precisely this reason that the novel is such an interesting genre, and a genre that has been central for so-called "ethical criticism." [53] [54] My intention is, however, to inflect such ethical criticism politically, in a time of emergencies, crises, and exceptions, in order to see how the narratives of care I consider can become meaningful today, as political narratives about biopolitics, the novel, and their shared fate in the twenty-first century.[55]

After Ethics: Reading Sebald's Images

> I can't stomach any kind of notion that serious fiction is good for us, because I don't believe that everything that's wrong with the world has a cure, and even if I did, what business would I, who feel like the sick one, have in offering it? It's hard to consider literature a medicine ...[56]
>
> —Jonathan Franzen, *How to Be Alone*

As a way into the rest of the book, and at the threshold of the biopolitical issues to which I arrive in Chapter One, I propose to explore briefly how a pharmacological theory of care and of literature could inform, and ultimately lead out of, the ethical criticism that has been dominant in literary studies until 2001. As I have said, Derrida points out in his 1968 text "Plato's Pharmacy" that *pharmakon* means both cure and poison. Therefore, it becomes impossible to decide in Plato's *Phaedrus* whether the author is talking about the curative or empoisoning aspects of, for example, the *technè* of writing. This point is repeated more explicitly in the *Republic*, which both rejects writing and painting as poisonous, and embraces them as useful falsehoods for governing.

One might have reservations about Plato's rejection of writing and painting in the *Republic*, or about what appears to be (though Derrida draws this into question) his negative evaluation of writing in the *Phaedrus*. But that should not prevent one from doing justice to the position that underlies both: *clearly, Plato believed that art has the capacity to change people*. His position in the *Republic*, and Derrida's position in his text about the pharmakon, could ultimately be rephrased as follows: if one believes that art has the capacity to make people worse, then one must believe that it has the capacity to make people better; and vice versa. That would be a pharmacological theory of art.

The theory could inform some discussions in what has come to be called "ethical criticism," which was part of the widespread and interdisciplinary "turn to ethics" in the humanities, the social sciences, and even the sciences during the late 1990s. Consider, for example, the case of the German novelist W. G. Sebald. I do not know what Sebald believed about art and its capacity to transform people. But given his argument in the academic essay "Air War and Literature,"[57] that in order for the Germans to be able to come to terms with the violence they suffered during the Second World War through the Allied bombings of German cities like Hamburg and Dresden, this violence needs to be "represented," it seems that he must have believed to some extent that art can make us better: that it can help us live with a traumatic experience. To do so, however, would also mean to consider—following the pharmacological theory of art—that such representations might *not*:

they might also make us worse, and produce more trauma. It is from this perspective that the role of images in Sebald's work could be reconsidered.

One characteristic feature of Sebald's novels is that they combine the literary and the visual. Their text is accompanied by images that are presented without captions in the novels' pages. Sometimes these images relate directly to the text. In other cases, the connection is less clear and it is largely up to the reader to gather what aspect of the text the image might visualize. Even when the relation between the image and the text is clear, however, the images retain a high degree of indeterminacy. Given that Sebald's texts are supposedly "fictions," one can never be entirely certain that the "thing" represented in the "image" is exactly that "thing" that is talked about in the text, or whether the image merely functions to add some semblance of reality, of materiality (a materiality that cannot but remain spectral, given that it is provided by an image), to a textual thing that is otherwise doomed to remain a thing of words. Although the images on the one hand seem to add reality to the text, their very inclusion within a literary text can also be said to subtract reality from the image, resituating both text and image within a zone of "spectral materialism" that critical theorist Eric Santner has argued to be typical of Sebald's work.[58]

Sebald's work also includes, however, texts that are different from the novels: academic writings. Some of those writings also contain images, and it is the difference between the images in these academic texts and the images in the novels that interests me. Sebald's last work, a text entitled "Air War and Literature" that was published as part of an English translation entitled *On the Natural History of Destruction*, is an academic essay about Germany's incapacity to represent, and therefore work through, the violence it suffered in the Allied bombings of its major cities towards the end of the Second World War. It is a provocative essay that has stirred much controversy. Like Sebald's novels, the text of the essay is accompanied by images that, in this case, clearly visualize what Sebald is writing about in the essay. And although the presence of images in Sebald's *literary* work never made me question the ethics of Sebald's artistic practice—they never made me ask, for example, about the possible *violence* that Sebald's inclusion of images might do to those represented in the images, to the readers taking in those images, or indeed to Sebald himself who is including those images in his writing—, the images in *On the Natural History of Destruction did* make me raise that question—perhaps because some of them are indeed not meant for sensitive viewers.

One can consider, for example, Sebald's description of the Allied bombings early on in the essay. Presumably, the descriptions offered are meant to make up for what Sebald in the essay is criticizing, namely the shocking absence within German literature of such descriptions of the violence that Germany suffered. After describing the hurricane-like firestorm destruction caused by the bombings, Sebald writes:

> Residential districts so large that their total street length amounted to two hundred kilometers were utterly destroyed. Horribly disfigured corpses lay everywhere. Bluish little phosphorous flames still flickered around many of them; others had been roasted brown or purple and reduced to a third of their normal size. They lay doubled up in pools of their own melted fat, which had sometimes already congealed.[59]

This description is followed on page 29 by another one, which Sebald borrows from Friedrich Reck (one of the rare authors who did represent the situation):

> Friedrich Reck describes a group of forty to fifty such refugees [i.e., refugees from the destroyed German cities] trying to force their way into a train at a station in Upper Bavaria, As they do so, a cardboard suitcase "falls on the platform, bursts open and spills its contents. Toys, a manicure case, singed underwear. And last of all, the roasted corpse of a child, shrunk like a mummy, which its half-deranged mother has been carrying about with her, the relic of a past that was still intact a few days ago."

The final description I will give comes from the second part of the essay, in which Sebald discusses the cleaning-up program after the bombardments. Convicts were sent in to clear away the dead bodies. Sebald notes that they

> could reach the corpses in the air raid shelters of the death zone only with flamethrowers, so densely did the flies swarm around them, and so thick were the floors and steps of the cellars with slippery finger-length maggots.[60]

Sebald quotes some of these passages as rare instances in German literature where Germany's suffering because of the Allied bombings is actually represented.

I think it is debatable whether descriptions such as this actually contribute to the Germans' coming to terms with the violence they suffered. The question poses itself most extremely with respect to the image that, in one of the cases just quoted, accompanies the text: the photograph of the burnt bodies reproduced on page 28. I do not know whether Sebald in the two other cases also had a photograph at hand representing the scene that is described. Given that he shows us the burnt bodies described in the first passage, one expects that if he had, he would likely also have included a photograph of the "roasted corpse of a child on the train platform," or of the "finger-length maggots" crowding the stairs to the bomb shelters. Thankfully, we are spared these curative treats.

The status of the images in Sebald's academic essay is clearly different from that of the images in his novelistic work. In the former case, the images are brought in as evidence of what Sebald (or the authors he is quoting) is/are describing. Although this might to a certain extent also be the case in the novels, to argue that the images "quoted" in the novels would function as "evidence" for the stories told in the novels would no doubt do a violence to the images "quoted" in Sebald's academic essay. I do not know of any other image in Sebald's novelistic work that is as shocking as the image of the burnt bodies quoted in *On the Natural History of Destruction*. The image is of an extraordinary violence that in no way compares to any of the other images in his *oeuvre*.

The question that I want to raise, at the ethical threshold of this political investigation into narrative care, has to do with Sebald's reproduction of this particular image: *do we really need this image, or such images?* If (big IF) we need descriptions such as the ones that Sebald, and the authors Sebald is quoting, provide—descriptions of the horrors caused by the Allied bombings of Germany—, do we really need images to further illustrate these horrors? Although I understand that the existence of these images can provide evidence that might be crucial in countering claims that would deny the violence that the Germans suffered, I also wonder what is actually achieved by their reproduction in Sebald's text *at the level of working through these experiences*.

I guess I am not sure about their effect. I am not sure whether it does us, or the Germans, any good having these scenes described and these images reproduced. I am ultimately not saying this out of some kind of prudishness towards these descriptions and these images. My wavering comes from a genuine *pharmacological* concern with literature/photography and the effects these representative practices have on human beings. Like Plato, and Derrida's Plato, I think that representation can change human beings, not only for the better but also for the worse. Therefore, the line between better and worse becomes a risky one to walk, and although Sebald's novelistic writings do a great job in terms of working through the horrors of the Second World War and the sufferings they produced, his academic essay "Air War and Literature" in my view fails precisely where the novelistic work succeeds. This failure is due to the fact that the essay represents too directly the trauma that is to be worked through. Sebald's novels never reach the straightforwardness of the academic essay—and that is why they are successful.

Sebald's project is an important one—one that I care about—and it is because I care about it that I argue his project fails in the academic essay where it is successful in the novels. The difference between this failure and this success in part depends on the regime of visibility Sebald sets up in these different works—upon what is seen and what remains off-scene in these two different types of texts. But that is only one part of the story.

J. M. Coetzee and the Obscene

An ethical argument for the off-scene, then, for what should remain off-scene if one wants to prevent the work of art from making people worse. This argument—Platonic, and moralist/humanist—is not exactly mine, but Elizabeth Costello's, and Costello herself can be said to be borrowing it from discussions about the ethics of representation going back at least as far as Plato (more on this below).

Costello is a character invented by the South African, now Australian, novelist J. M. Coetzee (to whom I will return in Chapter One). In a chapter in the novel *Elizabeth Costello* entitled "The Problem of Evil," Costello travels to Amsterdam to speak at a conference on the problem of evil, more precisely on the topic of "Witness, Silence, and Censorship." Costello's heart "misses a beat" when she notices in the conference program that the novelist around whose work her talk revolves, a man named Paul West, is scheduled to speak at the conference as well.[61]

In her talk, Costello had planned to challenge West on his novel *The Very Rich Hours of Count von Stauffenberg*, which describes in excruciating detail the execution of those who plotted an attack against Hitler. The chapter that offended Costello provides

> an account of what they [i.e., those who would have witnessed this horrible event, had there been any witnesses] had seen, down to the words the hangman spoke to the souls consigned to his hands, fumbling old men for the most part, stripped of their uniforms, togged out for the final event in prison cast-offs, serge trousers caked with grime, pullovers full of moth-holes, no shoes, belts, their false teeth and their glasses taken from them, exhausted, shivering, hands in their pockets to hold up their pants, whimpering with fear, swallowing their tears, having to listen to this coarse creature, this butcher with last week's blood caked under his fingernails, taunt them, telling them what would happen when the rope snapped tight, how the shit would run down their spindly old-man's legs, how their limp old-man's penises would quiver one last time.[62]

Presumably, there were no such witnesses; and yet, novelist Paul West decides to become such a witness when he writes an imaginative account of this event.

Costello's question is: why would one decide to write such a scene? Why would one decide to invest one's talent in this? In a word, she thinks the chapter is "*obscene*."[63] It is obscene because the things it relates

> ought not to take place, and then obscene again because having taken place they ought not to be brought into the light but covered up and hidden for ever in the bowels of the earth, like what goes on in the slaughterhouses of the world, if one wishes to save one's sanity.[64]

I take it that Costello is not arguing against historical evidence. She is not arguing that if there were evidence of the execution, if there had been a witness for example who had typed up her or his account, this account should be destroyed. She is merely saying that if such an account exists, it should be buried in the archives. It should not be reproduced as front-page news and it certainly should not be reproduced in fiction. That is, "if [big IF] one wishes to save one's sanity."

The latter condition turns out to be the key humanist (not only moralist, but also rationalist) supposition around which Costello's position revolves. There should be limits to representation, she argues, because "she is no longer sure that people are always improved by what they read."[65] Since she believes that art has the capacity to make people better, that means it also has the capacity to make people worse, and this "also" heightens the responsibility of the novelist, presumably because the novelist would not want to make people worse. It is for this reason, "to save our humanity," that Costello argues certain things should remain "obscene, meaning off-stage"[66]:

> To save our humanity, certain things that we may want to see (may want to see because we are human!) must remain off-stage. Paul West has written an obscene book, he has shown what ought not to be shown.[67]

"Ought not" because it does not make people better, but worse. Interestingly, Costello's argument does not only apply to West's readers; it also applies to West himself, who "risks a great deal by venturing into forbidden places."[68] Inverting the imagery of Plato's cave allegory, but preserving its logic, she argues that "we should not go into that cellar [i.e., the cellar in which the plotters were executed, but also the cellar of the obscene], any of us."[69] She thus proposes a kind of censorship in order to save our humanity.

Costello's argument and proposition are hardly new. One can think here of Susan Sontag's plea for an "ecology of images" in *On Photography* (where one would have to take into account Sontag's revisions of that earlier argument in the post-9/11 book *Regarding the Pain of Others*)[70]; or of Judith Butler's recent essay on photography and the Abu Ghraib prison tortures entitled "Torture and the Ethics of Photography: Thinking with Sontag."[71] Coetzee's Elizabeth Costello appears to be stuck in what Sontag in a critique of her own early work calls a "conservative critique of the diffusion of … images," namely a plea for a "Committee of Guardians" that is going to "ration horror."[72] The reference is, clearly, to Plato; Costello appears to be stuck "In Plato's Cave," to recall the title of the first essay in *On Photography*. At the end of "The Problem of Evil," the reader is left with Costello's request—or plea, as she puts it—to her fellow novelist Paul West: "Let me not look. … Do not make me go through with it!"[73] If you want me to keep my sanity, and remain human, *do not make me look*.

At first sight, this might sound like the argument for the off-scene that I developed earlier. However, I am turning to Coetzee because Coetzee's text, "The Problem of Evil," importantly does *not* stay stuck in the same conservatism as the novelist it represents. Indeed, although *Costello* might refuse to represent the chapter in Paul West's novel that she finds so offensive, the horrible content of that chapter does make its way into *Coetzee*'s chapter—albeit in a summarized form—in the paragraph describing the execution that I quoted above. It is a paragraph that, even though it is invented, hits me like the descriptions I quoted from Sebald's essay "Air War and Literature"; especially the last lines of Costello's summary: "how the shit would run down their spindly old-man's legs, how their limp old-man's penises would quiver one last time." However, the effect is ultimately *different* because *it is embedded within the structure of the novel.* It is *narrative* that adds some kind of dimension that makes the horror of the scene described easier to digest—it is *narrative* that accomplishes the curative effect of this otherwise poisonous scene. The chapter in its entirety can thus be read as an example of narrative care.

There is no guarantee, as Costello's critique of West shows, that narrative will accomplish this. Indeed, for Costello, West's narrative clearly did not. But as the pharmakon that it is, narrative does have this capacity. And, Costello suggests, it is up to the writer—whose role thus becomes analogous to Plato's statesmen or doctors—to use narrative in a beneficial way, aware of the vicissitudes of the pharmakon.

But this cannot be the last word on the matter either (writers as statesmen or doctors? you must be kidding!). For there is one enigma that, in both my reading of Sebald and of Coetzee, has not been considered and that relates to the concerns that are at the heart of this book. How does the novel as a genre relate to the biopolitical history of the Second World War—of fascism and the camps—that both Sebald's academic text and Paul West's novel expose? What kind of questions might a serious consideration of this history raise about the politics of the novel as a typically modern genre? In my reading, both Sebald's fiction and Coetzee's novel become haunted by the history of the Second World War. Is Sebald reinventing the genre of the novel in his fiction partly in response to the history of the camps? Why? Is it simply because trauma poses a limit to representation, as has been argued over and over again? And what about, say, Elizabeth Costello's reflections on realism that make up one chapter of Coetzee's book? Could the biopolitical history of the camps be at stake there as well? These questions are ultimately about how the experience of the Second World War, perhaps the most intensely biopolitical event of the twentieth century, resides within the novel—within *these* novels, as well as *others*. Is it simply present there as a private or collective trauma that, at the level of content, needs to be worked through? Or is it also present at the level of form, as a reflection on the origins of the rise of the novel as a genre? If both the camps and the novel find each other in modernity, is there a logic that connects them?

It is this—to some, no doubt, preposterous—question that the four novels I look at appear to be asking. As I will show, however, and as my reading of Sebald and Coetzee has already shown, the novel clearly also exists *beyond* the dark complicities that are hinted at here. If there is arguably a connection between the biopolitical experience of the camps and the novel, there is also a connection between the novel and care—between the novel and a critical aesthetics of existence. It is here that the novel-form appears to struggle with its political origins, and develops into something else. Such a struggle has been inscribed in the genre from the beginning. *Narrative Care* shows how four contemporary novels put the history of this struggle on the map for us: by rewriting key texts from the novel's history (Defoe's *Robinson Crusoe*, Shelley's *Frankenstein*) and addressing key aspects of the novel's aesthetic trajectory (realism, authenticity), these novels put their very own cultural production into a fascinating perspective—one that, though it does not deny the novel's status as a dark apparatus of capture, also theorizes it along brighter, more colorful lines: as a practice of care. It is this *pharmacology*, which identifies the genre, that the image on the cover of this book is meant to evoke.

Notes

1 J. M. Coetzee, *Slow Man* (New York: Viking, 2005).

2 Timothy Bewes, "The Novel as an Absence: Lukács and the Event of Postmodern Fiction," in *Novel* 38: 1 (2004): 7.

3 See Frédéric Worms, *Le moment du soin: À quoi tenons-nous?* (Paris: PUF, 2010), 219–25. Worms has also edited, with Lazare Benarayo, Céline Lefève, and Jean-Christophe Mino, the collection *La philosophie du soin: Éthique, médecine, et société* (Paris: PUF, 2010). Worms' work is very focused on ethics and differs from the work I undertake here.
4 See Arne De Boever, *States of Exception in the Contemporary Novel: Martel, Eugenides, Coetzee, Sebald* (New York: Continuum, 2012).
5 Worms, *Moment*, 38.
6 See *When the Levees Broke: A Requiem in Four Acts*, DVD, directed by Spike Lee (New York: HBO Video, 2006).
7 See Naomi Klein, *The Shock Doctrine: The Rise of Disaster Capitalism* (New York: Picador, 2007).
8 For an example of a recent conference on life, see: http://www.h-net.org/announce/show.cgi?ID=178065
9 See Giorgio Agamben, *Homo Sacer: Sovereign Power and Bare Life*, trans. Daniel Heller-Roazen (Stanford: Stanford University Press, 1998).
10 See Eric Santner, *On Creaturely Life: Rilke, Benjamin, Sebald,* (Chicago: University of Chicago Press, 2005).
11 See Judith Butler, *Precarious Life: The Powers of Mourning and Violence* (New York: Verso, 2004).
12 See Nikolas Rose, *The Politics of Life Itself: Biomedicine, Power, and Subjectivity in the Twenty-First Century* (Princeton: Princeton University Press, 2007).
13 See Melinda Cooper, *Life as Surplus: Biotechnology and Capitalism in the Neoliberal Era* (Seattle: University of Washington Press, 2008).
14 I would argue that literature's role in both texts is problematic. In the first chapter of my *States of Exception*, I suggested that Santner risks to confuse literature with theology in *On Creaturely Life*; his more recent (and excellent) *The Royal Remains: The People's Two Bodies and the Endgames of Sovereignty* (Chicago: University of Chicago Press, 2012) does more justice to the particularity of the literary. Worms' book is ultimately a book of philosophy that keeps its analyses of novels, films, and artworks down to a minimum.
15 See John D. Engel, Joseph Zarconi, Lura L. Penthel, et al., *Narrative in Health Care* (Oxford: Radcliffe, 2008); Michael White and David Epston, *Narrative Means to Therapeutic Ends* (New York: Norton, 1990); Gary M. Kenyon, *Storying Later Life* (Oxford: Oxford University Press, 2010); Andy Clark, *Natural-Born Cyborgs: Minds, Technologies, and the Future of Human Intelligence* (Oxford: Oxford University Press, 2003).
16 Catherine Malabou, *What Should We Do With Our Brain?*, trans. Sebastian Rand (New York: Fordham, 2008).
17 One hypothesis that should also be considered is that the issue of biopolitics and especially of care is simply more pressing in Western democracies, in which the rise of the welfare state and its subsequent

destruction through neoliberal policies have slowly but surely contributed to the erosion of care.

18 Jean Baudrillard, *The Agony of Power*, trans. Ames Hodges (Los Angeles: Semiotext(e), 2010), 88.

19 See Isabelle Stengers, *Au temps des catastrophes: Résister à la barbarie qui vient* (Paris: La Découverte, 2009), esp. 129–31.

20 See Vandana Shiva, *Biopiracy: The Plunder of Nature and Knowledge* (Brooklyn: South End, 1997).

21 See Dominique Lecourt, *Humain, posthumain: La technique et la vie* (Paris: PUF, 2003).

22 Lecourt, *Humain*, 65.

23 See Bernard Stiegler, *Taking Care of Youth and the Generations*, trans. Stephen Barker (Stanford: Stanford University Press, 2010).

24 See Bernard Stiegler, *Ce qui fait que le vie vaut la peine d'être vécue: De la pharmacologie* (Paris: Flammarion, 2010).

25 A key component in the analysis, represented by the book he published in between, is political economy. See Bernard Stiegler, *Pour une nouvelle critique de l'économie politique* (Paris: Galilée, 2009).

26 Giorgio Agamben includes literature in his enumeration of apparatuses in: *What is an Apparatus? And Other Essays*, trans. David Kishik and Stefan Pedatella (Stanford: Stanford University Press, 2009), 14.

27 Jacques Derrida, *Dissemination*, trans. Barbara Johnson (Chicago: University of Chicago Press, 1981), 70.

28 One famous example is the—to modern ears highly problematic—myth of metals: "a Phoenician story" about people being born with bronze/iron, silver, or gold in their veins. It's a story that the guardians use to justify their organization of the citizens' sexual relations. Like doctors, statesmen thus take recourse to drugs to practice their *technè* or art. See Plato, *Republic*, trans. G. M. A. Grube (Indianapolis: Hackett, 1992), 91.

29 Jacques Derrida, *Rogues: Two Essays on Reason*, trans. Pascale-Anne Brault and Michael Naas (Stanford: Stanford University Press, 2005), 24.

30 See Jacques Derrida, *The Beast and the Sovereign*, Vol. I, trans. Geoffrey Bennington (Chicago: University of Chicago Press, 2008).

31 Derrida, *Beast*, 371, 399, 400.

32 See Arne De Boever, "Biopolitics in Deconstruction" and "Derrida's Theory of the Novel": http://derridaseminars.org/workshops.

33 I quote here from the edited French manuscript of the first five session of the seminar, distributed to the participants in the translation workshops.

34 Derrida, *Dissemination*, 136.

35 My questions are thus more general than those already covered, for example, in Geoffrey Sill's *The Cure of the Passions and the Origins of the English Novel*. As Nicolle Jordan points out in a review of the book titled "Passion as Pharmakon: A Theme in Medicine, Theology, and the Novel" (*The Eighteenth Century* 45: 3 (2004): 285–91), Sill studies

the eighteenth-century novel as an aesthetic technique of existence, specifically a technique of managing the passions (which he distinguishes, not entirely convincingly, from emotions). Daniel Defoe's novel *Robinson Crusoe* takes up a central place in Sill's narrative. In *Narrative Care*, I widen Sill's argument; when I consider the novel as an aesthetic of existence, I have something more emancipatory in mind than a technique to manage one's passions. Perhaps that is the emancipation of the care of the self in the twenty-first century.

36 Ibid., 136.

37 Eric Myer has done something of the kind in "'The Nature of the Text': Ford and Conrad in Plato's Pharmacy" (*Modern Fiction Studies* 36: 4 (1990): 499–512). Although Myer does not talk about biopolitics, he does graft together Derrida's discussion of the pharmakon with close-readings of fiction (both short stories and a novel).

38 I have discussed the connection between Foucault's work on biopolitics and his late work on the care of the self elsewhere. See Arne De Boever, "Bio-Paulitics," in *Journal for Cultural and Religious Theory* 11.1 (2010): http://www.jcrt.org/archives/11.1/boever.pdf and "The Allegory of the Cage," in *Foucault Studies* 10 (2010): 7–22: http://rauli.cbs.dk/index.php/foucault-studies/article/viewFile/3124/3288

39 Others have explored this connection: Stephen Dougherty, "The Biopolitics of the Killer Virus Novel," in *Cultural Critique* 48 (2001): 1–29; and in particular Alex Houen, "Sovereignty, Biopolitics, and the Use of Literature," in *Theory & Event* 9: 1 (2006): 1–33.

40 See, for example, Dorrit Cohn, "Optics and Power and the Novel," *New Literary History* 26: 1 (1995): 3–20, which focuses on disciplinary power and the novel; Dieter Freundlieb, "Foucault and the Study of Literature," in *Poetics Today* 16: 2 (1995): 301–44, which explores the connection between archeology, genealogy, and literature, and ultimately turns to the aesthetics of existence to discuss the problem of literary self-formation. As far as books go, I can refer the reader to Simon During, *Foucault and Literature* (London: Routledge, 1992).

41 Edward Said, *On Late Style: Music and Literature Against the Grain* (New York: Pantheon, 2006), 4.

42 Said, *Late*, 4.

43 Ibid., 5.

44 Ibid.

45 John Marks has discussed the link between Jacob and Foucault in "Michel Foucault: Biopolitics and Biology," in *Foucault in the Age of Terror: Biopolitics and the Defense of Society*, ed. Stephen Morton and Stephen Bygrave (New York: Palgrave Macmillan, 2008), 88–105.

46 Said, *Late*, 5.

47 Ibid., 3.

48 Ibid., 7.

49 My focus is obviously on the contemporary novel. Nancy Armstrong has given a more nuanced account of how the tensions I discuss are played out in the history of the novel. Writing about the history of the novel from 1719 to 1900, she argues that the earliest novels were a means of supplementation that gave birth to the literary individual within a governmental world; later on, however, the novel succumbed to governmentality, and became a means of disciplinary power—self-expression was replaced by self-government. Contemporary experiments with the novel could then be read within this history as oscillating between the novel's supplemental and disciplinary tendencies. See Nancy Armstrong, *How Novels Think: The Limits of Individualism from 1719–1900* (New York: Columbia University Press, 2005).

50 See Ian Watt, *The Rise of the Novel: Studies in Defoe, Richardson, and Fielding* (Harmondsworth: Penguin, 1970).

51 It may be that Paul Auster's recent work, which includes more explicitly political fiction, will change this. Consider, for example, his brilliant novel *Invisible* (New York: Picador, 2010).

52 In terms of its process, the narrator's project thus reflects on what all of the other novels I discuss are doing: to reflect on care and biopolitics, *Slow Man* re-enacts Defoe's *Robinson Crusoe*, *Never Let Me Go* re-enacts Shelley's *Frankenstein*, and in *The Book of Illusions*, Hector Mann's films are re-enacted. Christian Moraru has considered the significance of strategies of rewriting in: *Rewriting: Postmodern Narrative and Cultural Critique in the Age of Cloning* (Albany: SUNY Press, 2001).

53 For more on ethical criticism and the ethical turn, see Todd F. Davis and Kenneth Womack (eds.), *Mapping the Ethical Turn: A Reader in Ethics, Culture, and Literary Theory* (Charlottesville: University Press of Virginia, 2001); Marjorie Garber, Beatrice Hanssen, and Rebecca L. Walkowitz (eds.), *The Turn to Ethics* (New York: Routledge, 2000).

54 In this sense, my approach owes much to books such as Armstrong's *How Novels Think*, which argues that novels at once create debates and are created by them.

55 For another critic who speaks of the novel as pharmakon, see Adrián Pérez Melgoza, "Macedonio Fernández's Narrative Pharmakon: The Shared Project of 'Adriana Buenos Aires' and 'Museo dela Novela de la Eterna,'" in *Latin American Literary Review* 35: 70 (2007): 5–30.

56 Jonathan Franzen, *How to Be Alone* (New York: Farrar, Strauss, and Giroux, 2002), 73.

57 W. G. Sebald, "Air War and Literature," in W. G. Sebald, *On the Natural History of Destruction*, trans. Anthea Bell (New York: Random House, 2003), 1–104.

58 Santner, *On Creaturely Life*. I have commented on this aspect of Sebald's writing in the final chapter of my *States of Exception*.

59 Sebald, "Air War," 27–8.

60 Ibid., 35.
61 J. M. Coetzee, *Elizabeth Costello* (New York: Viking, 2003), 161.
62 Coetzee, *Costello*, 158.
63 Ibid.
64 Ibid., 159.
65 Ibid., 160.
66 Ibid., 168.
67 Ibid., 168–9.
68 Ibid., 173.
69 Ibid., 173.
70 See Susan Sontag, *On Photography* (New York: Farrar, Straus, and Giroux, 1977); Susan Sontag, *Regarding the Pain of Others* (New York: Farrar, Straus, and Giroux, 2003). Indeed, Sontag has also written about the notion of the obscene in her essay "The Pornographic Imagination," in Susan Sontag, *Styles of Radical Will* (New York: Delta, 1969), esp. 57.
71 See Judith Butler, "Torture and the Ethics of Photography: Thinking with Sontag," in Judith Butler, *Frames of War: When is Life Grievable?* (New York: Verso, 2009), 63–100.
72 Susan Sontag, "Looking at War," in *The New Yorker*, 9 December 2002: 84.
73 Coetzee, *Costello*, 179.

1

J. M. Coetzee's *Slow Man* as "a Biologico-Literary Experiment"

But we are grown people, so why are we letting someone we barely know dictate our lives? That is what I ask myself.[1]

—J. M. Coetzee, *Slow Man*

A Novel of Care

J. M. Coetzee's *Slow Man* opens with a gripping scene. Biking on Magill Road in Adelaide, Australia, the novel's main character Paul Rayment—"Rayment" rhyming not with "payment" but with the French *vraiment* ("really," literally "true-ly"), as the novel explains[2]—is caught from the right by a blow, "sharp and surprising and painful, like a bolt of electricity, lifting him up off the bicycle."[3] He has been hit by the car of a young man called Wayne Blight. When he is conscious for a few moments in the hospital, a doctor informs him that if he wants them to save his leg, "we are going to have to amputate."[4] "We don't have a choice Paul," the doctor says. "It is not one of those situations where we have a choice."[5] And so Paul's right leg is amputated above the knee, and he turns from an independent older man into someone who is entirely dependent on others. This situation is the springboard for the novel's investigation of care, a word that recurs obsessively throughout the book.[6]

The novel's opening scene recalls a scene from the New Testament's Acts of the Apostles, which involves another Paul, at that point still called Saul (Coetzee quotes from Paul's letters in the novel's fifth chapter). While traveling from Tarsus to Damascus to fight the Christians, Saul is blasted off his horse:

> Now as he journeyed he approached Damascus, and suddenly a light from heaven flashed about him. And he fell to the ground, and heard a voice saying to him: "Saul, Saul, why do you persecute me?" And he said, "Who are you, Lord?" And he said, "I am Jesus, whom you are persecuting; but rise and enter the city and you will be told what you are to do."[7]

Saul does not lose a leg in the accident, but he does lose his eyesight. After three days of darkness, however, God sends him a messenger called Ananias, who restores it. As a consequence of this event, Saul will change his name to Paul and convert, turning into the most famous militant of early Christianity.

This second story has received some airplay in the post-secular age: critical theorists such as Alain Badiou, Giorgio Agamben, and Slavoj Žižek have recovered it as a story through which they reflect on philosophical notions such as the event, the subject, or community.[8] In *Slow Man*, Coetzee rewrites this theological story in order to reflect on care—initially, on *the subject's relation to the welfare state*. The theological story about Paul and the birth of the church, that ancient institution of pastoral care, is morphed in Coetzee's novel into a story about the caring administrations of the modern state. However, although Paul Rayment rages against the welfare state, it is important to note that he does not rage against Christian care or caritas: like Coetzee's earlier novel *Elizabeth Costello*, *Slow Man* attempts to separate a Christian notion of care from the care practiced by the welfare state. But, as Paul quickly learns, this care is not easily practiced. Indeed, we might have entirely forgotten how to do so. How to distinguish it, for example, from "love"? How to distinguish "love" from "eros"? One could also add, as I will do below, the notion of "philia"—"love," "friendship"—to the discussion.

At this point in the novel, one of Coetzee's other characters, the novelist Elizabeth Costello shows up. As a result, the problematic of care is transposed onto a meta-fictional level, thereby turning *Slow Man* into a reflection about the novel's (or writing's) relation to care, something that Jacques Derrida was arguably already addressing in "Plato's Pharmacy."[9] *Slow Man*'s references to Daniel Defoe's *Robinson Crusoe*—a recurring theme in Coetzee's *oeuvre*—reinforce this meta-fictional turn and invite one to reflect on the novel's relation to the *history* of care, from pastoral care to the welfare state, that *Slow Man* lays out.[10] Indeed, when the novel characterizes its own project as a "biologico-literary experiment,"[11] this raises *political* questions about the power of the governing author, the status of the character-subject, and the particular regime of authority that the novel practices. It is within this context that the novel mobilizes the question of care, and of narrative care, in all of its complexity.

The Welfare State

> We are not succumbing to oppression or exploitation, but to profusion and unconditional care—to the power of those who make sovereign decisions about our well-being. From there, revolt has a different meaning: it no longer targets the forbidden, but permissiveness, tolerance, excessive transparency—the Empire of Good. For better or worse.
>
> Now you must fight against everything that wants to help you.[12]
>
> —Jean Baudrillard, *The Agony of Power*

Shortly after his accident, Paul receives a visit from "a social worker, Mrs. Putts or Putz."[13] She is a representative of the welfare state. "You're still a young man, Mr. Rayment," she tells him.

> You will want to remain independent, and of course that's good, but for quite some time you are going to need nursing, specialized nursing, which we can help to arrange. In the longer term, even once you are mobile, you are going to need someone to be there for you, to give you a hand, to do the shopping and the cooking and cleaning and so forth.[14]

The problem is that there is no such person. Paul is divorced, estranged from his wife, and has no children or family to take care of him. As far as he is concerned, he just wants to take care of himself. Mrs. Putts, however, suggests that he "will need a care-giver."[15] But that is not what Paul has in mind.

Almost comically so, he attempts to steer clear from the welfare state's administrations, fighting against everything that wants to help him (to recall the sentence from Baudrillard that I quoted at the beginning of this section). He refuses, for example, a prosthesis: "*I don't want a prosthesis*," he insists; "I would prefer to take care of myself."[16] Paul's most important concern—what he cares about most—appears to be "to stay on the right side of Mrs. Putts": "Mrs. Putts is part of the welfare system. Welfare means caring for people who cannot care for themselves."[17] Paul does not want to fall into this category, and he thinks he will be able to convince Mrs. Putts that he does not. He fantasizes, even, about the fact that it may be possible that "he overestimates Mrs. Putts' concern."

> When it comes to welfare, when it comes to care and the caring professions, he is almost certainly out of date. In the brave new world into which both he and Mrs. Putts have been reborn, whose watchword is *Laissez faire!*, perhaps Mrs. Putts regards herself as neither his keeper nor her brother's keeper nor anyone else's.[18]

But no such luck: "When the ambulancemen bring him home, Sheena [the nurse Mrs. Putts has arranged for him] is ready and waiting."[19]

As was perhaps to be expected, Paul cannot stand Sheena who "calls the bedpan his potty" and "calls his penis his willie."[20] After only one week, he "telephones Mrs. Putts. 'I am going to ask Sheena not to come back,' he says. 'I cannot abide her. You will have to find someone else.'"[21] His subsequent reliance on temporary and irregular help does not improve his situation. But then Mrs. Putts' second candidate shows up: a Croatian nurse named Marijana Jokic. Her "caring skills"[22] are excellent; her "regimen of care"[23] is one into which he can settle. Continuing to refuse a prosthesis, he learns to rely on crutches and his "Zimmer-frame": "a four-footed aluminium stand for use around the flat."[24] At first sight, none of this seems to change his belief that one day he will be entirely self-reliant again. When Marijana asks him "So who is going to take care of you?," he casually replies: "Oh, I'll take care of myself."[25] But as he realizes his dependence on Marijana's administrations, that phrase—"I'll take care of myself"—begins to take on new meaning: thoughts of suicide pass through his mind. He considers the kind of caring that is practiced "with a shotgun."[26]

It is shortly thereafter, on the day when Marijana proposes to dust his books, that something changes within this precarious relation of care. For when he sees Marijana take care of his books, "an interest that had not amounted to more than curiosity [a word that is etymologically related to care], turns into something else."[27] Paul begins to desire Marijana, in spite of the fact that she is married and with children. He is visited by his friend Margaret McCord, who had an affair with him several years ago. She unambiguously proposes sex, but he does not pursue her offer, most likely because the one he really wants is Marijana. What Marijana promises is "no cure, just care":

> Perching down on his bedside, pressing down on his groin with her left hand, Marijana watches, nodding, as he flexes, extends, and rotates the stump. With the lightest of pressure she helps him to extend the flexion. She massages the aching muscle; she turns him over and massages his lower back.[28]

It is not a sex act, perhaps, but it is certainly described like one.[29] And thus, over time, Paul's comical resistance against the welfare state turns into a love for Marijana.

Of course, this love risks to upset the entire regimen of care into which he has so comfortably settled. After meeting Marijana's son Drago one day, Paul proposes to put up the money for his college education. When Marijana asks him "why?," he answers: "I love you. That is all. I love you and I want to give you something. Let me."[30] "The next day", the following chapter begins, "Marijana does not arrive."[31] With his confession, Paul has extended the relation of care beyond where it is able to stretch. It is at this point in the novel that one of Coetzee's other characters, the novelist Elizabeth Costello, shows up and that *Slow Man*'s reflections on care are taken to a different level.

What is the novel's description of the relation between Paul and Marijana about? It is not as if Paul comes to love, through her, the administrations of the welfare state. To say the least, he remains very critical of it. Paul Rayment's story is in this sense not a conversion story, like the story of that other Paul. However, the relation of the modern-day Paul to the ancient Paul is also more complicated, because although Paul Rayment resists the administrations of the welfare state, he does not resist a theological, pastoral notion of care. It is as if he is trying to *recuperate*, while *resisting* the welfare state, a practice of care from the welfare state's theological origins.

Indeed, that is the notion of care that informs his desire to take care of Marijana's son, and later on in the novel of her other children[32]: the kind of care that Jesus would approve of.[33] A kind of charity or caritas, a notion that has been circulating in Coetzee's novels for a while. Although no critics (to my knowledge) have considered Coetzee's *oeuvre* through the lens of the notion of care,[34] care is central to many of his books, including *Life and Times of Michael K* (think, for example, of Michael K's care for his dead mother or his care for his pumpkin seedlings), *Waiting for the Barbarians* (think of the Magistrate's care for a captured barbarian woman), and *Disgrace* (think of Lucy and Lurie's care for abandoned, sick, or old animals).[35] It is Coetzee's novel *Elizabeth Costello*, however, that puts the notion of care and the question of caritas explicitly on the page towards the end of a chapter titled "The Humanities in Africa."

In this chapter, novelist and animal rights activist Elizabeth Costello recalls visiting an old and sick family friend called Aidan Phillips—a gentleman who, in his spare time, used to paint. On one of these visits, Phillips—who has difficulties speaking because of a laryngectomy—, slips her a note saying "Wish I could paint you in the nude … Would have loved that."[36] In response Costello does something that surprises not only Mr. Phillips but also herself: "I loosened the wrap [of her garment] and shrugged it off my shoulders and took off my brassiere and hung it on the back of the chair and said, 'How's that, Aidan?'"[37] Describing what she did as "a blessing"[38] rather than "*[c]ock-teasing*"[39] (although she acknowledges there was an element of the latter in it as well), she characterizes her act as an act "of humanity,"[40] which she considers in relation to both the Christian and the ancient Greek traditions.

Consider the scene's follow-up: exposing herself to Mr. Phillips again on another occasion, she also performs oral sex on him. Here is the insight that comes to her during the act:

> As for her, Elizabeth, crouched over the old bag of bones with her breasts dangling, working away on his nearly extinct organ of generation, what name would the Greeks give to such a spectacle? Not *eros*, certainly—too grotesque for that. *Agape*? Again, perhaps not. Does that mean the Greeks would have no word for it? Would one have to wait for the Christians to come along with the right word: *caritas*?[41]

Rehearsing the semantic field of "love" to which I alluded in the introduction to this chapter, Costello ultimately arrives at the Christian term "caritas": a term that is central to the discourse of Paul, and to the New Testament at large. As such, it is not surprising that it would turn into a crucial notion in Coetzee's *Slow Man*.

Although Paul Rayment resists the caring administrations of the welfare state, he thus appears to be open—and to promote, even—the care of caritas that is associated with the Christian theology to which the opening scene of *Slow Man* alludes. The suggestion could be that such a practice of care, such caritas, has gotten lost in the caring administrations of the modern welfare state. With the transition from care in Paul's time to care in Paul Rayment's time, humanity has lost the practice of caritas. Furthermore, *Slow Man* shows how Paul's relation of care develops into eros, and poses problems because it does so. However, eros might ultimately not be what Paul is after. At the end of the day, what he wants appears to be different: he wants to become the godfather of Marijana's children, so that he can "extend a protective hand over them": "I want to bless them and make them thrive."[42] The problem is, however, that his *vocabulary* fails him. If it is already difficult to explain these different nuances of care to a native English-speaker, it is much harder even for him, who does not speak English like a native speaker (as Costello reproaches him later in the novel)[43] to explain to Marijana, whose English is much worse than his, how this kind of care is different from eros. Read in this way, *Slow Man* would be recovering certain practices of care, specifically caritas, in an age in which they have gone lost.

One should not forget, of course, that as such this becomes part in Coetzee's novel of a resistance against the administrations of the welfare state. The novel reveals itself to be a plea for private, family or family-like care, practiced outside of the administrations of the welfare state. That seems to be what enables Paul to retain a certain degree of independence: to be able to *give* in a meaningful way while he *receives* Marijana's care.[44]

Coetzee's novel thus raises powerful questions about different care-taking practices today. It asks about the loss of caritas with the emergence of the modern welfare state. In addition, it asks whether this loss ultimately dismantles the caring relation, which is one of giving and receiving. Paying taxes, the novel might thus be considered to suggest, is ultimately *not* a meaningful activity; supporting the education of the son of the nurse who is taking care of you *is*. To be taken care of by a nurse whose salary is paid by your tax-money might even be humiliating: for there is no personal relation and both the care-giver and care-taker feel entirely dependent on the welfare state. If there is a personal relation and one is able to give something back to one's care-taker, this feeling of dependence is attenuated and one is able to receive care because one is also giving it. This also entails a risk, however, for it creates conditions in which the care-giver and the care-taker are more closely linked than might be good for them. It creates a relation in which both are actually *involved* in the relation, unlike when they are taken care of by the welfare state (which does not care, or does not care in the same way a person does).

It might thus be that the caring relation can ultimately not be taken over by the state. Instead, the alienation of the state marks the end of the caring relation (care cannot survive such alienation). However, within such a perspective, Coetzee's novel does not represent a leap into "privatized"[45] (and still impersonal) care either. Instead, care is managed in Coetzee's novel within the family, and within a modern-day family of immigrants (Paul is ultimately not a part of Marijana's family, he is an immigrant among immigrants), which is a different kind of private care, with its own set of problems. This discourse is translated in the novel into questions about national community as well.[46] Could a system of care, such as the one Paul and Marijana somehow achieve—with all the risks it involves—be implemented at the level of the nation-state, without producing the alienation of the modern welfare state? Did such a system of care used to exist? Does it still exist, within certain communities? Or is it a fantasy that can as such exist only within the imagination of a novel? Can it perhaps only exist as a fantasy within the limits of the modern novel? Coetzee's novel invites one to reflect on the welfare state's modes of administering care and the risks it includes. They are opposite to the risks within the relation between Paul and Marijana. Whereas Paul and Marijana are too close, the state leaves them too distant.

From Pastoral Care to Biopolitics

All of these questions are highly relevant today, against the background of the ongoing healthcare debates both in the United States and abroad. *Slow Man* also investigates them in a historical fashion by linking the contemporary story of Paul Rayment to the theological story of Paul. The story of Paul's resistance against the modern welfare state is linked to a pastoral care that is associated in the novel with the New Testament. This is not, of course, a new connection. Michel Foucault already considered it in his lecture courses on biopolitics during the second half of the 1970s.[47] In order to understand where Foucault is coming from when he arrives at his discussion of pastoral care, and so as to ultimately do justice to his position on the welfare state (which has often been misrepresented), this chapter section develops a brief history of Foucault's engagement with biopolitics, both in the first volume of *The History of Sexuality* and in his lecture courses. I include such a history to present my understanding of Foucault's theory of biopolitics. As will be clear, Foucault's concept will be considerably stretched in this chapter and the following, when I discuss it in relation to the practice of novel-writing. In the context of this chapter, it is from a consideration of this history next to Coetzee's point about caritas that a pharmacological theory of care for our time can emerge.

As is by now well known, Foucault first talks about biopolitics in his lecture course *"Society Must Be Defended."*[48] There, Foucault states:

> At this point [in the early nineteenth century], the discourse whose history I would like to trace abandons the initial basic formulation, which was "We have to defend ourselves against our enemies because the State apparatuses, the law, and the power structures not only do not defend us against our enemies; they are the instruments our enemies are using to pursue and subjugate us". That discourse now disappears. It is no longer: "We have to defend ourselves against society", but "We have to defend society against all the biological threats posed by the other race, the subrace, the counterrace that we are, despite ourselves, bringing into existence".[49]

"At this point," Foucault continues, "we see the appearance of a State racism: a racism that society will direct against itself, against its own elements and its own products. This is the internal racism of permanent purification."[50]

The importance of this passage is revealed in the last lecture of the course, where Foucault talks about state racism again, now linking it to biopolitics. In this lecture, he describes what he refers to as "one of the basic phenomena of the nineteenth century," namely "power's hold over life."[51]

In the nineteenth century, "the biological came under State control" and Foucault sees in this development "one of the greatest transformations" that political right underwent at that time:

> I wouldn't say exactly that sovereignty's old right—to take life or let live—was replaced, but it came to be complemented by a new right which does not erase the old right but which does penetrate it, permeate it. This is the right, or rather precisely the opposite right. It is the power to "make" live and "let" die. The right of the sovereignty was the right to take life or let live. And then this new right is established: the right to make live and to let die.[52]

Distinguishing this new right from disciplinary power "which is addressed to bodies,"[53] Foucault goes on to note that this "new nondisciplinary power is applied not to man-as-body but to the living man, to man-as-living-being; ultimately, if you like, to man-as-species."[54] It is a power that targets the people as population. As such, he describes it as a "'biopolitics' of the human race."[55]

This analysis, which in the lecture course revolves around state racism, is repeated in the fifth part of *The History of Sexuality: An Introduction*. In this instance, however, the discussion revolves around sex. Titled "Right of Death and Power over Life," this part of the book fleshes out the historico-political analysis that was already developed in *"Society Must Be Defended."* "Since the classical age", Foucault writes, "the West has undergone a very profound transformation of power."[56] There has been a shift in the history of power,

> or at least a tendency [of power] to align itself with the exigencies of a life-administering power and to define itself accordingly. This death that was based on the right of the sovereign is now manifested as simply the reverse of the right of the social body to ensure, maintain, or develop its life.[57]

Today, we are dealing with a power that

> exerts a positive influence on life, that endeavors to administer, optimize, and multiply it, subjecting it to precise controls and comprehensive regulations. Wars are no longer waged in the name of a sovereign who must be defended; they are waged on behalf of the existence of everyone; entire populations are mobilized for the purpose of wholesale slaughter in the name of life necessity; massacres have become vital. It is as managers of life and survival, of bodies and the race, that so many regimes have been able to wage so many wars, causing so many men to be killed.[58]

Here too, Foucault distinguishes such a politics from disciplinary power—from what he calls "an *anatomo-politics of the human body*."[59] The new power is described in this text as "*a biopolitics of the population*."[60]

Although racism is still mentioned[61] as an important site of biopolitical analysis,[62] most of Foucault's analysis revolves around sex. At the crossroads of the disciplines of the body (anatomo-politics) and the regulation of populations (biopolitics), sex assumes unprecedented importance "as a political issue"[63]:

> It fitted in both categories at once, giving rise to infinitesimal surveillances, permanent controls, extremely meticulous orderings of space, indeterminate medical or psychological examinations, to an entire micro-power concerned with the body. But it gave rise as well to comprehensive measures, statistical assessments, and interventions aimed at the entire social body or at groups taken as a whole. Sex was a means of access both to the life of the body and the life of the species. It was employed as a standard for the disciplines and as a basis for regulations.[64]

These analyses of a biopolitics of race and sex have proved extremely productive, most recently not so much in terms of what they can contribute to the study of race and sex but in terms of the general theoretical framework they provide to study contemporary techniques of power. Although the *biopolitical* component of this framework appears to be more or less accepted across the board, scholars have argued *over just about everything else that comes with it*: biopolitics' historical origins; the meaning of the "life" that it targets; its dissociation from sovereignty; the meaning of the "politics" that it names; and so forth.

Part of this is no doubt due to the fact that Foucault never properly completed his work on biopolitics. Although he announces at the beginning of both his 1977–8 lecture course *Security, Territory, Population* and his 1978–9 lecture course *The Birth of Biopolitics* that this year, he would study what he had "somewhat vaguely" referred to as "bio-power,"[65] he would never tackle the issue of biopolitics head-on. Instead, the 1977–8 lecture course focused on the pastorate and governmentality. The following year, the course focused on neoliberalism.[66] It is ultimately left up to Foucault's audience to figure out how these topics relate to the issue of biopolitics.

If Foucault were alive today, he would undoubtedly point out the need to update his analyses of biopolitics—dating from the mid to late 1970s—in response to contemporary times. Several scholars have tried to do so: building on Wendy Brown's work on governmentality, Judith Butler has challenged Foucault's analytical distinction between sovereignty and governmentality and his call for us to "cut off the head of the king"[67] in political thought and analysis. If the post-September 11 era has shown us anything, it is that sovereignty is not quite dead yet.[68] In order to analyze a political phenomenon such as the Guantánamo Bay detention center, one needs to think sovereignty and governmentality *together*.[69] From a different perspective, Michael Dillon and Luis Lobo-Guerrero have looked at how the scientific redefinition of life since the 1970s has challenged Foucault's notion of biopolitics. Given the new understandings of life today—and given that power has morphed in response to these developments—surely one's understanding of biopolitics ought to transform as well. This imperative informs much of the analyses I present here, and especially the ways in which I use the term "biopolitics" in this book.

Given my analysis of *Slow Man*, it is interesting to note how in *Security, Territory, Population* the question of biopolitics transforms into an investigation of what Foucault calls governmentality and pastoral care. Foucault's point is powerful: working within the transition of sovereignty to governmentality that he laid out in previous courses—a transition of emphasis that does not overcome one model of power into another, as he insists—Foucault points out that modern power's success depends on its *governing less*. There is an economic rationale that comes to inform governance: economy becomes the episteme of governance. Power understands that it is not necessarily successful by implementing *more* laws; or by trying to save *all* of its subjects from dying of famine; or by investing *all* of its energies in defending its *territory*. Instead, power's keyword becomes "security," which is guaranteed by *frugal* government: by ensuring the freedom of subjects and goods, within the limits of programmed relations.

Successful governance therefore becomes possible "by a sort of '*laissez-faire*,'" Foucault says, "a certain 'freedom of movement (*laisser-passer*)', in the sense of 'letting things take their course.'"[70] A famine sometimes does not need to be prevented entirely (indeed, preventing it entirely might cost the state so much that it goes bankrupt). Instead, famine needs to be prevented to such an extent that the state does not go bankrupt and the people do not revolt. Following a cost-benefit analysis, one should in part *let things run their course*. In such a system, power is not exercised through laws, as Foucault insists in the *History of Sexuality*, but through norms. It is within the realms where we think we are free—that is, where power refrains from *positively* implementing itself—that we turn out to be most controlled.

Within such a context, power becomes more and more interested in domains that traditionally fall outside of the law, such as sex and race. Reproduction and health, for example, rise to power's center of attention. The question of modern health care, and of a state that takes care of the health of its population—in other words, the question of the welfare state and its representatives, such as Mrs. Putts—can be traced back to these seventeenth- and eighteenth-century developments. But, Foucault asks in his fifth lecture, what are the origins of these developments?

Here, he turns to the central concern of the course, namely "pastoral power."[71] Although Foucault uncovers some discussion of pastoral power in the Greeks, its development only really takes off with Christianity, a religion which "constitutes itself as a Church, that is to say, as an institution that claims to govern men in their daily life on the grounds of leading them to eternal life in the other world, and to do this not only on the scale of a definite group, of a city or a state, but of the whole of humanity."[72] Foucault is interested in this "government of souls"[73] as the origin of governmentality and, ultimately, biopolitics. However, with the government of souls we are still a long way removed from the biopolitical government of, say, the health of populations. Indeed, the pastorate will have to enter into a crisis in order for the properly biopolitical government of men to come about.

From the perspective of pharmacology, which will take up a more and more central place as we move along, it is worthwhile noting that some of the practices that are being discussed in the course as part of the pastoral care developing into biopolitics, return in Foucault's late work on the care of the self as potentially *curative* practices that constitute the broad range of techniques of the self that Foucault characterizes as an aesthetics of existence. This seems to suggest there is something in the development of biopolitics that can be recuperated from it, as a practice that is potentially curative. How might this insight relate to the reflection on the welfare state that I began above?

For this, I want to turn to a lecture from March 7, 1979 which is part of Foucault's 1978–9 lecture course at the Collège de France titled *The Birth of Biopolitics*. In it, as I have noted, Foucault was supposed to address the topic of biopolitics, which he had launched several years before and had promised to return to in his subsequent courses. And indeed, in his opening lecture Foucault announces that "I thought I could do a course on biopolitics"[74] this year. However, Foucault never delivered. Instead, the course focuses on neoliberalism. As Foucault acknowledges at the beginning of the March 7 lecture: "I would like to assure you that, in spite of everything, I really did intend to talk about biopolitics, and then, things being what they are, I have ended up talking, maybe for too long, about neo-liberalism."[75]

The reasons why Foucault is interested in neoliberalism are worth considering. "[W]hat is currently challenged," Foucault writes, "is almost always the state: the unlimited growth of the state, its omnipotence, its bureaucratic development, the state with the seeds of fascism it contains, the state's inherent violence beneath its social welfare paternalism."[76] He distinguishes between "two important elements which are fairly constant in this theme of the critique of the state"[77]: the first is the "intrinsic power of the state in relation to its object-target, civil society."[78] He is referring to what is perceived to be the state's hegemonic power to take over entirely its outside, namely civil society. The second element that returns again and again in what Foucault refers to as "state phobia" is

> that there is a kinship, a sort of genetic continuity or evolutionary implication between different forms of the state, with the administrative state, the welfare state, the bureaucratic state, the fascist state, and the totalitarian state all being, in no matter which of the various analyses, the successive branches of one and the same great tree of state control in its continuous and unified expansion.[79]

Foucault lays bare precisely the conflation of fascism and the welfare state that other scholars are also interested in.

Given Foucault's general take on the state, one would perhaps expect him to side with the anti-statism he is discussing. But that is not what happens in the lecture. Instead, Foucault goes on to severely criticize the two elements in state phobia that he has been discussing—the state's hegemonic relation to civil society, and the conflation of fascism with the welfare state—for putting in circulation "an inflationary critical value."[80] His critique is powerful and could be leveled directly against one of the anti-statists whose work will be discussed in Chapter Two, Giorgio Agamben:

> As soon as we accept the existence of this continuity or genetic kinship between different forms of the state, and as soon as we attribute a constant evolutionary dynamism to the state, it then becomes possible not only to use different analyses to support each other, but also to refer them back to each other and so deprive them of their specificity. For example, an analysis of social security and the administrative apparatus on which it rests ends up, via some slippages and thanks to some plays on words, referring us to the analysis of concentration camps. And, in the move from social security to concentration camps the requisite specificity of analysis is diluted.[81]

As Foucault sees it, the inflationary critique "allows one to practice what could be called a general disqualification by the worst."[82]

This constitutes an inflation not simply of the state but also of critique itself, for "it enables one to avoid paying the price of reality and actuality inasmuch as, in the name of this dynamism of the state, something like a kinship or danger, something like the great fantasy of the paranoiac and devouring state can always be found."[83] In such a fantasy, "there is no longer any need to analyze actuality."[84] This "elision of actuality" troubles Foucault, who insists again and again on the importance of the actual in his late work.[85]

Turning to the origins of this inflation of the state in neoliberalist discourse from 1930 until 1950, Foucault ultimately arrives at his own position. The passage is powerful:

> Well, against this inflationary critique of the state, against this kind of laxness [i.e., confusing fascism with the welfare state], I would like to suggest some theses which have been present, roughly, in what I have already said, but on which I would like to take a bit of a bearing. In the first place is the thesis that the welfare state has neither the same form, of course, nor, it seems to me, the same root or origin as the totalitarian state, as the Nazi, fascist, or Stalinist state. I would also like to suggest that the characteristic feature of the state we call totalitarian is far from being the endogenous intensification and extension of the mechanisms of the state; it is not at all the exaltation but rather a limitation, a reduction, and a subordination of the autonomy of the state, of its specificity and specific functioning … I am saying that we should not delude ourselves by attributing to the state itself a process of becoming fascist which is actually exogenous and due much more to the state's reduction and dislocation.[86]

In short, fascism and the (welfare) state are different.

It might not exactly be a defense of the welfare state, but it certainly is not anti-statism either. Instead, Foucault dismantles what he calls the "inflationary critique" of the state in order to call for a more careful analysis of actuality. Such a position suggests that he attributes some value, some currency, to the state—or at the very least to critique: to a critique that would not inflate the state but be able to see the difference between different forms of the state. The poison is thus *not* identical to the cure. Indeed, Foucault appears to go even further (and beyond Derrida?), suggesting that the one should *not at all* be tainted by the other.

Whereas *Slow Man*, a novel, rages against the welfare state and points out its potentially poisonous dimension—the fact that it has erased the practice of caritas from the history of care—, Foucault acknowledges the relation between theological care and the modern welfare state, but takes it up for the welfare state, against conflations of the welfare state and fascism. It is perhaps not yet a defense of the potentially curative aspects of the welfare state, but the position could certainly be read as the beginning of *a pharmacology of the welfare state* and its administrations: yes, there is poison in the welfare state, but that does not mean there is no cure.

It is already one thing for a novel to engage with these theoretical questions—and some might argue that novels should steer clear from pursuing them. Indeed, why treat these questions in the form of a novel? What could a novel possibly *add* to the theoretical investigation that Foucault offers in his course? This is where we reach the final stage of my argument: I want to suggest that by addressing these questions within the form of a novel, *Slow Man* is inviting us to consider the relation between these questions and the birth of the novel. In the following section of this chapter, I show that *Slow Man* takes the theoretical insights that I have developed to a new level when it considers their relevance for writing and for the history of the novel as a genre.

Elizabeth Costello's "Biologico-Literary Experiment"

After Paul has confessed his love to Marijana, and transgressed the limits of their relation of care, she does not return to work. But that does not mean that he returns to being on his own. Indeed, on the first day of Marijana's absence, Paul receives a visitor: it is Elizabeth Costello, the novelist. She is also a character from one of Coetzee's other novels, as I have already discussed. Costello's entrance upon the scene marks a strange break in the novel, and one through which all of the issues I have discussed so far suddenly become tied to the practice of novel-writing, and to the history of the novel as a genre. Indeed, it is at this point that several odd references earlier on in the novel to language, writing, chapters, and so on, begin to make sense.

From the opening scene of Paul's accident, there is a curious concern with language—with letters and with words. On his way to the hospital and the operating table, Paul hears the "*clack clack clack*" of a type-writer in the background. On page 14, the novel—which is focalized through Paul—suddenly includes a reference to "the opening of the chapter": "From the opening of the chapter, from the incident on Magill Road, he has not behaved well."[87] It is as if there is an awareness in the novel, and in Paul as well, that his life is being written, that his being is a being of language, that his life is structured in chapters, paragraphs, sentences.

This is also Costello's contribution to the novel. Entering upon the scene as "a doubting Thomas … wanting to explore for myself what kind of being you are,"[88] she reveals herself, on the one hand, to be the author out of whose imagination Paul's life has sprung. "'You came to me', she says,"[89] adding that she is not entirely in control of the lives she writes. Instead, she has to put up with her imagination's order of the day (there is some degree of *passive exposure* in the writing process; she is not *entirely* responsible for Paul's accident). However, that does not take away the feeling that Costello is in control of Paul's life, that she invented everything that has been happening to him since the beginning of the novel:

> Heavily, she reseats herself again, squares her shoulders, and begins to recite: "*The blow catches him from the right, sharp and surprising and painful, like a bolt of electricity, lifting him off the bicycle.* Relax!, *he tells himself as he tumbles through the air*, and so forth."[90]

Those are the opening lines of Coetzee's novel and of Paul Rayment's life. He has no life outside of this book. In that sense, he is different from Costello, who lives in another one of Coetzee's novels as well.

However, *Slow Man* also includes the suggestion that even though Costello may be a novelist, she and Paul are in the same boat. She, too, is ultimately a character in someone else's imagination. Thus, they become companions, stuck with each other and sharing the same, strange fate. Paul wants to get rid of her, but as Costello points out, it does not work like that: "For the foreseeable future, I am to accompany you."[91] Even though Paul has never met Costello before, they have thus become companions and he will have to put up with her until further notice.

The situation is frustrating and reinforces, in a way, something that has been recurring throughout the book, namely a reflection on automata. Paul thinks of himself as a "wooden puppet"[92] early on in the novel. A little later, he insists in a discussion with Marijana's daughter Ljuba about his prosthesis that "I have no screws in me. If I had screws I would be a mechanical man. Which I am not."[93] These references, which need to be read with reference to Paul's newly acquired status of dependence after the accident, also resonate with the profession of Marijana's husband, Miroslav "Mel" Jokic. As Costello explains, "[h]e was a technician, specializing in antique technology. He reassembled, for instance, a mechanical duck that had lain in parts … for two hundred years, rusting. Now it quacks like a regular duck, it waddles, it lays eggs."[94] In Australia, the man works for a *car* company (his wife is in the *care* business). The novel's suggestion that Costello is writing Paul's life reinforces the suggestion that Paul, contrary to his own insistence, is a mechanical man, one whose life is being written by someone other than himself. That other one might be Costello. Or it might be that Costello's life, too, is being written by that other person (and so on and so forth). Suddenly, the novel's questions about care and about whether life with one leg is worth living take a different turn: what about a life that is not a life of flesh and blood, but character-life? What kind of life is this? Is this a life worth living?[95]

This question, in turn, powerfully connects with Foucault's theorization of governmentality, as a power that operates through *laissez-faire*, by allowing its subjects and goods to move freely within the limits of certain programmed regulations. By playing out its reflection on pastoral care and the welfare state at a meta-fictional level, *Slow Man* invites the reader to reflect on the novel's relation to the history of care that it has laid out. Indeed, given that Foucault, when he is discussing the rise of governmentality and biopolitics, is mainly talking about the seventeenth, eighteenth, and especially the nineteenth centuries, it is worth noticing that the rise of governmentality coincides with the rise of the novel, starting with what is generally taken to be the first novel in English, Daniel Defoe's *Robinson Crusoe*. This novel, first published in 1719, might very well have to be reread in this light, as a novel that is not so much about Crusoe establishing sovereignty over his island and over Friday, but as a text that, as the very first English-language novel, already reflects on its author's governmental power-relation to its characters.[96] As the first English-language novel, and as the literary form par excellence of the modern era, *Robinson Crusoe* might thus capture something of the developments in power that Foucault is describing.

Early on in *Slow Man*, Paul mentions Robinson Crusoe, saying that "I am not Robinson Crusoe"[97]—and indeed, Paul and Crusoe are of course very different characters. On what grounds does Paul insist on the difference? Unlike Crusoe, Paul has friends. He simply *prefers not to* ask them to take care of him. There is some tragic irony to the Crusoe-statement, given that his struggle to remain independent from the welfare state in spite of having lost a leg resonates with Crusoe's situation: it is as if Paul, after having been shipwrecked, chooses to be on Crusoe's island when there is some degree of land and civilization in close reach.

However, I would argue that the irony also has a meta-fictional twist: Paul is very much like Robinson Crusoe in the sense that his life is also the life of a character in a novel. Crusoe may have been the master of his island, but his life was still being written by Defoe. In spite of all his attempts to attain sovereignty, his precious self-governance was still exposed to the whims and wants of Defoe. Crusoe's relation to Friday, whom is described in Defoe's novel as "my New Companion"—"I was greatly delighted with him and made it my Business to teach him every Thing, that was proper to make him useful, handy, and helpful; but especially to make him speak, and understand me when I spake, and he was the aptest Schollar that ever was"[98]—, can thus easily be read as an allegory of the author's relation to the character, in which Crusoe, like Elizabeth Costello, is himself caught up.[99] The author, then, becomes aligned with government, in Foucault's history; the characters with modern subjects. In such a history of the novel, the novel comes to exist in close proximity to biopolitics.

One might argue that I am making too much of a single reference to Robinson Crusoe in *Slow Man*. But I am confronting this thematic because it is a recurring concern in Coetzee's *oeuvre*. Indeed, Coetzee has produced a contemporary rewriting of the Crusoe story, a high postmodernist tale that revolves exactly around the strange concerns with authorial power and character-life that I am laying out. Published in 1986, that story—titled *Foe*—does not yet address quite as forcefully the biopolitical concerns related to pastoral care and the welfare state that are central to *Slow Man*. In Coetzee's Nobel Lecture "He and His Man"—which can be read as a summary statement of Coetzee's writerly project—, Robinson Crusoe is a central reference as well.[100]

So as to give a just little more literary critical substance to the (for some readers no doubt rather fantastic) hypothesis that I am uncovering in Coetzee's work, I propose to turn to an early example of novel theory that Coetzee has mentioned on occasion,[101] Ian Watt's *The Rise of the Novel: Studies in Defoe, Richardson, and Fielding*. Reading Watt's classic text, one notes that Watt's descriptions of what he considers the novel as a genre to accomplish, resonate with Foucault's theorization of governmentality and biopolitics (even though Watt is, of course, no Foucauldian in his approach to the novel-genre). Watt argues in this book that "[t]he novel is in nothing so characteristic of our culture as in the way that it reflects [the] characteristic orientation of modern thought."[102] But what is this orientation? Defoe and Richardson are praised as "the first great writers in our literature" because "they did not take their plots from mythology, history, legend, or previous literature."[103] Instead, plot becomes "total[ly] subordinat[ed] to the pattern of the autobiographical memoir."[104] The novel's characteristic tense is "the present tense."[105] With the rise of the novel, everyday life—the present—works its way into the text. Such a shift from myth, history, legend, or previous literature to an original, life-like tale is connected with a shift from universals to particulars. With the novel, literature suddenly becomes interested in the lives of particular individuals. Watt's account also reveals, however, that the individuality of these figures is only illusory. He notes, for example, that although a character in a novel is given a name that sounds like an ordinary, realistic one, this name is at the same time "subtly appropriate and suggestive"[106] (his example is Richardson's Mrs. *Sin*-clair). His general point is clear though: writing a novel becomes equal to "the production of what purports to be an authentic account of the actual experiences of individuals."[107] In this mindset, the writer's "exclusive aim is to make words bring his object home to us in all its concrete particularity whatever the cost in repetition or parenthesis or verbosity."[108]

It certainly sounds like a governmental project: as a literary form, the novel, and its desire to write the lives of ordinary people, could only be born from a similar mentality as the one Foucault describes in his lectures on governmentality and biopolitics. To govern the lives of ordinary people—to program their freedom of movement, regulate their health and reproduction, foster their life until the point of death—is both the project of governmentality and in a certain sense that of the novel. From this perspective, one can indeed think of the novel as what Costello calls a "biologico-literary experiment"[109]: in it, writers are experimenting with the governmentality that would become the political order of the day. The novel is exposed as a tense experiment in the governance of the present.[110]

Given that this mentality originates in pastoral care (associated with the caritas that Costello and Paul are attached to) and will ultimately translate into the welfare state (which Foucault defends), the novel thus takes up an important position within these developments, as a literary form of governmentality that is in between caritas and the welfare state. This is exactly where Coetzee situates it in *Slow Man*. But it is an insight that informs his more explicit rewritings of the Robinson Crusoe story as well.

In *Foe*, Coetzee rewrites the Robinson Crusoe story from the perspective of a woman who is cast away on Crusoe's island. Many have considered the novel from a postcolonial or feminist perspective, but the most convincing reading, in my view, comes from those critics who look at the text as a metafictional allegory of the writing situation—Lewis MacLeod's article "Do We of Necessity Become Puppets in a Story?" is exemplary here, and anticipates in many ways the argument that I am making about *Slow Man*.[111] *Foe* is ultimately a novel about a character, Susan Barton, who is trying to come to terms with what it means to have no substance other than textual substance. She suffers—like many characters in eighteenth-century fiction; but *from being a character*. Thus, she begs the author in *Foe*, a man called Daniel Foe, to press on with his writing so that her life will no longer be "drearily suspended."[112] This relation between author and character is cast in the novel as a legal and political relation. Still strongly invested in sovereignty—this is one of the main differences between *Foe* and the much later *Slow Man*—the novel explicitly takes the law as one of its central themes: first, Cruso's (Coetzee's spelling) law on the island; and once Susan and Friday have returned to England, the law represented by the bailiffs occupying Foe's house. But there is also the law of Foe's writing, which Susan would like to break but cannot. It is perhaps this law that ultimately comes closest to God's law, the law of the conjurer ("the brewer," as suggested on page 75; or "the author," page 91), who employs a secret code of writing that the characters cannot read. "May it not be," Susan muses, "that God continually writes the world and all that is in it?"[113] And, in a series of questions that resonate with the conversations between Paul and Elizabeth Costello in *Slow Man*: "[w]ho am I and who indeed are you? … I am doubt itself. Who is speaking me? Am I a phantom too? To what order do I belong? And you, who are you?"[114]

These questions—characteristic of high postmodernist fiction—are central to *Slow Man* as well, but they are worked out more powerfully there, in the context of an investigation of pastoral care and biopolitics. Indeed, having gone through Ian Watt's theory of the novel and Coetzee's earlier *Foe*, one begins to get a sense of the political swing of Paul's suggestion that his life might be no more than a novelist's "biologico-literary experiment." As such, this experiment is not represented too positively in *Slow Man*. I argue that by associating the novel with Foucaultian biopolitics, *Slow Man* appears to adopt Foucault's critique of biopolitics, which translates itself in the novel as a rage against Costello and the welfare state. Although Foucault is highly critical of biopolitics, he would not quite follow Paul all the way, as my references to Foucault's discussion of the welfare state have shown. And indeed, it is not as if Paul does not benefit from the welfare state and the novel either. As he notes at several points throughout the book, if it were not for the welfare state, he would never have met Marijana. He owes his entire life—its sorrows but also its pleasures—to the novel. It is through the novel that he is capable of recovering caritas from the administrations of the welfare state. That is, of course, not nothing. In the final section of this chapter, I want to consider in more detail the practices of care that the novel uncovers within the limits of biopolitics.

The Politics of Companionship

> A phrase from catechism class a half-century ago floats into his mind: *There shall be no more man and woman, but…* But what—what shall we be when we are beyond man and woman? Impossible for the mortal mind to conceive. One of the mysteries.
>
> The words are St Paul's he is sure of that—St Paul his namesake, his name-saint, explaining what the afterlife will be like, when all shall love with a pure love, as God loves, only not as fiercely, as consumingly.[115]
>
> —J. M. Coetzee, *Slow Man*

The phrase is indeed from Paul's Letter to the Galatians. Paul, however, finishes the sentence: "There is neither male nor female;" he writes, "for you are all one in Christ Jesus."[116] In Coetzee's novel, Christ Jesus is Paul Rayment. Elizabeth Costello describes herself in relation to him and his peculiar being as a doubting Thomas. Paul aligns himself with Jesus when he talks about caritas and the fact that he does not "want to hurt Jesus any more by [his] actions"—from now on, he only wants to extend a protective, blessing, helping hand.[117] Within the logic of this parallel, this means that beyond man and woman, there is Paul: a character in a novel. In this realm of being, it is no longer a question of male or female, or master or slave (this is why feminist or postcolonial readings of *Foe*,[118] which insist on either women or colonial subjects as "the other" in Coetzee's writings, ultimately miss the point): the issue is that of character-being, in which all of us become one. *There shall be no more man and woman, but*… characters. That is what is "[i]mpossible for the mortal mind to conceive." It is character-being that is presented here as "one of the mysteries." It is, Coetzee suggests, ultimately in the being of the character that our human condition is most deeply, most intensely explored. In this sense, the character—familiar, yet at the same time utterly strange; *uncanny*—is one of fiction's greatest mysteries. How to explain the liveliness of its life, the fact that one cares about characters, sometimes more so than about real people, in spite of the fact that they are not real (as we know very well…)?[119] What questions for ethics and politics does the aesthetic being of the character pose?

The question might appear silly to many readers, but it is central to Coetzee's creative project; my argument in this chapter is that, given the novel's relation to governmentality and biopolitics, it matters a great deal more than has been acknowledged. Given the novel's complicity with governmentality, the situation of the character can be said to allegorize the modern, biopolitical condition—that is, the condition of being subjected to the government of life in its most intimate details—in its full pharmacological swing. One's pull into literature could then be explained from two directions: *from above*—we all enjoy being authors, being in the position of government, and seeing how character-lives unfold within the novel's programmed regulations[120]; and (second) *from below*—we identify with characters, we recognize in their governed lives our own biopolitical condition. The novel enables us, in other words, to experience the essentially modern condition of both being the subject of and being subjected to. This split, which Stathis Gourgouris has argued to be characteristic of modernity,[121] defines the novel better than any other literary genre, precisely because it deals with the lives of ordinary people. In this sense, the novel marks the point where myth turns into something else, or where the lives of ordinary individuals become mythical.

Coetzee himself explores these questions most succinctly in a text that has received relatively little commentary so far,[122] namely his Nobel Lecture

"He and His Man." It is a brilliant statement of his literary program, and one that is prefaced, very tellingly, by a quote from Defoe's *Robinson Crusoe* (it is the passage in which Crusoe describes Friday as his new companion that I have quoted earlier on). The text is set in England, and begins with a discussion of "decoy ducks or duckoys,"[123] ducks that are used to capture other ducks. Fed by hand, these ducks are sent out to other countries where they mingle with ducks in worse circumstances, and "fail not to let them know, in a form of language which they make them understand, that in England from where they come the case is quite different"[124]: there, they are fed by hand, and properly cared for. And so these other ducks follow them back to England, where they are captured. It is a preface to another story about executions in Halifax:

> Custom had it in Halifax, though, that if between the knocking out of the pin and the descent of the blade the condemned man could leap to his feet, run down the hill, and swim across the river without being seized again by the executioner, he would be let free. But in all the years the engine [of execution] stood in Halifax this never happened.[125]

Both these stories are written by a character referred to in the lecture as "his man."

After the Halifax story, however, we shift to "he," who "sits in his room by the waterside in Bristol and reads this."[126] He used to live in more summery climes—there is a reference to the "skin of his face" being "almost blackened by the trip sun."[127] When the text includes a reference to a parrot, squawking "Poor Robin! … Poor Robin Crusoe! Who shall save poor Robin?," the reader understands that we are dealing with yet another version of Robinson Crusoe in Coetzee's *oeuvre*. There is the mention of a wife, as well as of "poor Friday."[128]

However, as the reference to his man reveals, something interesting is going on: Crusoe, the archetypical *character*, is turned here into an *author*. "He does not read," Coetzee writes,

> he has lost the taste for it; but the writing of his adventures has put him in the habit of writing, it is a pleasant enough recreation. In the evening by candlelight he will take out his papers and sharpen his quills and write a page or two of his man … this busy man of his.[129]

Crusoe is compared here to the author—I worked within this comparison earlier on when I suggested Defoe's novel can be read as a meta-fictional allegory of the author/character relation, with Crusoe being the author and Friday the character—, but one who has a "man" working for him, a "busy man" who sends him reports. This sounds like Elizabeth Costello receiving reports about Paul Rayment. They come to her, from outside her command. And so he sets out to invent his man, this man who sends him reports—"what species of man can it be who will dash so busily hither and thither across the kingdom, from one spectacle of death to another ... sending in report after report?"[130]

And then, a few lives of his man are invented: it is Coetzee's most explicit demonstration of the governmental, biopolitical logic of novel-writing yet. "Make him prosperous," the first narrative goes; "then bring his happiness suddenly to an end."[131] "[Give] him much happiness, until the plague descends upon the city" where he is living.[132] "It is an allegory!" a character in this second narrative is crying—and indeed, that is what the reader must have gathered by now. Robinson Crusoe, the character in Defoe's novel, is cast as a novelist who is writing the lives of characters such as himself, "poor Robin Crusoe." But, the text continues, there is one thing about this whole arrangement that is hard to understand: "How then has it come about that this man of his, who is a kind of parrot and not much loved, writes as well as or better than his master? For he wields an able pen, this man of his, no doubt of that." Quoting from his man's reports, he notes that "[o]nly when he yields himself up to this man of his do such words come."[133] If one is dealing here with a Hegelian master–slave dialectic, as some critics have suggested with reference to the meta-fictional dimension of Coetzee's *oeuvre*, this is the moment of reversal where it is revealed that the master in fact depends upon the slave, who performs the labor and is a much happier character. His man in fact rises above him when it comes to writing, even if he is the writer. Crusoe the character rises above Crusoe the author, undoing the upgrade from character to author that the lecture seemed to accomplish.

In the final instance, however, both Crusoe the author and Crusoe the character are Coetzee's inventions, of course, in the same way that Costello and Paul Rayment are both Coetzee's inventions. In this sense, they are all in the same boat. It is this metaphor of seafaring that ultimately comes to dominate the lecture. For he begins to ask himself whether he and his man will ever meet (a fascinating, M. C. Escher-like question: will Crusoe the author ever confront Crusoe the character?). "How are they to be figured, this man and he? As master and slave? As brothers, twin brothers? As comrades in arms? Or as enemies, foes?"[134]

> But he fears that there will be no meeting, not in this life. If he must settle on a likeness for the pair of them, his man and he, he would write that they are like two ships sailing in contrary directions, one west, the other east. Or better, they are deckhands toiling in the rigging, the one on a ship sailing west, the other on a ship sailing east. Their ships pass

> close, close enough to hail. But the seas are rough, the weather is stormy: their eyes lashed by the spray, their hands burned by the cordage, they pass each other by, too busy even to wave.[135]

It seems that, according to this text at least, there will be no meeting. The closest they can come to it is likely in novels such as *Foe* or *Slow Man*, which directly address this problematic. Ultimately, the realm of fiction and the realm of real life, although closely connected allegorically, can never meet. Instead, they pass each other by, too busy to even acknowledge each other. Of course, with a text such as *Slow Man*, one is forced to slow down and acknowledge the passing—and something is glimpsed in these moments. Although this something might appear to belong in the high postmodernist era, and although it might appear to be the stuff that only fictions are made of, I have tried to show in this chapter that this something is also politically significant, and provides insights into our modern, biopolitical condition. This point is made in much more explicitly biological terms by Kazuo Ishiguro's novel *Never Let Me Go*, which will be the focus of the next chapter.

Before the novel is entirely identified with a logic of governmental biopolitics that Foucault's work (as well as the work of others writing in his tracks) has taught us to approach with suspicion, it is worth noting Crusoe's remark that "the writing of his adventures has put him in the habit of writing, it is a pleasant enough recreation." Here, we move towards Foucault's aesthetic of existence, which invites us to read Defoe's novel in a different light, as a novel not simply of imprisonment but also of individuation. This story is well known—it is, indeed, the traditional reading that *Robinson Crusoe* has received.[136] In *Slow Man* as well, something becomes possible through writing, through the novel: for Paul ultimately takes his leave from Costello, to go his own way. That is what several characters in the novel, including Costello herself, had been urging him to do. He himself, speaking in line with his resistance to the welfare state and the governmental logic of biopolitics, states that "there is no need for us to adhere to any script; we are free agents."[137] Echoing the doctor's remark early on in the novel that "it is not one of those situations where you have a choice," Marijana's son, Drago, tells him that "you can choose."[138] Has Paul undergone a development by this point? Has he changed? His basic attitude—his wanting to be independent, and his resistance against the welfare state and its administrations of care, including the governmentality of the novel—has not. But there are some insights precisely about the novel's complicity with biopolitics, and then also about caritas and the management of care, that he would otherwise not have had. The novel is thus also a care-*ful* practice that resists its complicity with governmentality.

It is in this context that Marijana's profession ultimately becomes meaningful: as Costello explains, "[s]he spent two years at the Art Institute in Dubrovnik and came away with a diploma in restoration"[139]—so she is actually an art restorer. No wonder that Paul can settle into her administrations. A work of art himself, he could not have been in better hands. And although Coetzee's novel draws out the cruelties of an author inventing a character like Paul Rayment, who in the opening pages of *Slow Man* suffers such a terrible fate (it sounds like *narrative cruelty* rather than *narrative care*), the novel also shows that something becomes possible through these cruelties—something that exceeds the fantastic nature of the violence that the novel also wields. Indeed, given the characters that Coetzee makes his readers put up with (they are rarely likable) one might begin to wonder about the "ethics" that informs his narrative practice, specifically about whether it can at all be associated with narrative care.

But surely, one must resist, in one's theorization of care, an understanding of care that would only be limited to the beautiful, the interesting, the wealthy, and so on—a gentrified notion of care. Indeed, it may very well be that care properly conceived is precisely care for and by those by whom one would prefer not to be accompanied. In this sense, to read Coetzee's novels is to undergo a profound experience of care: for in order to take in the compelling beauty of the work, one must put up with dislikable characters, whose company one would, under normal circumstances, prefer to avoid. And yet, one sticks with them, one comes to care for them and to be taken care by them nevertheless. It is in this way, too, that Coetzee's work presents its readers with an ethics of companionship, one that, considered in the way I have done here, takes on a deeper, political meaning that I will continue to explore in the next chapters.

Notes

1 J. M. Coetzee, *Slow Man* (New York: Viking, 2005), 111.
2 Coetzee, *Slow*, 192.
3 Ibid., 1.
4 Ibid., 5.
5 Ibid.
6 See Eric Paul Meljac, "The Poetics of Dwelling: A Consideration of Heidegger, Kafka, and Michael K," in *Journal of Modern Literature* 32: 1 (2008): 75n. 4.
7 Acts 9.3–6 (Revised Standard Version).
8 See Alain Badiou, *Saint Paul: The Foundation of Universalism*, trans. Ray

Brassier (Stanford: Stanford University Press, 2003); Giorgio Agamben, *The Time that Remains: A Commentary on the* Letter to the Romans, trans. Patricia Dailey (Stanford: Stanford University Press, 2005); Slavoj Zizek, *The Puppet and the Dwarf: The Perverse Core of Christianity* (Cambridge, MA: MIT Press, 2003).

9 For this, see the introduction to this book.

10 For other explorations of the novel's relation to the welfare state, see: Bruce Robbins, *Upward Mobility and the Common Good* (Princeton: Princeton University Press, 2008); Michael Szalay, *New Deal Modernism* (Durham, NC: Duke University Press, 2005). See also *Occasion* 1 (2009): http://arcade.stanford.edu/journals/occasion/, on "States of Welfare."

11 Coetzee, *Slow*, 114.

12 Jean Baudrillard, *The Agony of Power*, trans. Ames Hodges (Los Angeles: Semiotext(e), 2010), 88.

13 Coetzee, *Slow*, 16.

14 Ibid.

15 Ibid., 17.

16 Ibid., 10.

17 Ibid., 22.

18 Ibid., 22–3.

19 Ibid., 23.

20 Ibid.

21 Ibid., 24.

22 Ibid., 28.

23 Ibid., 32.

24 Ibid., 35. Both the crutches and the Zimmer-frame are, of course, prostheses of a kind; the Zimmer-frame recalls Immanuel Kant's reference to a *Gängelwagen* or "walking frame" in his text "What is Enlightenment?" Kant refers to it there when he is arguing that enlightened subjects should learn to walk alone, without the help of a frame. See Immanuel Kant, "What is Enlightenment?," in Michel Foucault, *The Politics of Truth* (Los Angeles: Semiotext(e), 2007), 29–37. Michel Foucault's most extended analysis of this text, where he discusses Kant's use of the word *Gängelwagen*, is part of his lecture course on *The Government of Self and Others*. See Michel Foucault, *Le Gouvernement de soi et des autres: Cours au Collège de France, 1982–1983* (Paris: Gallimard, 2008).

25 Coetzee, *Slow*, 43.

26 Ibid., 44.

27 Ibid., 50.

28 Ibid., 63.

29 Kirby Dick's documentary film *Private Practices: The Story of a Sex Surrogate* (New York: Zeitgeist, 1986) approaches precisely this borderline between care and eros.

30 Coetzee, *Slow*, 76.

31 Ibid., 79.
32 Paul offers to pay for the college education of Drago, Marijana's son; when Marijana's daughter, Blanka, is accused of shoplifting, he settles the matter with the shopkeeper by buying 500 dollars worth of gear.
33 See ibid., 156.
34 There is a small section on Heidegger and care in Charles Sarvan, "'Disgrace': A Path to Grace?," in *World Literature Today* 78: 1 (2004): 28. Eric Paul Meljac has also commented on the importance of care in Coetzee's work in "The Poetics of Dwelling."
35 See J. M. Coetzee, *Life and Times of Michael K* (New York: Penguin, 1985); J. M. Coetzee, *Waiting for the Barbarians* (New York: Vintage, 2000); J. M. Coetzee, *Disgrace* (New York: Vintage, 1999).
36 J. M. Coetzee, *Elizabeth Costello* (New York: Viking, 2003), 147.
37 Coetzee, *Costello*, 148.
38 Ibid.
39 Ibid., 149.
40 Ibid., 150.
41 Ibid., 154.
42 Coetzee, *Slow*, 156.
43 Ibid., 231.
44 In addition to Heidegger's discussion of "*Dasein*'s Being as Care" in *Being and Time* (Martin Heidegger, *Being and Time*, trans. John MacQuarrie and Edward Robinson (New York: Harper Perennial, 2008), 235), the questions about taking, giving, and receiving care that I raise here also resonate with the problematic of the gift as it has been developed in a closely related series of anthropological writings on the subject, starting with Marcel Mauss' essay on the gift. I have discussed the relevance of these writings (ranging from Mauss to Claude Lévi-Strauss and Jacques Derrida) for Coetzee's novel *Disgrace* in the third chapter of my *States of Exception in the Contemporary Novel: Martel, Eugenides, Coetzee, Sebald* (New York: Continuum, 2012).
45 I use the word here to refer to health care offered by private companies.
46 Although I do not have time to discuss this aspect of the novel in full, I want to single out two possible sites of analysis: first, there is the fact that Drago, Marijana's son, forges some of the historical photographs in Paul's collection documenting Australia's history of immigration, by photoshopping into them the faces of his family members (see Coetzee, *Slow*, 245). Second, the novel contains a long discussion between Costello and Paul about Paul's origins, the fact that he ultimately remains a foreigner in Australia. The discussion focuses on language, and draws out the novel's meta-fictional point: Paul does not speak from the heart, he speaks like a book; Costello proposes to teach him to speak from the heart (see ibid., 231).
47 I thus link Coetzee's work here to biopolitics; other Foucauldian aspects

of his *oeuvre*, for example the importance of discipline in his novels, have been discussed. See, for example, Patrick Lenta, "Discipline in *Disgrace*," in *Mosaic* 43: 3 (2010): 1–16. Some critics have talked about Coetzee in relation to biopolitics, but the focus here has been on the work of Giorgio Agamben. See Catherine Mills, "Life Beyond Law: Biopolitics, Law and Futurity in Coetzee's *Life and Times of Michael K*," in *Griffith Law Review* 15: 1 (2006): 177–95; Duncan McColl Chesney, "Toward an Ethics of Silence: Michael K," in *Criticism* 49: 3 (2007): 307–25.

48 Michel Foucault, *"Society Must Be Defended": Lectures at the Collège de France 1975–1976*, trans. David Macey, ed. Arnold I. Davidson (New York: Picador, 2001).

49 Foucault, *"Society,"* 61–2.

50 Ibid., 62.

51 Ibid., 239.

52 Ibid., 241.

53 Ibid., 242.

54 Ibid., 242.

55 Ibid., 243.

56 Michel Foucault, *The History of Sexuality: An Introduction*, Vol. I, trans. Robert Hurley (New York: Vintage, 1990), 136.

57 Foucault, *History*, 136.

58 Ibid., 137.

59 Ibid., 139.

60 Ibid.

61 Ibid., 149–50.

62 Contrary to what Giorgio Agamben claims in the introduction to *Homo Sacer: Sovereign Power and Bare Life*, Foucault *does* dwell here (albeit very briefly) on the question of Nazism and the camps, and I explore this connection in more detail in the next chapter. See Giorgio Agamben, *Homo Sacer: Sovereign Power and Bare Life*, trans. Daniel Heller-Roazen (Stanford: Stanford University Press, 1998), 4.

63 Foucault, *History*, 145.

64 Ibid., 145–6.

65 Michel Foucault, *Security, Territory, Population: Lectures at the Collège de France 1977–1978*, trans. Graham Burchell, ed. Arnold I. Davidson (New York: Picador, 2007).

66 See Michel Foucault, *The Birth of Biopolitics: Lectures at the Collège de France 1978–1979*, trans. Graham Burchell, ed. Arnold I. Davidson (New York: Picador, 2008).

67 Foucault, *History*, 89.

68 I will return to this point in my book *Plastic Sovereignties: Giorgio Agamben and the Politics of Aesthetics*.

69 See Judith Butler, "Indefinite Detention," in Judith Butler, *Precarious Life: The Powers of Mourning and Violence* (New York: Verso, 2004), 50–100.

70 Foucault, *Security*, 41.
71 Ibid., 123.
72 Ibid., 148.
73 Ibid., 151.
74 Foucault, *Birth of Biopolitics*, 21.
75 Ibid., 185.
76 Ibid., 186–7.
77 Ibid., 187.
78 Ibid.
79 Ibid.
80 Ibid.
81 Ibid. 188.
82 Ibid.
83 Ibid.
84 Ibid.
85 I have discussed the importance of this notion, and the problems of translation it poses, in "The Allegory of the Cage," *Foucault Studies* 10 (2010): 7–22: http://rauli.cbs.dk/index.php/foucault-studies/article/viewFile/3124/3288
86 Foucault, *Birth of Biopolitics*, 192–3.
87 Coetzee, *Slow*, 14–15.
88 Ibid., 81.
89 Ibid.
90 Ibid.
91 Ibid., 84.
92 Ibid., 27.
93 Ibid., 56.
94 Ibid., 86.
95 Some of my readers might think such questions are silly, but Coetzee is fascinated by them, as evidenced by his review of Defoe's *An Essay on the History and Reality of Apparitions*: J. M. Coetzee, Rev. of Defoe, Daniel. *An Essay on the History and Reality of Apparitions*, in *Common Knowledge* 15: 1 (2009): 92–3.
96 Gregg Lambert has suggested this can be expanded into a reflection on Crusoe's aesthetics of existence as well—think of Crusoe's diary writing, for example, which is included in Defoe's novel.
97 Coetzee, *Slow*, 14.
98 Daniel Defoe, *Robinson Crusoe* (New York: Random House, 2001), 194.
99 The discussion of allegory in relation to Coetzee's work is long standing and I cannot possibly summarize it here. Suffice it so say that I am moving away from postcolonial or feminist allegorical readings in order to consider Coetzee's work as a meta-fictional allegory—that too, has of course been done. Mark Sanders summarizes some of the debates in

his review of Derek Attridge's *J. M. Coetzee and the Ethics of Reading*, in *Modern Fiction Studies* 53: 3 (2007): 641–5.

100 See J. M. Coetzee, "He and His Man": http://nobelprize.org/nobel_prizes/literature/laureates/2003/coetzee-lecture-e.html

101 See Joanna Scott, "Voice and Trajectory: An Interview with J. M. Coetzee" in *Salmagundi* 114/115 (1997): 97–8.

102 Ian Watt, *The Rise of the Novel: Studies in Defoe, Richardson, and Fielding* (Harmondsworth: Penguin, 1970), 22.

103 Watt, *Rise*, 14.

104 Ibid., 15.

105 Ibid., 25.

106 Ibid., 20.

107 Ibid., 28.

108 Ibid., 30.

109 Coetzee, *Slow*, 114.

110 Watt's insistence on the "present tense" cannot be given enough emphasis in this context. It is worth noting that the organizers of the second Seminar of Experimental Critical Theory at the University of California, Irvine chose to title the seminar, which dealt with biopolitics, *Present Tense* (http://uchri.org/Initiatives/SECT/2/). Though the title is obviously a reference to our explosive contemporary biological and political situation, it is worth noticing the connection between the title and the simple form of the verb, whose use Watt considers to be characteristic of the novel.

111 See Lewis MacLeod, "'Do We of Necessity Become Puppets in a Story?': or Narrating the World: On Speech, Silence and Discourse in J. M. Coetzee's *Foe*," in *Modern Fiction Studies* 52: 1 (2006): 1–18.

112 J. M. Coetzee, *Foe* (New York: Penguin, 1986), 63.

113 Coetzee, *Foe*, 143.

114 Ibid., 133.

115 Coetzee, *Slow*, 33.

116 Gal. 3.28 (Revised Standard Version).

117 Coetzee, *Slow*, 156.

118 Fiona Probyn summarizes some of these debates in her article "J. M. Coetzee: Writing with/out Authority," in *Jouvert: a Journal of Postcolonial Studies* 6.3 (2002): english.chass.ncsu.edu/jouvert/v7is1/probyn.htm

119 On this, see Blakey Vermeule, *Why Do We Care about Literary Characters?* (Baltimore: Johns Hopkins University Press, 2009).

120 This is, most likely, also why we read the news, where the lives of people are narrativized as if they are part of a novel. The newspapers are, in this sense, the most extreme expression of language's relation to modern, biopolitical governmentality. A particularly keen insight into this is delivered by works of fiction that explore the ways in which journalists "make" the news, that is, create the stories on which they ultimately come to report—thus, we ultimately do not read real-life stories, but stories

that are made up with real life. The 2011 scandal with the British tabloids illustrates this well.

121 See Stathis Gourgouris, *Does Literature Think? Literature as Theory for an Antimythical Era* (Stanford: Stanford University Press, 2003).

122 I can refer to two relevant ones. See Gareth Cornwell, " 'He and His Man': Allegory and Catachresis in J. M. Coetzee's Nobel Lecture," in *English in Africa* 33: 2 (2006): 97–114. Cornwell considers *Slow Man* in this article as a novel about "a struggle of control [between Rayment and Costello] over the unfolding plot" (100). See also Derek Attridge, "A Writer's Life," in *The Virginia Quarterly Review* 80: 4 (2004). Attridge relates the lecture to *Elizabeth Costello* and the issue of realism that the book raises, but he pursues the ethical, not the biopolitical track.

123 Coetzee, "He and His Man," 2.

124 Ibid., 2.

125 Ibid., 3.

126 Ibid.

127 Ibid.

128 Ibid.

129 Ibid., 4.

130 Ibid.

131 Ibid.

132 Ibid., 4–5.

133 Ibid., 6.

134 Ibid., 8.

135 Ibid. The passage is reminiscent of Maurice Blanchot's récit *The One Who Was Standing Apart From Me* (*Celui qui ne m'accompagnait pas*—the original French title includes the reference to the word "companion"). The reference to Blanchot is on the mark, since he arguably belongs to a wave of French authors who have challenged and reinvented the genre of the novel: one can think also of his contemporaries, Georges Bataille and Pierre Klossowski. As Susan Sontag in an essay about Natalie Sarraute and the *nouveau roman* points out, that wave of authors was followed by a second one "of books written in the 1950s, by (among others) Michel Butor, Alain Robbe-Grillet, Claude Simon, and Nathalie Sarraute": Susan Sontag, *Against Interpretation* (New York: Delta, 1964), 104. I will return to Robbe-Grillet in Chapters Three and Four.

136 Patrick Hayes rehearses the reading in his discussion of *Foe*, with reference to Watt's account of the novel's relation to individualism, in "'An Author I have not Read': Coetzee's *Foe*, Dostoevsky's *Crime and Punishment*, and the Problem of the Novel," in *Review of English Studies* 57: 230 (2006): 273–90. On page 283, Hayes importantly refers to Coetzee's mention of Watt in an interview from 1997. See also Edith W. Clowes, "The Robinson Myth Reread in Postcolonial and Postcommunist Modes," in *Critique* 36 (1995): 145–59.

137 Coetzee, *Slow*, 102.
138 Ibid., 179.
139 Ibid., 86.

2

Bare Life and the Camps in Kazuo Ishiguro's *Never Let Me Go*

To write is certainly not to impose a form (of expression) on the matter of lived experience. Literature rather moves in the direction of the ill-formed or the incomplete ... Writing is a question of becoming, always incomplete, and always in the midst of being formed, and goes beyond the matter of any livable or lived experience. It is a process, that is, a passage of Life that traverses both the livable and the lived. Writing is inseparable from becoming: in writing, one becomes-woman, becomes-animal or vegetable, becomes-molecule to the point of becoming-imperceptible.[1]

—Gilles Deleuze, *Essays Critical and Clinical*

It is time to remember that some explosions are not in fact terrorist—explosions of rage, for example. Perhaps we ought to relearn how to enrage ourselves, to explode against our culture of docility, of amenity, of the effacement of all conflict even as we live in a state of permanent war.[2]

—Catherine Malabou, *What Should We Do With Our Brain?*

Exploding Care

Kazuo Ishiguro's novel *Never Let Me Go* tells the intertwined life-stories of Kathy, Tommy, and Ruth, ranging from their early childhood and adolescence at Hailsham boarding school until their deaths (in the case of Ruth and Tommy) or "late" life (in the case of Kathy, who narrates the book).[3] Like the other children at Hailsham, Kathy, Tommy, and Ruth are clones whose destiny in life is to ultimately donate their organs to regular human beings who are in need of them. Before they become donors, each of them spends some time as a carer, taking care of other clones who have donated. The duration of this period depends on how good they are at caring. Although some donors can donate up to four times before "completing," most of them die long before, sometimes even as early as after the first donation (as in the case of Chrissie, an older Hailsham student they meet at the Cottages, once they have left Hailsham).

Cloned from the genetic material of "junkies, prostitutes, winos, tramps" and "convicts,"[4] the clones take on a contested place in a society that depends on them for its health but would prefer to deny them a humane way of life. That is what Hailsham, in contrast to the "government homes"[5] referred to in the closing chapters of the novel, intends to provide. At the boarding school, the students receive a humanistic education. Although the facts about their lives are explained to them little by little, the instructors prefer to shelter the students from the less likeable truths of their existence, which risks giving free rein to students' imagination. However, although education might make the students aspire to a better life, all the books in the world cannot change the path that has been set out for them. At the end of the day, each and every one of them must care, donate, and complete. That is the narrative they must stick to. *Never Let Me Go* tells the story of how the clones, during their short life-span, confront these issues.

Although Ishiguro's novel might be a novel about clones, the questions that the clones confront about life, death, humanity, authority, and so on are universal questions that haunt all of us, clones and regular people.[6] Indeed, from the novel's very first page, which sets the novel firmly in England in the late 1990s, the suggestion appears to be that the story that follows applies to us. It is not a science-fiction story that we will be able to comfortably enjoy because it takes place in the future, at a remove from us. Instead, the novel appears to present itself as a novel about the present (more specifically, the recent past) and *about us*. The clones' situation thus becomes *our* situation. This makes it all the more disturbing that although there is no clear source of authority in the novel that forces the clones to stick to the life they live, the clones do not resist. With the exception of Tommy, who from a very early stage appears to be raging against his sorry fate, the clones strike one as lambs that are led to the slaughter with remarkable ease. Is Ishiguro saying something about our current political condition as well, in the first decade of the twenty-first century?

In the context of my investigation of narrative care, the most unsettling aspect of his lack of resistance may be that "care" appears to play into it. As Tommy asks towards the end of the novel, why do donors ultimately need carers?[7] Of course, one can see how, from a humane perspective, it is important to have a carer. But having a carer changes nothing about the clones' fate: ultimately they must still donate and complete. Moreover, it might be that it is in part because they have carers that donors do not resist. The care they receive dulls the pain of their existence, and it might be that if it were not for this care, their pain would develop into something more explosive that would overthrow the dubious biopolitical system that the novel represents. From this perspective, care seems to be complicit with the system Tommy is raging against. It must be investigated as a technique of domination.[8] However, it might also be that Tommy's rage *is* a form of care: a non-gentrified form of care that enables subjects to resist, without rejecting, the forms of care they receive. In his reading of *Never Let Me Go*, Bruce Robbins has suggested that anger might thus be part and parcel of our relation to the welfare state.[9] That would be a *pharmacology of care* that is not opposed to explosions of anger.

One of the most interesting aspects of Ishiguro's novel is that it ultimately relates this entire problematic of care and biopolitics to the practice of novel-writing itself. Clones thus become aligned with characters, and the novel as well as the novelist with the society that produces them. Ishiguro's suggestion, in this context, is harsh. Following Hailsham instructor Miss Lucy, who compares Hailsham to a concentration camp, one could in this case compare the novel to a camp, and character-life to what Giorgio Agamben in his philosophical study of the Auschwitz concentration camp has called bare life: an inhuman kind of life in between human and animal life that he characterizes as pure biopolitical substance. Given *Never Let Me Go*'s multiple references to literary history, and the fact that the novel is also a re-writing (as critics have noted[10]) of Mary Shelley's *Frankenstein*, this suggestion also reflects back on the history of the novel as a genre. If Shelley's novel were somehow an allegory of the writing situation, what questions does this raise about the authority of the novelist, the political regime of the novel, and the scripted lives of the characters who are caught up in it?[11]

Ultimately, these are questions about the biopolitics of the novel, and the limits and limitations of thinking the novel as a regime of care. Nevertheless, as Tommy's outbursts of anger show, *Never Let Me Go* also leaves room within its complicity with biopolitics for resistance. As I will show, however, this resistance does not quite develop yet into what Michel Foucault in his late work called an aesthetics of existence.

Biopolitics in *Never Let Me Go*

Never Let Me Go is narrated by Kathy and begins with reminiscences about her early childhood at Hailsham boarding school. As in other, similar accounts, the tone in these pages is emphatically nostalgic, with Kathy thinking back to Hailsham as a kind of ideal place, remarking even "how lucky"[12] she, Tommy, and Ruth have been to live there. It is by no means strange to find such a statement and tone in an account of this kind (it becomes especially understandable when we find out, later in the novel, that Hailsham has been closed). However, given that Kathy will turn out to be talking about a boarding school that is preparing generations of clones to care, donate, and complete, Hailsham begins to look a little like a candy house in which Hansel and Gretel are fattened to be eaten.[13] Life at Hailsham resembles life at any high school or boarding school of the time: with the girls observing the boys and vice versa, the boys playing soccer while the girls are talking about the boys, and the boys bullying one particular boy—Tommy—who in this case stands out because of his outbursts of anger. Tommy's explosions of rage are in many ways the mystery of Ishiguro's book, one that remains opaque even to Tommy himself but that Kathy perhaps comes closest to understanding in the novel's closing pages, when she suggests that somehow, Tommy always seemed to have known they were being fooled.

In the novel's opening chapters, speculations about Tommy's anger serve as a vehicle for Kathy to explain some of the ethics—habits, rules and regulations—that shape community life at Hailsham. Thus, the reader learns about the "Guardians"[14] watching over the clones (philosophically inclined readers might hear echoes of Plato and his *Republic*, a classic in the history of utopia, and one in which eugenics is a central topic). We also learn about the art "Exchanges"[15] that take place at the school and the "Gallery"[16] of student artwork curated by the school's headmistress, a Belgian or French woman referred to as "Madame."[17] The fact that these words are capitalized suggests that they function within the community of Hailsham as god-terms: they have been around forever, they cannot be touched. They are the cornerstones of life at Hailsham. Except for Tommy, all the students appear to be buying into them with much enthusiasm. It is only around the figure of Tommy, who is not as creative as the others and therefore does not participate in the art exchanges and does not contribute to the gallery, that these foundations begin to tremble. All of the others have built their lives upon them, and as a result their lives make sense. Indeed, since none of them have a life outside of Hailsham, it is the *only* life that makes sense to them.

One striking aspect of Hailsham life is that it is very precious, in spite of its hardships. It is perhaps especially in a state of hardship that certain aspects of a life that might seem ridiculous to an outsider become precious. One notes, for example, Kathy's strong attachment to the objects that are acquired at the Exchanges, or also at the "Sales"[18] that take place at the school. To an outsider, it seems clear that the objects that are being sold at the school and that Hailsham students find so precious are cast off items from a donations store. And yet, deprived of objects and of a private life in general as they are, Hailsham students get excited about these objects as if they were the most precious things in the world (and they are, of course, to *them*). When one does not have much, anything can turn into such a precious object. Human beings arguably need objects like that in order to make life meaningful: to create a world of their own and make their existence cohere. It is an aesthetics of existence of a kind, but one that is practiced in this case in the most dire circumstances, in full denial of the reality that constitutes it.

When one of these objects goes lost, as happens for example with a music tape that Kathy is particularly attached to, all of existence enters into a state of crisis, in the same way that a child cannot be consoled when it has lost what psychoanalyst D. W. Winnicott calls a transitional object.[19] Only *that* object will be able to make up for the loss, and without it, existence cannot be complete. This shows that life at Hailsham is precariously balanced between belief, its material support system, and the risk of them being unsettled.

Such an existence could be characterized as "literal." Consider, for example, that when Kathy loses her tape, she somehow thinks she will find it back in Norfolk, which is described by one of their teachers as "the lost corner"[20] of England. Since the "lost and found" section at Hailsham is also called "the lost corner," Kathy somehow establishes an association between the two. Interestingly, the novel confirms this madness: she will indeed find the tape back during an excursion to Norfolk, when she will even wonder, with Tommy, whether the tape she finds there may be *the exact same tape* that she lost. It is a reflection on the relation between the original and the copy (the clone), but it also testifies to the highly scripted life of Hailsham students—a life that the novel, because it confirms it, seems to be complicit with (more on this later). Hailsham life is in fact so scripted that it risks to collapse under any kind of critique. It is a world that can only exist on the condition that one does not ask too many questions.

That this precious, precarious, "literal" life is intensely biopolitical[21] is revealed along the way, as the reader slowly but surely finds out that Kathy as well as all the other students at Hailsham are clones. As I have explained in the previous chapter, I adopt the term "biopolitics" from the work of Michel Foucault, who defines it in his lecture courses at the Collège de France in the context of his analysis of the shifting modes of power from the seventeenth century to the time when he was lecturing, the mid 1970s. Distinguishing between the ancient power of sovereignty, symbolized by the sword and defined by the right to take life, and modern governmentality, which does not so much *take* life *but* fosters and generates it until the point of death, he uses the term "biopolitics" to refer to modern governments' increased interest in the biological life of their people, of the people as population. This involves an increased interest in the population's health and reproduction, for example, or in the circulation of consumer goods such as food. I have already addressed the exchange of goods at Hailsham, and the emotional dimension of this economy as an instance of such regulation. The more shocking aspect of the novel, however, are the chapters in which the school's biopolitical regime is described.

Because the students' sole purpose is to ultimate donate their organs to regular human beings who are in need of them, it is of the utmost importance that they stay focused on "keeping yourselves well, keeping yourselves very healthy inside."[22] This entails, as we all know (this is one of the uncanny ways in which the clones' biopolitical existence overlaps with our own), not smoking: "I don't know how it was where you were," Kathy writes, thus explicitly involving the reader in the narrative, "but at Hailsham the guardians were really strict about smoking"[23]:

> I'm sure they'd have preferred it if we never found out smoking even existed; but since this wasn't possible, they made sure to give us some sort of lecture each time any reference to cigarettes came along. Even if we were being shown a picture of a famous writer or world leader, and they happened to have a cigarette in their hand, then the whole lesson would grind to a halt. There was a rumour that some classic books—like the Sherlock Holmes ones—weren't in our library because the main characters smoked too much, and when you came across a page torn out of an illustrated book or magazine, this was because there'd been a picture on it of someone smoking.[24]

When Miss Lucy (one of the teachers) tells the students it is important they keep themselves healthy inside, none of them asks "Why?" And so, the mystery of their existence remains unexplained to them. The students simply agree with the values that these lessons pass on, thus unknowingly growing into the healthy donors they are set to become.

One other biopolitical aspect of their existence, and one that is linked to the story about Kathy's tape, is that none of the clones can reproduce. One evening, when Kathy is playing a song on the tape titled *Never Let Me Go*, she is dancing with a pillow, imagining that the baby that is referred to in the song is a little baby, and holding the pillow as if it were a little baby. Madame witnesses this scene from the corridor, and when Kathy sees her standing there she notices that Madame is crying. It is not entirely clear at this moment why, but one gathers that it might very well have been because Madame *knows* that none of the girls at Hailsham are able to have children (the real reason is explained by Madame herself later in the novel, on page 272: it is because she saw a brave new world advancing, and a girl holding on to the old one in which she could not remain). At the time when the discussions about smoking and sex are taking place, however, none of the students knew "that none of us could have babies."[25] This is something that is only revealed to them at a later time.

It is because of this reason, most likely, that Miss Lucy—the Hailsham instructor who is most conflicted about the school's project—comes to compare Hailsham to a concentration camp. When she is talking "about soldiers in World War Two being kept in prison camps" one day, "[o]ne of the boys asked if the fences around the camps had been electrified, and then someone else had said how strange it must have been, living in a place like that, where you could commit suicide any time you liked just by touching the fence."[26] How strange indeed! "It's just as well", Miss Lucy says after a moment of reflection, "the fences at Hailsham aren't electrified. You get terrible accidents sometimes."[27] The remark is spoken quietly, and while Kathy picks it up few of the other students do. But it is an important observation, of course, and one that enables the reader to see the relation between Hailsham's highly scripted mode of existence and the camps. Of course, critics will say that life at Hailsham, with the various comforts it still includes, can in no way be compared to life in the camps; and of course, they are right. But surely one can also see what Miss Lucy is alluding to here: a certain *logic* that existence at Hailsham and existence in the camp (if it can still be called that) share. In addition, one finds out through this remark that there are fences around Hailsham. It raises the question of whether anyone has actually ever seen such a fence, or tried to cross it. There is some discussion in the novel about the woods separating Hailsham from the rest of the world. Stories circulate that are meant to keep the kids out of the woods. But during her entire time at Hailsham, Kathy never seems to have tried to get into the woods, and out of Hailsham. Clearly, the "education" she was receiving was working.

It is indeed through Miss Lucy, who will ultimately leave Hailsham, that some of the realities of the students' scripted lives are revealed. When one day, shortly after the concentration camp episode, two students are dreaming about becoming movie stars in the United States, she interrupts them to clarify, in very explicit terms, the following:

> None of you will go to America, none of you will be film stars. And none of you will be working in supermarkets as I heard some of you planning the other day. Your lives are set out for you. You'll become adults, then before you're old, before you're even middle-aged, you'll start to donate your vital organs. That's what each of you was created to do. You're not like the actors you watch on your videos, you're not even like me. You were brought into this world for a purpose, and your futures, all of them, have been decided.[28]

Not much upward mobility here, not much aesthetics of existence. Kathy's life has already been decided for her, it is set out for her, regardless of what her personal aspirations might be. She was created to do something. Whatever potentiality she carries within her is not hers to realize. Instead, it has been committed to a specific actualization in which she has no say. At least, that is what Hailsham has her believe.

Nevertheless, there are rumors—and these increase after they have left Hailsham and moved to the Cottages, a residence for upper-level students—about donors getting what is called a deferral, and being able to postpone donating for three to four years. Here, one might wonder about the effects of such a story about respite: is it not precisely such stories, about the possibility of an escape route somewhere, that make us keep the horrible realities we suffer intact? Is it not the promise of escape, of another possible existence, that makes us undergo our sometimes sorry fates? Rather than actually trying to change them?[29] Indeed, Kathy's existence in later life is largely driven by this story about deferrals. The logic that Hailsham students have worked out, without ever talking about this much, goes as follows: if you are highly creative, and contribute a lot of work to Madame's Gallery, thus making your name known with the higher echelons where your existence is being decided, and if you can move those higher echelons not just with your art but with a love-story—that is, by proving that you and another clone are truly in love—then it is possible that you and your partner will be granted a deferral.

Of course, when Kathy and Tommy meet up with Madame towards the end of their lives to discuss the possibility of deferral, it turns out this entire story is fabricated. Neither art nor love can save them from the fate that has been set out for them. It is a revelation that drives Tommy angry, and triggers one of the outbursts of rage from which he used to suffer. But somewhere, the reader also thinks: *now* you realize? *This* is when you realize that your life is unfair, that you kept undergoing humiliation after humiliation in the hope that one of those fairy tales you have been telling yourself would work out?[30]

Why do the clones not resist? Given that there does not seem to be a violent center of authority in the novel forcing them to go through the lives that have been set out for them, why do they not simply say "no" and escape? Why does Tommy, who perhaps comes closest to doing so, not run away? Is it only because he has no family out there, no world out there in which he thinks he could survive? Are we *that* afraid of turning our backs on our relatively comfortable existences? Miss Lucy's comparison of Hailsham to the camps invites one to link these questions to the camps (as has been done): how is it that the Germans were able to organize the extinction of human beings on such a mass scale? Why did so many people say "yes" when they were told to leave their lives behind, and to get on a train to go work in some other country, far away from their homes? Psychologists such as Stanley Milgram have developed elaborate experiments to investigate the human being's will to obey, the ways in which the human animal has been disciplined into docility, amenity, the avoidance of conflict. It seems that at least for Hailsham students (with the exception, perhaps, of Tommy), there was not even the possibility of saying "no," perhaps because in spite of all of the reading they were doing and the alternative literary worlds they were exploring, there was no other sufficiently *real* place out there from where they could confidently resist.

The Novel as a Camp

> … and therefore—once again!—fascism.[31]
>
> —Susan Sontag, *Against Interpretation*

Never Let Me Go presents the reader with a suggestion that I also uncovered in J. M. Coetzee's *Slow Man*, namely the fact that the novel as a genre may be complicit with the power that Foucault called governmentality and biopolitics. As I suggested in the previous chapter, given that the novel as a genre emerges at the same time when governmentality and biopolitics develop, it makes sense to consider that the novel, as a characteristically modern genre, might be the literary expression of a political logic that developed simultaneously to it. I argue that something had to break within human beings' political imagination in order for the novel as a literary form to become possible—in order for the human being to try its hand at a form of fiction that would concern the lives of ordinary people. It is a major shift in the imagination if one comes to think of it: from the lives of mythical, historical, and legendary figures or the lives of characters from older stories, the human imagination moves to the creation of everyday characters, *people like us*, and the fates of their private lives (their births and deaths, their happiness and their sickness, their loves, their work, and so on). It is as if what used to be merely an exercise of *fiction* suddenly becomes *real*.

Slow Man—and Coetzee's *oeuvre* as a whole—develops this suggestion in part through its multiple and elaborate references to Daniel Defoe's *Robinson Crusoe*, often taken to be the first novel in English. Indeed, Defoe's novel can be read, as Defoe himself pointed out, not simply as a story about human individualism in the modern age, but also as an allegory about imprisonment that implies to the modern age as well. In this sense, it resonates with Michel Foucault's theories about disciplinary power and the modern state's practices of surveillance. However, in the fact that the novel meticulously describes the techniques that Crusoe uses to govern himself on the island, Defoe's story could also be read—as Gregg Lambert has suggested[32]—as the first biopolitical novel, a novel that walks the thin and treacherous line between biopolitics' government of bodies and souls, which goes back (as I have discussed in the previous chapter) to the pastoral care of early Christianity, and the aesthetics of existence that Foucault theorizes in his late work. In addition, and as Coetzee's novel *Foe* has drawn out, the novel can be read as a meta-fictional allegory about the relation between authors and characters.

Never Let Me Go contributes to this revisionist history of the novel not simply through the multiple references to literary works that it includes—it is, in many ways, a hyper-literary novel that involves all of literary history in its project—but also through the fact that it can be read as a rewriting of Mary Shelley's *Frankenstein* (1817).[33] First published some hundred years after Defoe's novel, Shelley arguably returns to Defoe's initial meta-fictional allegory, now in the romanticist context of an investigation into the Promethean excesses of science. Her novel is about a scientist who creates a living being using parts of dead bodies, and by using the electricity produced by lightning.[34] It is obviously an allegory about the novelist trying to bring her or his characters to life, and in this sense the novel can be read as a reflection on the project of the novel as such. It subordinates plot entirely to the biographical, life-writing element in fiction. In addition, the novel reflects, of course, and in this particular aspect it furthers Defoe's *Robinson Crusoe*, on the quality of the character-life that is being created.

What is the life of a living dead man, of a man consisting of the parts of other dead men? Is it the life of a monster? Can we care for this kind of life? Does it care? Or is it a sorry existence that we would prefer not to have any business with? If the latter, then why *do* we care about literary characters? How are they any different? Are not they too curiously put together, alive but not quite—living, but not a life that we would consider worth living? These are, of course, also the questions that haunt Ishiguro's clones, who are "like" characters. In the last instance, these questions also come to apply to us. For who is to say that we are any different? What agency do we ultimately have? Or more precisely, how do we use it? Do we share our sorry fates with literary characters? Is that why we are so interested in them, spend so much of our time with them?

Ishiguro's particular contribution, which is reinforced, in my opinion, through the novel's intertextuality with Shelley's text about science, is that, when considered from this perspective, the modern novel could be described as a camp.[35] As Giorgio Agamben writes in *Homo Sacer: Sovereign Power and Bare Life*, whenever a structure is created in which the life of the individual becomes indistinguishable from the law, one finds oneself in the presence of a camp.[36] Once again, critics might disagree with this and argue that this does an injustice not just to the extremeness of the camp, but also to the genre of the novel. And although I am inclined to agree on both counts, I also argue that there is a continuity that must be considered here, and that Ishiguro forces us to consider. If we would *not* raise this question, we would simply be like the clones in his book, for whom there is no why. Indeed, the shadow that the camp in *Never Let Me Go* casts not just over this particular novel but over the history of the novel as a genre, is present—albeit in a largely occluded way—in Ian Watt's *The Rise of the Novel*, with which I have already been working in the previous chapter.

Here is how Watt presents the book in the first sentence of his preface: "In 1938 I began a study of the relation between the growth of the reading public and the emergence of the novel in eighteenth-century England; and in 1947 it eventually took shape as a Fellowship Dissertation for St John's College, Cambridge."[37] Hiding in the space between Watt's two clauses is the Second World War and the experience of the camps; and indeed, these events will not receive much airplay in Watt's study. They do return, however, in a crucial paragraph towards the end of Watt's fourth chapter, which deals in part with Defoe's novel. "The Second World War," Watt writes,

> brought us closer to the prophetic nature of Defoe's picture of individualism. Camus used Defoe's allegorical claim for *Robinson Crusoe* as epigraph for his own allegory, *La peste* (1948): "It is as reasonable to represent one kind of imprisonment by another, as it is to represent anything that really exists by that which exists not." At the same time André Malraux wrote that only three books, *Robinson Crusoe*, *Don Quixote*, and *The Idiot*, retained their truth for those who had seen prisons and concentration camps.[38]

The next sentence is infected by this mentioning of the concentration camps: "Defoe's concentration on isolated individuals, it would seem, is closer to the view of life held by many writers today than to those held in the intervening centuries."[39] Although this is, of course, not Watt's suggestion, I would argue that there is indeed some kind of echo, some kind of resonance, between Defoe's "concentration" on individuals and the "concentration camps." The modern novel could indeed be described as a concentration camp in which the author's law coincides to the letter with the lives of the individuals being described. A literature of universals shifts to a literature of particulars, and with that the philosophical structure that Agamben calls "camp" has come into being.[40]

This might raise some questions, at first sight, given that Agamben in his work on the camp insists on tying the camp to the logic of sovereignty, leaving Foucauldian governmentality largely aside (he does insist on the connection between sovereignty and biopolitics). This is only a minor reservation, however: although it is true that Agamben is foregrounding the importance of sovereignty in part in response to Foucault's reduced attention to it—in the first volume of the *History of Sexuality*, Foucault is famously calling for the head of the king to finally be cut off in political thought and analysis—, it is not as if Foucault ever said that sovereignty was to be abandoned or as if Agamben is not interested in governmentality.[41] Rather, we are talking about a question of emphasis here. As Foucault saw things in the 1970s, governmentality was the dominant mode of power exercise. Sovereignty had moved to the background. As Agamben sees things in the late 1990s, and then especially after the September 11 terror attacks from 2001, sovereignty has re-entered upon the political scene, and needs to be given serious consideration if one wants to understand the exercise of power in the contemporary age. Not everyone agrees with him on this, and one might indeed bicker about the issue for a long time. What interests me, however, is the logic that Agamben lays bare, and the way in which it resonates with the practice of novel-writing.

Already in the opening paragraph of Agamben's book, one finds something extremely interesting from the literary critical perspective, namely the fact that in his rehearsal of the ancient Greek distinction between *zoe*, or the simple fact of living as shared by animals, humans, and gods, and *bios*, or the form of living of an individual or a collective, Agamben includes the gods as sharing in the simple fact of life. Indeed, as Paul Veyne has discussed in his book *Did the Greeks Believe in their Myths?*, the ancient Greek structure of belief is highly complex, and includes the possibility of believing that the gods live on Mount Olympus while not expecting to actually find them there. Veyne speaks, in this context, of the "constitutive imagination," and with that term, of course, he comes closer to a history of secular storytelling in which the birth of the novel as a genre participates.[42] By speaking about the simple fact of living of the gods, it becomes possible to speak about the simple fact of living of characters, and to investigate the biopolitical mode of their existence.

Indeed, when Agamben at the very end of his book lists a number of figures of what he calls bare life, it seems that literary characters could easily have fit in here. By bare life, Agamben refers to an inhuman form of life in between human and animal life. It is politicized *zoe*, the life that comes into being when life (*zoe*) is separated from its form of life (*bios*) and the simple fact of living is politicized (into bare life, mere life, or naked life). Bare life is coupled in Agamben's book to sovereign power. Indeed, he suggests that the essential activity of sovereign power is the production of bare life. Although the concentration camp is the site where this becomes most explicit, and where the hidden logic of modern politics if most drastically exposed, Agamben traces the logic of sovereignty back to Ancient times, finding figures of bare life in the most diverse contexts and situations.

Consider, for example, Agamben's reference to the work of anthropologists Georges Dumézil and Károly Kerény on the Flamen Diale:

> one of the greatest priests of classical Rome. His life is remarkable in that it is at every moment indistinguishable from the cultic functions that the Flamen fulfils. This is why the Romans said that the *Flamen Diale* is *quotidie feriatus* and *assiduus sacerdos*, that is, in an act of uninterrupted celebration at every instant. Accordingly, there is no gesture or detail of his life, the way he dresses or the way he walks, that does not have a precise meaning and is not caught in a series of functions and meticulously studied effects.[43]

Agamben follows up by observing that "[i]n the life of the *Flamen Diale* it is not possible to isolate something like a bare life. All of the *Flamen*'s *zoe* has become *bios*; private sphere and public function are absolutely identical."[44] The Flamen Diale *is* bare life, in other words, *and nothing else*. As such, this priest arguably captures the life of the character, or at the very least a certain way of writing, reading, and theorizing about characters. Indeed, do not readers—or at least literary critics—to a certain extent expect that every gesture or detail of a character's life, including the way he or she dresses or even walks, has a precise meaning, and is caught in a series of functions and effects that can be meticulously studied? Is this not how we tend to read novels—in the expectation that everything that is present on the page ultimately adds up to a meaningful whole? Of course, writers, readers, and critics have resisted such a way of reading to focus, for example, only on the pleasure of the text: its presentation rather than its representation, its sensuous whole rather than its intellectual construct. But I am suggesting those resistances be considered in the context of the novel's connection to biopolitics and specifically the camp that Ishiguro is forcing us to confront.

In his analysis of the camp, Agamben is interested in the "total politicization of everything … even the life that had been private."[45] This leads, in his opinion, to the production of a bare kind of life that, considered as such, does not deserve to live. Even if one might be reluctant to tie characters to this kind of life, one can surely see how Ishiguro's clones fit this bill. The whole debate around their education focuses, precisely, on whether cloned life deserves to life, and to live in a more humane way than it has done so far. We do not learn much about the life of clones outside of Hailsham, but in the closing chapters of the novel it is suggested that they live in "government homes" where life is much worse than at Hailsham.[46] Hailsham was closed, however, not so much because people stopped believing that it was important to provide clones with a more humane way of living, but because a scientist called James Morningdale "wanted to offer people the possibility of having children with enhanced characteristics. Superior intelligence, superior athleticism, that sort of thing."[47] It is because of this *eugenic* aspiration and the risk of humanity being overcome by superhumans that projects such as Hailsham are ultimately abandoned in favor of keeping bare life firmly in its place. Thus, it is ultimately human sovereignty that is defending itself through these movements, and that is producing bare life to keep itself intact.

The project fits Agamben's theory of the camp very neatly. An Agambenian theory of the novel would not only align the novel with the camp, but also the life of characters—character-life—with bare life. Characters would thus become situated in "a limit zone between life and death, inside and outside, in which they are no longer anything but bare life."[48] Pushing matters a bit, one could conceive of the novel as an apparatus of "life-support technology," focused on "artificial respiration, maintenance of cardiac circulation through intravenous perfusion of adrenaline, technologies of body temperature, and so on."[49] The character then becomes aligned with the overcomatose person that Agamben discusses in his book—a "neomort," a *faux vivant*.[50] This would be a theory of the novel as a camp, and of the character as the bare life that is caught up within it. If Watt argues that the novel is the characteristic literary form of modernity, and if Agamben argues that the camp is the characteristic political structure of modernity, should we not then also consider the argument that there might be a connection between the novel and the camp? That is what Ishiguro's *Never Let Me Go* suggests.

Aesthetics of Existence

Of course, Ishiguro's interest in the camps and the events of the Second World War is not limited to this. He had already explored the relation between a certain kind of cloned life, namely the life of a butler, and the concentration camps in *The Remains of the Day*.[51] In *The Unconsoled* as well (which is more of a Cold War novel), Ishiguro is exploring the strange world of fiction in which characters are caught up. Watt's reference to Defoe's statement about *Robinson Crusoe* as a story about imprisonment is entirely on the mark in both these cases. To consider the novel critically means to confront these complicities.

However, that cannot be the last word on the novel. It is not because one is complicit with something that one is entirely saturated by it. Indeed, in order to be effective, any action (gesture, statement, et cetera) arguably needs to be complicit with something—otherwise it risks falling outside of the logic of the world altogether, and remaining unheard (it could become heard at a later time; but it finds no audience in the present). In *Never Let Me Go* as well, complicity does not amount to saturation. Kathy's voice is dominant, and her investment in caring does not falter. But there is her love for Tommy, and her interest in Tommy's tantrums. These are, as Robbins has noted, a line of flight in the book[52]—they are an exit point, the only moments within the Hailsham hell when a *critical* way out appears to be possible (deferral also marks a way out, but one that is entirely *within the order of things*). The only problem is that Tommy himself does not quite rise to the level of his anger. Kathy understands it best, it seems, when she summarizes it at the end of the novel as an anger that was directed, all this time, against the system that was fooling them. But Tommy himself is not sure about this, and puts it aside as being less meaningful than Kathy thinks.

He does raise, however, another suggestion that casts some suspicion on the notion that is central to my book, namely care. Why do we ultimately need carers, he asks? Everyone ultimately donates and completes anyway. It is just something that softens the blow, sweetens the pill. Kathy, an excellent carer herself, insists on the importance of it. And of course, she is right from a humane perspective: if Hailsham is closed down, if they are all being raised in horrible "government homes," then caring might be the precious little humanity that is left to them. However, as such it becomes part of the problem: for if caring softens the blow and sweetens the pill, one wonders whether in this sense it does not contribute to the system against which Tommy rages? Tommy might be on the track of this when, towards the very end of his life, he begins to separate himself from Kathy. Supposedly, this is because he does not want her to see him waste away after his fourth donation and complete. But one also gathers that a gap has inserted itself between the two lovers, one that has to do with the fact that she is a carer and he a donor, in other words the fact that she is contributing to the system from which he suffers. They belong, ultimately, in different classes, and whereas he is the one who donates and dies, she appears to be *on the side of the system*. That is, ultimately, the most disturbing thing about Kathy's entire account, which is related in such a careful and composed way that one does indeed begin to doubt whether Kathy is human.[53] Why is she not more critical of Hailsham and of the entire system of which it is a part? Why does she not explore more than she does? Why do these characters keep swallowing and swallowing, until they have become too fat to move and are ready for the slaughter? Surely, that is not what the fairy tale taught us.

Ishiguro's novel thus casts some suspicion on the notion of care, and specifically on the idea of an institution—a school or by extension a state—that claims to care for you. Bruce Robbins has considered the novel in this light as a novel about the welfare state and its caring administrations. In an article titled "Cruelty is Bad: Banality and Proximity in *Never Let Me Go*," he reads Tommy as a figure who, like Coetzee's Paul Rayment, rages against the welfare state and its administrations. Through Tommy, Ishiguro might thus be making the case for another kind of care, namely anger: "One of the must subtly shocking aspects of *Never Let Me Go* is the way its dark satire of the welfare state's anger-management program also creates a space in which readers can be asked to countenance and even admire cruelty."[54] Hailsham is a model for a welfare state "that bribes us with minor restitutions and supplements so as to divert us from deep and systematic injustice, which is to say from our legitimate causes for anger."[55] Kathy appears to have been entirely saturated by this logic. In the case of Tommy, however, things are different. This leads Robbins, in the concluding paragraph of his essay, to make a case for cruelty:

> Cruelty is bad. All things considered, civility would be preferable. But here at least cruelty and incivility also seem to be part of a more expansive and counter-intuitive political vision, one that allows us to consider caring here as possibly conflicting with caring there, that allows us to consider the welfare state as a distanced, anger-bearing project in which anger is a necessary part of a genuine concern for people's welfare.[56]

Note that the argument does not go against the welfare state and its administrations. But it does not go against anger against the welfare state either. Instead, the "*nuclear* criticism" that might have tempted other critics here—*explode* the welfare state and its administrations! *Get rid of* biopolitics!—develops into a "*pharmacological* criticism" that considers both pros and cons, contextualizes welfare (here/there), and develops a non-idealized theory of caring that includes anger and cruelty.[57] Sometimes, in order to care, one must be angry or cruel. Sometimes you must resist what tries to help you.

This idea is powerfully evoked in the conclusion of Catherine Malabou's book *What Should We Do With Our Brain?*, which I have quoted at the beginning of this chapter. "It is time to remember," Malabou writes,

> that some explosions are not in fact terrorist—explosions of rage, for example. Perhaps we ought to relearn how to enrage ourselves, to

> explode against our culture of docility, of amenity, of the effacement of all conflict even as we live in a state of permanent war.[58]

The passage—which resonates with Hailsham's culture of docility, amenity, and the effacement of all conflict—becomes highly relevant in my discussion of Ishiguro's book, especially because Malabou's work inscribes itself in Foucault's work on biopolitics. Malabou's argument about the brain can productively be read as a rewriting of Foucault's biopolitical argument about sex and race as I began to present it in the previous chapter.

When Stephen Riggins asks Foucault in an interview titled "The Minimalist Self" whether since the nineteenth century, anything has replaced sex as "*the* secret of life," Foucault replies that he does not think so: "I think that people still consider, and are invited to consider, that sexual desire is able to reveal what is their deep identity."[59] What if we were to ask this question again, today? Might it be that the brain has replaced sex as the secret of life? And if this is the case, then how might Foucault's analyses of sex apply to the contemporary interest in the brain? In what follows, I would like to read Malabou's book as a continuation of Foucault's work on biopolitics, which focused on the analysis of sex and race, in order to ultimately see how Malabou's insistence on rage fits into this, and into my discussion of Tommy's tantrums in *Never Let Me Go*. However, to focus *only* on biopolitics in this context would mean to miss the ways in which Malabou's theory of the brain—summed up by the motto "the brain is a work, but we do not know it!"—*also* continues Foucault's late work on the aesthetics of existence and the care of the self. My aim is thus to explore how Malabou's book, read in light of Foucault's work on biopolitics, proposes a care of the brain that invites us to rethink our conceptualizations of care—and specifically, the politics of care—today, in order to ask, finally, about the aesthetics of existence in Ishiguro's novel.

Throughout *The History of Sexuality*, and especially in the book's closing pages, Foucault makes a simple but powerful point: if one wants to understand the politics of sex, one should look *not* for the reasons for which sexuality was "being repressed"[60] *but* for the reasons for which it "was constantly aroused."[61] He urges his readers to analyze what one could call a sex-"*effect*,"[62] that is, the ways in which sex does not pre-exist sexuality as a biological category that would be outside of power but is rather "a complex idea that was formed inside the deployment of sexuality."[63] His point is not that "sex did not exist"[64]. He is *not* speaking of sexuality *as if there were no sex*. His point is, rather, that *there is no true sex*. Instead, "sex is the most speculative, most ideal, and most internal element in the deployment of sexuality organized by power in its grip on bodies and their materiality, their forces, energies, sensations, and pleasures."[65] Through a historical reversal,

> we have arrived at the point where we expect our intelligibility to come from what was for many centuries thought of as madness: the plenitude of our body from what was long considered its stigma and likened to a wound; our identity from what was perceived as an obscure and nameless urge.[66]

In short: from sex. *Nothing could be more ridiculous.* "We must not think that by saying yes to sex, one says no to power,"[67] he writes, continuing:

> [O]n the contrary, one tracks along the course laid out by the general deployment of sexuality. It is the agency of sex that we must break away from, if we aim—through a tactical reversal of the various mechanisms of sexuality—to counter the grips of power with the claims of the bodies, pleasures, and knowledges, in their multiplicities and their possibility of resistance.[68]

Fast-forward to the so-called neurological turn in the sciences, the social sciences, and the humanities today: the brain appears to have taken the place of sex as the site where human beings will discover their true selves (which may very well be posthuman, but so be it: that too, was part of Foucault's philosophy[69]). However, do we *truly* need a *true* brain, as Foucault already asked about sex (do we need a true sex?) in his introduction to the memoirs of the nineteenth-century French hermaphrodite Herculine Barbin?[70] And is it true that "our 'liberation'" is somehow "in the balance" in all this brain talk (which can be sexy, too!)?[71] Foucault's answer to all these questions would likely be "no." But this "no" needs to be supplemented—as philosophers such as Bernard Stiegler have argued—with the more affirmative tone of his later work on *The Care of the Self* (Stiegler is partly following Félix Guattari and his work on ethico-aesthetic paradigms for existence).[72] Malabou accomplishes such a balance—between biopolitics and the care of the self—in *What Should We Do With Our Brain?* Although Ishiguro's novel puts one on the threshold of such an aesthetics of existence, it is ultimately accomplished, I argue, not in Kathy's writing nor in Tommy's anger, but in our reading both of these together.

How can the practices of care—the techniques of taking care of oneself—that Foucault discusses in *The Care of the Self* be disentangled (to echo Foucault's "What is Enlightenment?"[73]) from the intensification of power-relations that he analyzed earlier in his work on biopolitics? How can one be pro-care, but remain critical of biopolitics? Clearly, everything will depend on the *kind* of care one practices. Malabou's *What Should We Do With Our Brain?* can be read as a meditation—and a highly provocative one—on such practices of care. Given the passage on anger that I quoted earlier on, for

Malabou care is not simply a practice that is complicit with biopolitics. It is not simply a technique of "bowing one's head with a smile." Instead, it is explosive: it rages, it struggles. It says "no." In a word: in Malabou's vision, care is *plastic*. This relation between care and plasticity deserves to be explored in more detail.

Malabou's association with care arrives through art, specifically through the work titled *Take Care of Yourself* by the French artist Sophie Calle with which I began the introduction to this book. One of the women that Calle wrote to for her project was Malabou. The philosopher responded with a letter in which she develops a theory—inspired by Søren Kierkegaard's *Repetition*, which was also written after a break-up—of how Calle's lover lacks "being somebody" and feels he must lose Calle in order to "be somebody." Like Calle's project, the letter is a little cruel: it mercilessly lays bare the psyche of Calle's lover—*and for everyone to see!*[74]

At this point in time, Malabou's book on the brain had already appeared. While I am unaware of Calle's exact reasons for contacting Malabou, it is not difficult to read Malabou's book on the brain as a manifesto of care. Its *Leitmotiv*, which Malabou borrows from Karl Marx' *The Eighteenth Brumaire of Louis Bonaparte*, calls for a careful kind of brainwork, a *brain care*: "The brain is a work," the book begins, "and we do not know it."[75] The first task of the book will be to awaken what Malabou calls a consciousness of the brain, more precisely a consciousness of how the brain, which is always in part genetically determined, is always also a work-in-progress. As such, it implicates anyone who has a brain in its development. *What Should We Do With Our Brain?* thus aims to make human beings *responsible* for their brain, in the sense that Marx wrote, at the beginning of the *Eighteenth Brumaire*, that "[h]umans make their own history, but they do not know that they make it"[76]—a sentence that resonates, of course, with my discussion of *Never Let Me Go*, in which the clones appear to have no other history than the one that is already laid out for them.

That is the sentence that Malabou supposedly quotes from Marx (she does not give a reference) in the opening paragraph of her book. It is worth noting, however, that Marx' sentence reads slightly differently: "Men make their own history," he writes,

> but they do not make it just as they please. They do not make it under circumstances chosen by themselves, but under circumstances directly encountered, given and transmitted from the past. The tradition of all the dead generations weighs like a nightmare on the brain of the living.[77]

One can see why, given Marx' insistence on the brain, Malabou would have been interested in this passage. In Malabou's adaptation of the sentence,

Marx' "history" morphs into the "brain." "[T]hey do not *make* history just as they please" becomes "they do not *know* that the brain is a work" (emphases mine).

The differences are illuminating: the first is a substitution that Malabou immediately justifies. She argues in the first and second paragraphs of her book for a deep "structural bond"[78] between the brain and history. "It's not just that the brain has a history … but that it is a history."[79] To say so means to insist, as she does in the second part of her motto, that the brain is a work: "Today … there exists a constitutive historicity of the brain. The aim of this book is precisely to awaken a consciousness of this historicity."[80] This leaves the reader with one major question, namely whether "a *consciousness* of this historicity" is the same as "*making* history" (emphases mine). This question boils down to the substitution—and identification?—of verbs in the second half of Malabou's motto: is "to know" the same as "to make"? Certainly, "knowing" is a form of "making," and "making" a form of "knowing"; but in terms of this book, and the emancipatory project it adopts, it is surely worth asking whether "knowing" can fully answer Malabou's promise of liberation, or whether the reader is ultimately left wanting for more "making"?

Malabou's central argument is that we need to become conscious of the brain's plasticity. For as long as we can remember, we have believed in a genetically determined brain. However, this rigid vision of the brain is only part of the truth. Recent research on the brain has shown that it in fact also contradicts rigidity—that it is *plastic* (that is, rigid *and* in the process of construction). In her much earlier book *The Future of Hegel*, Malabou already lists the three meanings she gives to this term: "plasticity" names the capacity to *receive* form; to *give* form; and, last but not least, to *explode* form. Plasticity is thus not just "the sensible image of taking form"[81]; it also refers to "the annihilation of all form (explosion)."[82] Although it is true that the brain is always in part genetically determined, it is not the case that "the brain is already made."[83] For this reason, Malabou can speak of a "plastic organic art"[84] of the brain. What should we do with this *bioart* of the brain, "with this potential within us? What should we do with this genetically free field?"[85] This is the question that "the idea of a truly *living* brain"[86] puts before us, and one of the reasons why Malabou's work on the brain resonates with Foucault's work on biopolitics and the question of *actualization* that fascinated Foucault.[87]

It is this, I argue, that ultimately resonates in the clones' fascination with their "possible"[88] in Ishiguro's novel. A "possible" is someone from whose genetic material one could have been cloned. Not someone from the low-life list of trashy characters that I quoted above, but a regular human being with a regular life in society. Pursuing Ruth's possible one day, the possibility of another life that this pursuit opens up is brutally shattered when the clones all agree that the person they have been tracking does not look like her in any way. However, it could also have gone the other way: the confrontation with one's possible might have made them realize that another life is possible, for they do not differ in any significant way—other than the fact that they cannot reproduce and have no family—from their originals. This is, according to Foucault, the fundamental experience of enlightenment: that one can be, think, or do otherwise than one has been trained to. Of course, it is precisely this that is impossible at Hailsham.

"We are living at the hour of neuronal liberation," Malabou writes, "and we do not know it."[89] Given how often this line is repeated throughout the book, it is hard to reach the book's closing sentence without knowing that the brain is indeed a work. Which leaves the reader with the question: *what now?* What to *do* with this knowledge? As Malabou explains, the knowledge that the brain is a work "implicate[s]" us;[90] it "seeks to give birth in everyone to the feeling of a new responsibility."[91] Although her Chapter One—on plasticity's fields of action: developmental, modulational, and reparative—moves towards answering this question, one still does not really feel at the end of this chapter (when Malabou states that "our brain … is what we do with it"[92]) that much guidance has been provided in terms of what to do with one's brain. It may be that this is simply not the philosopher's project—that the philosopher ultimately leaves it up to readers to make the leap into action for which the book has prepared them.

On the other hand—and Malabou's book insists on this—knowledge *is* action. When Malabou writes that "any vision of the brain is necessarily political,"[93] one understands that there is politics in the vision of the brain that is being laid out here. The brain as Malabou sees it—the *plastic* brain—is opposed to the image of the brain as a "central telephone exchange" and a "computer."[94] It is not a central, controlling organ as power would like us to believe. As Malabou points out, power has a stake in the production of such *brain images*, in the generation of such *brain effects*: referencing Foucault's work on governmentality and biopolitics, she notes that "power hasn't been united in a long time."[95] To think of the brain as the central, controlling organ keeps a certain ideology of power intact.

Malabou's vision of the plastic, living brain resists such *neuro-political ideology*. Indeed, "resistance" appears to be what is ultimately at stake in her book. With reference to Friedrich Nietzsche, she writes that

> What we are lacking is *life*, which is to say: *resistance*. Resistance is what we want. Resistance to flexibility, to this ideological norm advanced consciously or otherwise by a reductionist discourse that models and

> naturalizes the neuronal process in order to legitimate a certain social and political functioning.[96]

Malabou's use of the word "flexibility" reveals that with her book on the brain, she is also struggling against "the spirit of capitalism"[97]—another point of connection with Foucault's work on biopolitics. With the concept of plasticity, she tries to recover from the global dominance of capital a true transformational power that is covered over by plasticity's "mistaken cognate, *flexibility*."[98] She argues:

> The difference between these two terms appears insignificant. Nevertheless, flexibility is the ideological avatar of plasticity—at once its mask, its diversion and its confiscation. We are entirely ignorant of plasticity but not at all of flexibility. … To be flexible is to receive a form or impression, to be able to fold oneself, to take the fold, not to give it. To be docile, to not explode. Indeed, what flexibility lacks is the resource of giving form, the power to create or even to erase an impression, the power to style. Flexibility is plasticity minus its genius.[99]

By proposing a vision of the brain as plastic—as giving, receiving, and exploding form—Malabou thus resists capitalist flexibility. The passage I have just quoted reveals that "plastic material resists polymorphism" and "designates solidity as much as suppleness."[100] Plasticity is, Malabou insists, explosive: it can blow up; it is not eternally flexible.

Ultimately, it is this realization to which Malabou's book leads. Clarifying that "[d]espite the explosive resonance of the meanings of plasticity, this vision of things obviously does not correspond to a terrorist conception of the constitution of identity"[101]—"the explosions in question are clearly understood as energetic discharges, creative bursts that progressively transform nature into freedom"[102]—, she nevertheless closes the book with a plea for anger. Indeed, "rage" ultimately works its way into Malabou's plea for a care of the brain. Moreover, plasticity's genius—the point at which it is perhaps most crucially different from flexibility—may precisely lie in this rage, in this *care for rage*. It is only when rage will have completely disappeared that flexibility's hegemonic struggle will be complete. Might rage—*menis*, the first word of Homer's *Illiad*—perhaps also be the origin of Sophie Calle's work on the care of the self? According to Malabou, "we ought to relearn how to enrage ourselves."[103] That too—that *in particular*—is part of the care of the self, a not-so-obvious type of plastic care that prevents care from being entirely appropriated by biopolitics.

However, do we *truly* need a *true* brain? Does Malabou present plasticity as the truth of the brain? I adapt these questions from Foucault's introduction to the memoirs of the nineteenth-century French hermaphrodite Herculine Barbin. The problem with this introduction, as Judith Butler in *Gender Trouble* has shown, is that whereas Foucault in the *History of Sexuality* argues that *there is no sex outside of power*, in his introduction to Herculine's memoirs, he

> fails to recognize the concrete relations of power that both construct and condemn Herculine's sexuality. Indeed, he appears to romanticize h/er world of pleasures as the "happy limbo of a non-identity" (xiii), a world that exceeds the categories of sex and identity.[104]

Foucault thus sentimentally indulges "in the very emancipatory discourse his analysis in the *History of Sexuality* was meant to displace."[105] And so she sets out "to read Foucault against himself"[106] by asking, with respect to Herculine's text, "What social practices and conventions produce sexuality in this form?"[107] She continues:

> In pursuing the question, we have, I think, the opportunity to understand something about (a) the productive capacity of power—that is, the way in which regulative strategies produce the subjects they come to subjugate; and (b) the specific mechanism by which power produces sexuality in the context of this autobiographical narrative.[108]

It is by looking at "the concrete narrative structures and political and cultural conventions that produce and regulate the tender kisses, the diffuse pleasures, and the thwarted and transgressive thrills of Herculine's sexual world"—in short: by close-reading—that Butler will conclude that Herculine's narrative "takes place within an established set of literary conventions."[109] Herculine's sexuality is thus "'inside' a discourse which produces sexuality and then conceals that production through a configuring of a courageous and rebellious sexuality 'outside' of the text itself."[110] But this hardly qualifies, of course, as effective resistance. In Butler's book, it is ultimately performance that will enable the displacement of the norms by which this "inside" is governed.

Butler's critical questions could be applied to Malabou's book as well. On the one hand, the book clearly shows that *there is no brain outside of power*: power has a stake in our images of the brain; the brain does not exist as a biological a priori outside of power but is produced as an effect within a neuro-discourse. That does not mean, of course, that there is no brain; it simply means that there is no *true* brain… And yet, when Malabou proposes the hypothesis that the brain is plastic—a qualifier that comes close to Foucault's description of Herculine's sexuality as a "happy limbo of non-identity"—she appears to "[fail] to recognize," as Butler puts it with respect to Foucault, "the concrete relations of power"[111] that may have produced this hypothesis.

At this point, however, and against the point about the plastic brain as a "happy limbo of non-identity," one can immediately object that for Malabou, the plastic brain is just as much about solidity as it is about suppleness. In other words, the plastic brain is not a happy limbo of non-identity that can be perpetually molded into *whatever*. Instead, its plasticity resists. It is not polymorphous and eternally flexible. Secondly, at the very end of Malabou's book it appears that Malabou's "sketching an ideological critique of the fundamental concepts of the neurosciences … also involves an ideological critique of plasticity" itself:[112] "Indeed, so long as we do not grasp the political, economic, social, and cultural implications of the knowledge of cerebral plasticity available today, we cannot do anything with it."[113] As Marc Jeannerod asks in his introduction to Malabou's book: "Might we have a neo-liberal brain that would impose its model on our socioeconomic organization? Or, inversely, might the global economy's upheaval generate a conceptual change that would affect, by contagion, our view of the way the brain functions?"[114] In other words: how do Malabou and Malabou's theory of the brain relate to the power they criticize? The closing lines of the book appear to suggest that Malabou very much situates her book within the long history of thinking about the brain, since they are presenting the brain, in the final sentence of the book "as the image of a world to come."[115] Given that the world, as she argues earlier in the book, shapes the brain, this means that she ultimately presents the brain, too, as *to come*. Indeed, this might very well ultimately be the key feature of plasticity.

Following Foucault, I would argue that our liberation is *not* in the balance with all this brain talk. As Foucault argues with respect to sex, it is *not* by talking about sex that we will discover the truth about ourselves, and become free. Our liberation *is* in the balance, however, in the realization of sex's biopolitical production—in the knowledge that sex is a work, to project Malabou's statement about the brain back into Foucault. Sex is a work, but we do not know it. (We are all sex workers, but we do not know it…) If this was the "truth" that Foucault brought home to us (a peculiar truth, since it states that there is no truth at the bottom of sex), Malabou accomplishes something similar. Foucault claims that

> it is the agency of sex that we must break away from, if we aim—through a tactical reversal of the various mechanisms of sexuality—to counter the grips of power with the claims of the bodies, pleasures, and knowledges, in their multiplicities and their possibility of resistance.[116]

Malabou claims something similar about the brain. One should therefore take very seriously her insistence in the introduction to her book on a "plastic organic art"[117] of the brain: it is indeed in the realm of art, and specifically of bioart—conceived here in the broadest possible way, as including for example Sophie Calle's project on the care of the self—, that (in my view) the possibilities for *life* and *resistance* lie.

Here, too, Malabou's work resonates with that of Foucault, who in his late work on the care of the self developed a plea for precisely such an "art of existence"[118]: a *cura sui*, a *technè tou biou*[119]—in short, a *bio-technic*. Today, when care has once again emerged as a site around which what Nietzsche calls the "will to power" is played out, it is crucial to explore such an art of existence, and to practice the aesthetic education that seeks to inspire it.

In a way, one could argue that this is very much part of Hailsham's educational project—but it is part of it *in the wrong way*. Indeed, one of the most characteristic aspects of Hailsham life is that students are encouraged, strongly encouraged even, to be productive and to make art. They exchange their artwork amongst each other. Particularly good pieces from students at all levels are taken away for the gallery of Madame. This mysterious gallery plays a crucial role in Hailsham mythology, especially in the story about the deferral that emerges while Kathy is at the Cottages. According to this story, if one has made a name for oneself by contributing works to the gallery, and if one is truly in love with another clone, one's time of being a donor can be deferred by three to four years. As I noted earlier on, this turns out to have been a lie, but it is interesting to see the role that art plays in this set-up. Indeed, as I have said above, it appears to be through art and love that the students think they will be able to redeem themselves (do we not all hold on to the hope, somewhere, that we may be redeemed through our love and our work?). In reality, however, the art is collected to prove to financial donors and advocates of the Hailsham project that the students have souls, and deserve humane living conditions. And thus, Tommy keeps working away on his art—even after he has already gone through three donations—in order to prove that he is a good student, that he has something to offer to the world.

This is exactly the structure that produces bare life, where life has become separated from art and one is attempting to demonstrate the worth of one's life through something that is exterior to it. Instead, what Tommy fails to grasp is the political potential of the aesthetics of existence: if only he would have taken hold of his life as he takes hold of his art, of the elaborately detailed mythical animals he draws—how different his life could have been! If only all of the students had invested as much time in the art of living as they did in the art that they exchanged while they were at Hailsham! The only one, perhaps, who ultimately approaches the aesthetics of existence is Kathy, that excellent carer. She does end up writing the story of her life, and not just of her life but of the lives of all of them. However, as such a carer and practitioner of narrative care, her role is problematic, as I have shown, because it risks to be complicit with the system that Tommy rightfully contests. And so Kathy's aesthetics of existence turns out to be an ideological one that does not draw the system into question.[120]

However, it is when reading Tommy's bursts of anger—which never develop into an aesthetics of existence, an organized individual and collective form of resistance—*together with* Kathy's account that something else becomes possible, namely *an aesthetics of existence that could have developed from the anger* and from the separation between life and law that Tommy represents. Tommy's life does not coincide with the Hailsham life, his reality does not match the reality presented to him at Hailsham. In this sense, the figure of him raging against the school, his fellow students, his incapacity to make what is considered to be good art, splashing mud all over his favorite shirt, is reminiscent of the figure of Nietzsche, and the position that Malabou associates with him:

> What we are lacking is *life*, which is to say: *resistance*. Resistance is what we want. Resistance to flexibility, to this ideological norm advanced consciously or otherwise by a reductionist discourse that models and naturalizes the neuronal process in order to legitimate a certain social and political functioning.[121]

Tommy is the figure of such a life, but lacks its aesthetics. Whereas Kathy approaches its aesthetics, she lacks the life itself.

The two should never have let go of each other. It is only in their meeting that a narrative care on the far side of biopolitics becomes possible.

Notes

1 Gilles Deleuze, *Essays Critical and Clinical*, trans. Daniel W. Smith and Michael A. Greco (Minneapolis: University of Minnesota Press, 1997), 1.

2 Catherine Malabou, *What Should We Do With Our Brain?*, trans. Sebastian Rand (New York: Fordham University Press, 2008), 79.

3 The notion of a "late life" obviously rings false here, since the clones only have a very short life-span.

4 Kazuo Ishiguro, *Never Let Me Go* (New York: Knopf, 2005), 166.

5 Ishiguro, *Never*, 265.

6 There has been some critical debate about the implications of this point. Is Ishiguro saying that clones are like humans (see, for example, Richard F. Storrow, "Therapeutic Reproduction and Human Dignity," in *Law*

and Literature 21:2 (2009): 257–74)? Or that humans are like clones? The first would be a humanist argument, but a disturbing one given the clones' submissive attitude throughout the novel. The second would a posthuman one, but—paradoxically—one that risks to work in the service of a humanist presupposition: the clones are submissive because they are clones. Human beings would never act in this way. See, for example, Rebecca L. Walkowitz, who suggests that the point of Ishiguro's novel is that we "see humans as clones. That is, we are urged to see that even humans produced through biological reproduction are in some ways copies" ("Unimaginable Largeness: Kazuo Ishiguro, Translation, and the New World Literature," in *Novel* 40:3 (2007): 226). See also Martin Puchner, who argues that the novel's "ultimate goal is to question the status of the clone, and, by extension, of the human" ("When We Were Clones," in *Raritan* 27:4 (2008): 37).

7 See Ishiguro, *Never*, 282.

8 Wendy Brown makes this point in the introduction to her *States of Injury: Power and Freedom in Late Modernity* (Princeton: Princeton University Press, 1995), 15.

9 See Bruce Robbins, "Cruelty is Bad: Banality and Proximity in *Never Let Me Go*," in *Novel* 40:3 (2007): 289–302.

10 See, for example, Keith McDonald, "Days of Past Futures: Kazuo Ishiguro's *Never Let Me Go* as 'Speculative Memoir,'" in *Biography* 30: 1 (2007): 74–83.

11 My question pertains to the novel in particular. Of course, "[t]he idea of creating a living replica of an organism, an 'imitation of life', has been a goal of art, aesthetics, and image technology at least since Aristotle," as W. J. T. Mitchell notes (*Cloning Terror: The War of Images, 9/11 to the Present* (Chicago: University of Chicago Press, 2011), 22). He mentions, in this context, "[t]he routine invocation of the Frankenstein myth, the Pygmalion and Narcissus narratives, the legend of the Jewish golem, the artificial warrior animated from dead matter, all the way down to the modern robot and cyborg" (Mitchell, *Cloning*, 32): all of these examples testify to "the human fascination with the prospect of creating an artificial human life form" (ibid.). In this sense, art's connection with biopolitics is much older than the novel. With the novel, however, it takes on a particularly modern form—one that becomes highly significant today, in the age of biotechnology (the latter is central to Mitchell's book as well). Mitchell briefly mentions Ishiguro's *Never Let Me Go* early on in his book (ibid., 34–5).

12 Ishiguro, *Never*, 6.

13 Kathy's account might show that one is always nostalgic for the site of one's childhood, no matter the childhood's particular circumstances.

14 Ishiguro, *Never*, 6.

15 Ibid., 16.

16 Ibid., 30.
17 Ibid.
18 Ibid., 42.
19 See D.W. Winnicott, *Playing and Reality* (New York: Routledge, 2005).
20 Ishiguro, *Never*, 65.
21 Bruce Jennings has already used the term "biopower" in relation to Ishiguro's novel in: "Biopower and the Liberationist Romance," in *The Hastings Center Report* 40: 4 (2010): http://www.thehastingscenter.org/Publications/HCR/Detail.aspx?id=4770
22 Ishiguro, *Never*, 69.
23 Ibid., 67.
24 Ibid., 67–8.
25 Ibid., 73.
26 Ibid., 78.
27 Ibid.
28 Ibid., 81.
29 One could argue that this point matters especially in US society, which is driven by the story of the American dream, the "rags to riches" story that drives everyone's individual endeavor and prevents Americans from collectively rebelling against the conditions of their existence—for rebellion would only put you behind in relation to those others who do not rebel, and thus make it up the ladder faster than you; it puts you behind in the competition towards the realization of the dream. It is the belief in the dream, one could argue, that keeps the repressive apparatus from which Americans suffer intact; if only one could stop dreaming, and start acting, one might not realize the individual dream, but another dream that would transform everyone's world.
30 This reminds one of the search that drives Steven Spielberg's *Artificial Intelligence* (United States: DreamWorks, 2002), a story about a mechanical boy looking for the blue fairy in the hope that she will make him real. Of course, there is no such fairy… In this case, however, we are still dealing with a cybernetic machine. The situation gets all the more frustrating in *Never Let Me Go*, when the protagonists in question are not mechanical, but natural: cloned, but human beings nevertheless.
31 Susan Sontag, *Against Interpretation* (New York: Delta, 1964), 91.
32 Lambert intended to treat this topic in his contribution to a journal issue on biopolitics and the novel that Pieter Vermeulen and I had planned. Unfortunately, the issue never materialized.
33 Two critics come close to mentioning biopolitics in their discussions of Frankenstein: Sarah Guyer, "Testimony and Trope in Frankenstein," in *Studies in Romanticism* 45: 1 (2006): 77–115; Maureen N. McLane, "Literate Species: Populations, 'Humanities', and Frankenstein," in *English Literary History* 63: 4 (1996): http://knarf.english.upenn.edu/Articles/mclane.html Mark Hansen completely revisits McLane's claims about

Frankenstein as a "technophobic allegory" in "'Not thus, after all would life be given': Technèsis, Technology and the Parody of Romantic Poetics in Frankenstein," in *Studies in Romanticism* 36: 4 (1997): 575–609.

34 Remember here how Paul is thrown off his horse by lightning, and how Paul Rayment is thrown off his bike by a bolt of electricity produced by the car of Wayne Blight. Perhaps Coetzee, too, was alluding to the scene in Shelley's novel?

35 On this, see Shameem Black's excellent article "Ishiguro's Inhuman Aesthetics," in *Modern Fiction Studies* 55: 4 (2009): 785–807, in particular 789. Black mentions there Agamben's theory of the camp and links it to the life of the clones, casting them explicitly as bare life. This develops into Black's criticism of humanist art as "keep[ing] the students unaware of their own inhumanity—it masks their own mechanical condition and serves to further prepare them for lives of exploitation" (Black, "Ishiguro's," 790). Black notes later in the article that it is "particularly painful" that the profession that is indicted here—that of the humanist artist—"is in some sense Ishiguro's own": "As in *The Unconsoled*, which dramatizes the predicament of a bewildered musician, *Never Let Me Go* illuminates the problems that arise when art becomes a governing ideological force" (ibid., 793). My own reading of Kathy's narrative is wholly in line with this. Black ultimately proposes the notion of an "inhuman aesthetics" that would subvert the ideology of humanist art that the novel criticizes.

36 See Giorgio Agamben, *Homo Sacer: Sovereign Power and Bare Life*, trans. Daniel Heller-Roazen (Stanford: Stanford University Press, 1998), 174.

37 Ian Watt, *The Rise of the Novel: Studies in Defoe, Richardson, and Fielding* (Harmondsworth: Penguin, 1970), 7.

38 Watt, *Rise*, 138.

39 Ibid., 139.

40 Other theories of the novel are much more political: one can think, for example, of Georg Lukács' *Theory of the Novel* (London: Merlin, 1978), which takes the experience of the First World War as a central reference; or of Edward Said's *Culture and Imperialism* (New York: Knopf, 1993), a work of political, postcolonial criticism.

41 See Giorgio Agamben, *The Kingdom and the Glory: For a Theological Genealogy of Economy and Government*, trans. Lorenzo Chiesa with Matteo Mandarini (Stanford: Stanford University Press, 2011).

42 See Paul Veyne, *Did the Greeks Believe in their Myths? An Essay on the Constitutive Imagination*, trans. Paula Wissing (Chicago: University of Chicago Press, 1988).

43 Agamben, *Homo Sacer*, 182–3.

44 Ibid., 183.

45 Karl Löwith quoted in ibid., 121.

46 Hence, Kathy's remark that they were lucky—they constitute in a certain sense an elite among clones; if only they could overcome their "class"

position and align themselves with other clones in a shared struggle for different living conditions… Instead, they are focused on getting a deferral while the horrible lives of their brothers and sisters in the government homes continue.

47 Ishiguro, *Never*, 263–4.

48 Agamben, *Homo Sacer*, 159.

49 Ibid., 161. Particularly relevant in this context is the novel's suggestion about what happens after the fourth donation: "How maybe, after the fourth donation, even if you've technically completed, you're still conscious in some way; how then you find there are more donations, plenty of them, on the other side of that line; how there are no more recovery centers, no carers, no friends; how there's nothing to do except watch your remaining donations until they switch you off" (Ishiguro, *Never*, 279). "It's horror movie stuff," as Tommy says, but it is not that far from the reality that he is already living.

50 Agamben, *Homo Sacer*, 164.

51 I cannot do justice here to the wide range of articles that have appeared on this issue. Michel Terestchenko has recently discussed the butler's "blind obedience" in "Servility and Destructiveness in Kazuo Ishiguro's *The Remains of the Day*," in *Partial Answers* 5: 1 (2007): 77–89; Lisa Fluet connects the immaterial labor of the butler to that of the clones in *Never Let Me Go* in "Immaterial Labors: Ishiguro, Class, and Affect," in *Novel* 40: 3 (2007): 265–88.

52 I use the phrase "line of flight" after Gregg Lambert, who borrows it from Gilles Deleuze in his article "On the Uses and Abuses of Literature for Life: Gilles Deleuze and the Literary Clinic," in *Postmodern Culture* 8: 3 (1998): 1–37.

53 It might just be that she is British, but that is another issue.

54 Robbins, "Cruelty," 297.

55 Ibid.

56 Ibid., 301.

57 For a discussion of the difference between nuclear and pharmacological criticism, see my Chapter Three.

58 Malabou, *What Should We Do*, 79.

59 Michel Foucault, "The Minimalist Self," in *Politics, Philosophy, Culture: Interviews and Other Writings, 1977–1984*, ed. Lawrence D. Kritzman (New York: Routledge, 1990), 11.

60 Michel Foucault, *The History of Sexuality: An Introduction*, Vol. I, trans. Robert Hurley (New York: Vintage, 1990),148.

61 Ibid.

62 Ibid.

63 Ibid., 152.

64 Ibid., 151.

65 Ibid., 155.

66 Ibid., 156.
67 Ibid., 157.
68 Ibid.
69 See Michel Foucault, *The Order of Things: An Archeology of the Human Sciences*, trans. [not listed] (New York: Vintage, 1973), 386–7.
70 Michel Foucault, "Introduction," in *Herculine Barbin, Being the Recently Discovered Memoirs of a Nineteenth-Century French Hermaphrodite*, trans. Richard McDougall (New York: Pantheon Books, 1980), vii.
71 Foucault, *History*, 159.
72 See Bernard Stiegler, *Taking Care of Youth and the Generations*, trans. Stephen Barker (Stanford: Stanford University Press, 2010).
73 See Michel Foucault, *The Politics of Truth*, ed. Sylvère Lotringer (Los Angeles: Semiotext(e): 2007), 116.
74 See Sophie Calle, *Take Care of Yourself*, trans. Charles Penwarden et al. (Arles: Actes Sud, 2007).
75 Malabou, *What Should We Do*, 1.
76 Ibid., 1.
77 Karl Marx, *The Eighteenth Brumaire of Louis Bonaparte*, trans. [not listed] (New York: International Publishers, 1998), 15.
78 Malabou, *What Should We Do*, 1.
79 Ibid.
80 Ibid., 2.
81 Ibid., 5.
82 Ibid.
83 Ibid., 7.
84 Ibid.
85 Ibid.
86 Ibid.
87 See Arne De Boever, "The Allegory of the Cage: Foucault, Agamben, and the Enlightenment," in *Foucault Studies 10* (2010): 7–22: http://rauli.cbs.dk/index.php/foucault-studies/article/viewFile/3124/3288
88 Ishiguro, *Never*, 139.
89 Malabou, *What Should We Do*, 8.
90 Ibid., 11.
91 Ibid., 14.
92 Ibid., 30.
93 Ibid., 52.
94 Ibid., 33.
95 Ibid., 40.
96 Ibid., 68.
97 Ibid., 12.
98 Ibid.
99 Ibid. This quotation arguably also reveals interesting affinities between Malabou's thought on the brain and the work of Gilbert Simondon. I

do not have the space to explore this in full, but I have discussed the question of genius in relation to Simondon's pre-individual in "Agamben et Simondon: Ontologie, technologie, et politique," trans. Jean-Hugues Barthélémy, in *Cahiers Simondon* 2 (2010): 117–28. Interestingly, Simondon appears in a footnote in Mark Jerng's fine discussion of Ishiguro's novel "Giving Form to Life: Cloning and Narrative Expectations of the Human," in *Partial Answers* 6:2 (2008): 376n. 9. Later, Jerng alludes to Simondon when he puts forward an important point about individuation in the novel: "It is not that Ishiguro fails to portray these clones as human; rather, he writes a story that reverses the narrative trajectory of individuation. Ishiguro does not reveal the human as unfolding and developing from a given inert potentiality. This is a much more disturbing story because it withholds the reader's desire for emancipation: the clones do not rebel and thus 'become human'. Rather, they learn to make sense of their lives as clones" (Jerng, "Giving," 382).

100 Malabou, *What Should We Do*, 15.

101 Ibid., 74.

102 Ibid., 74.

103 Ibid., 79. Chapter 17 of Werner Herzog's *Grizzly Man* (Santa Monica: Lions Gate, 2005), in which Timothy Treadwell attacks "the individuals [of the Park Service] with whom he worked for thirteen years" (as Herzog explains in the voice over), is exemplary in this respect. Treadwell, who has been taking care of the coastly grizzly bears in Katmai National Park in Alaska, rages in this scene against the government, specifically the Park Service, which he considers to have misrepresented his protective, peaceful, and loving—in short: care-taking—presence in the park. In this grotesque scene of cursing, which Herzog all too easily reads as a mad performance ("the actor in the film has taken over from the filmmaker; I have seen this madness before—on the film set"), Treadwell's care-taking expresses itself as rage. As Herzog explains, this is a line he refuses to cross; but one wonders whether we might not *have to* cross it, if we do not want to end up in a society of "obedient individuals who have no greater merit than that of knowing how to bow their heads with a smile" (Malabou, *What Should We Do*, 79)?

In an article titled "Losing Face: Francis Bacon's *25th Hour*" (forthcoming in *Film-Philosophy*), I argue something similar about the famous chapter titled "Reflection" in Spike Lee's film *25th Hour* (United States: Touchstone, 2003). It would be all too easy, I think, to read "Reflection" as a scene of racism, reminiscent of the racist monologue in Tony Kaye's *American History X* (S.I.: New Line, 1999) that "Reflection" references. Instead, I argue that the politically incorrect anger that is expressed in "Reflection"—an anger that the film also associates with madness, given the personality disorder that the scene evokes—is in fact *a practice of care*, in the sense that it draws out how identity has become a vehicle of power in the post-September 11 era. As I argue there, Spike Lee's more recent *Inside Man* plays out a similar problem. Racism is very much at the heart of each of these films, but the position that the films take up with respect to this problem is much more complicated than a simple celebration of any identitarian category can account for.

104 Judith Butler, *Gender Trouble: Feminism and the Subversion of Identity* (New York: Routledge, 1999), 123.

105 Butler, *Gender*, 123.

106 Ibid., 124.

107 Ibid., 125.

108 Ibid.

109 Ibid., 126.

110 Ibid.

111 Ibid., 120.

112 Malabou, *What Should We Do*, 82.

113 Ibid.

114 Marc Jeannerod, "Foreword," in ibid., xii.

115 Ibid., 82.

116 Foucault, *History*, 157.

117 Malabou, *What Should We Do*, 7.

118 Michel Foucault, *The Care of the Self: The History of Sexuality*, Vol. 3, trans. Robert Hurley (New York: Vintage, 1988), 43.

119 Foucault, *Care of the Self*, 45.

120 I am opposing "aesthetic ideology" here to a critical "aesthetics of existence" that would be nurtured by an aesthetic education that differs from that which Kathy and co receive at Hailsham. I have explored the question of this other aesthetic education in Arne De Boever, "The Philosophy of (Aesthetic) Education," in *Everything is in Everything: Jacques Rancière Between Intellectual Emancipation and Aesthetic Education*, ed. Jason Smith and Annette Weissman (Zürich: Art Center Graduate Press/ JRP Ringier, 2011), 34–48.

121 Malabou, *What Should We Do*, 68.

3

Life-Writing in Paul Auster's *The Book of Illusions*

Everything that you write ... writes you as you write it.[1]

—J. M. Coetzee, *Doubling the Point*

In his novel Leviathan, *Paul Auster thanks me for having authorized him to mingle fact with fiction. And indeed, on pages 60 to 67 of his book, he uses a number of episodes from my life to create a fictive character named Maria. ... Since, in* Leviathan, *Auster has taken me as a subject, I imagined swapping roles and taking him as the author of my actions. I asked him to invent a fictive character which I would attempt to resemble.*[2]

—Sophie Calle, *Double Game*

Creation and Destruction

Paul Auster has always been interested in the writing of life. From his early autobiographical and biographical experiments in *The Invention of Solitude* to his later autobiography *Hand to Mouth*, and from his novel *Leviathan* to the more recent *The Book of Illusions*—both of which could be characterized as biographical fictions—, the question of life and its relation to writing has been at the center of Auster's projects. Consider, for example, the memorable opening lines of *Leviathan*, which put the problematic of life-writing—the impossibility of it—explicitly on the table:

> Six days ago, a man blew himself up by the side of a road in northern Wisconsin. There were no witnesses, but it appears that he was sitting on the grass next to his car when the bomb he was building accidentally went off. According to the forensic reports that have just been published, the man was killed instantly. His body burst into dozens of small pieces, and fragments of his corpse were found as far as fifteen feet away from the site of the explosion.[3]

How to reconstruct the life-narrative of this man? That is, of course, what Auster's novel will undertake. But the memory of this explosion and the life it has shattered will continue to haunt and frustrate the novel's biographical attempt.

The issue of life's relation to writing or to artifice in general is an old one, going back at least as far as Plato, and it concerns not only writers but also—and perhaps even more so—painters and sculptors (as Jacques Derrida in his text "Plato's Pharmacy" recalls).[4] The split between abstract and representational painting can be considered from this perspective: one should note, in this context, David Reed's reflections on the question in his writings on vampires (Auster has written about Reed in the essay "Black on White"[5]). But one can also think of such classics as E. T. A. Hoffmann's story "The Sandman"—Sigmund Freud analyzes the story at length in his essay "The Uncanny"—, the Pygmalion myth, the story of Pinocchio, the golem, or even Steven Spielberg's *Artificial Intelligence*: all of these testify to sculpture's obsession with life and with making art come to life.[6] In the biotechnological era, which is central to the concerns addressed in this book, we have come much closer to the possibility of actually realizing this. However, critics like Vandana Shiva remind us that there is much discussion about whether scientists can ever be said to have really invented life, since they are always starting from a basic material that precedes them. Their creations are hardly *ex nihilo*.[7]

There is indeed something politically suspicious about this history of art trying to make life. What makes Auster such an interesting novelist in the context of this study on biopolitics and the novel is the fact that he is very much aware of this. His awareness appears to come, in part, from his familiarity with the kind of French theory that informs this book. In addition, the biopolitical issue resonates with the postmodernist, meta-fictional concerns that are central to his *oeuvre*. As is well known, Auster is considered one of the icons of postmodernism in American literature. But he has also continued these concerns into the twenty-first century. Rather than marking them here as dated, as many contemporary readers of his *oeuvre* seem to do—his writing is not nearly as hot as fifteen years ago, when I first started reading his work—, I want to reconsider them in the context of this project on narrative care.

This chapter shows, specifically, that a biopolitical concern informs Auster's novel *The Book of Illusions*. The novel is about the life and work of filmmaker Hector Mann. At the same time, however, it is also about the life and work of its narrator, David Zimmer. In the case of both men, work becomes linked to life, and even survival. Mann abandons his creative work after his fiancée, Dolores Saint John, kills his pregnant ex-girlfriend, Brigid O'Fallon. Having buried Brigid in the hills north of Malibu, California, Hector can no longer go on with his life as before: he abandons filmmaking, changes his name, and sets out to become a nobody. Mann will return to filmmaking years later, however, after the death of his son. Faithful to his old oath that he would not make films again, he can do so only on the condition that no one will see the films, and that they will be destroyed after his death. Work, too, thus becomes linked to a practice of erasure and destruction—and all of this in order to make up for another destruction. It is not a particularly rational project, some readers might object, but reason is, of course, rarely what triumphs in these kinds of situations.

David Zimmer's work is closely related to his life as well. After his wife and children die in a plane crash, he authors the definitive work on Mann's films. Mann, who is presumed dead after his disappearance in 1929, reads the book and invites Zimmer to his ranch in New Mexico to watch the films he has made since 1929. Meanwhile, Zimmer is also at work on a translation of Chateaubriand's monumental autobiography *Mémoires d'outre-tombe*. Work clearly functions as a "medicine"[8] or pharmakon for Zimmer: it is a drug that is intended to cure him from his suffering. As such, this drug—which is like the other drugs he is taking in the book; he notes early on the novel that his salvation lies in "pharmacology"[9] and later too, the word "pharmacy"[10] is prominently featured in the novel—is also poisonous: he notes several times that he is so caught up within his work that he has come to resemble a dead man. The confrontation with Hector (himself something like a dead man given that no one has heard from him since 1929) will help Zimmer get out of this. But it is by no means an easy exit, and Auster's novel chronicles each and every one of its fantastic turns.

Hector's decision to burn his work recalls, as is noted in the novel, Franz Kafka's request to his friend Max Brod to have all of his manuscripts burnt.[11] Brod, of course, did not go through with it. But Hector's wife Frieda does. In fact, whereas Hector had requested only a burning of the films he made after 1929, she is hell-bent on burning every trace of Hector's life, including the old films, his notebooks, and the biography of Hector that his cameraman's daughter, Alma Grund, is writing. Frieda's burning thus turns into a holo-caust, an all-burning that raises some questions about the "act of breathtaking nihilism"[12] that informs Mann's art. Why did Mann ask Alma to write his biography, Zimmer wonders in the novel's closing pages? Why did Mann invite Zimmer to the ranch to watch the films he made after 1929? Might he have changed his mind about his project of destruction? Might he have given in on the radical and difficult path he had set out for himself? Hector's change of mind might become more understandable when it is considered next to the history of the Second World War and the Holocaust. The war is alluded to in the book only once, but the important dates in Hector's life all coincide with important dates in its history. Given how this history parallels the life-story of Mann, an Argentinian Jew, it is almost impossible not to think of the Holocaust when, in the closing pages of the book, all of Mann's work is burning.

What is *The Book of Illusions* saying, then, about Mann's project? About the project of his life, and his work? What is it saying about the relation between creation and destruction in Mann's life and work and about Zimmer's role as a witness in relation to both? How does this speak to the relation between art and life that is central to Auster's *oeuvre* as a whole? And what might be the biopolitical dimension of these questions?

Life-stories (Sadism and the Novel)

> [Pornography's] excesses belong to that timeless, locationless area outside history, outside geography, where fascist art is born.[13]
>
> —Angela Carter, *The Sadeian Woman*

In 1929, two months after releasing his last film—"*Double or Nothing*, the last of the twelve two-reel comedies he made at the end of the silent era"[14]—Hector Mann disappears from his California home never to be seen again. Sixty years later, in 1988, Hampton College professor of Comparative Literature David Zimmer publishes a book on Mann's films, which have by then become almost entirely forgotten. For the book, Zimmer notes, "the story of [Mann's] life was secondary"—instead, he "stuck to a close reading of the films themselves."[15] No life story, therefore, but a book of film criticism that establishes itself as the definitive text on Mann's work.

The book was "born out of a great sorrow,"[16] as Zimmer recounts, namely the death of his wife and children in a plane crash. After the loss, Zimmer gives in to drinking and the depression lasts until one night, watching one of Mann's films on television, Mann makes him laugh. The moment is crucial, because it makes Zimmer realize that there is still some life left in him. Very soon afterwards, he travels to various film archives in the US (starting with the one in Rochester, New York) and in Europe to watch all of Mann's films, and it is this work—which is obviously not just a work of criticism but also a work of mourning—that will turn into his book *The Silent World of Hector Mann*.

It is probably a good thing that Zimmer stuck to close-readings of the films, given that to write a book about Hector's life would have been rather difficult, if not impossible. Going over some profiles that were written about Hector between 1927 and 1928, Zimmer notes the contradictory information: whereas one of them includes a list of impressive credits going back to his work as a performer in Latin America, another has him stating that he did not do any work as a performer before arriving in Los Angeles. Whereas in one, he is quoted as speaking with a heavy Latin-American accent, another states that his English is impeccable, so good in fact that "you would swear he had been raised in Sandusky, Ohio."[17] In yet another profile, this remark is picked up by Mann, who suggests that Ohio is where he is from. Clearly, we are dealing with a man who is inventing multiple lives for himself. And indeed, he is living multiple lives—and at least *one life too many*.

While he is dating reporter Brigid O'Fallon, and spending every other night at her house, he also falls in love with actress Dolores Saint John, who has become (on Brigid's recommendation) the star actress of his films. Mann proposes to marry her and Saint John accepts, but Brigid is informed about none of this. Understandably, she is upset when Hector finally tells her. After surviving a suicide attempt, she discovers weeks later that she is pregnant. She informs Hector but he tries to block out the news, knowing that if he tells Saint John, their engagement will be off. When a manic Brigid shows up at Mann's house one day while he is away, and confronts Saint John with the fact that she loves Hector and is pregnant with his child, a panicked Saint John shoots Brigid in the face. The woman bleeds to death on Mann's carpet. To avoid persecution, Mann buries his pregnant ex in the hills north of Malibu, and the couple splits up. Saint John moves back to her parents' house, and Mann leaves his old life behind, moving north to do various odd jobs.

Mann has taken a life-changing decision. Since all he ever wanted was to become good at making movies, "therefore, that was the one thing that he would never allow himself to do again"[18]:

> You don't drive an innocent girl insane, and you don't make her pregnant, and you don't bury her dead body eight feet under the ground and expect to go on with your life as before. A man who had done what he had done deserved to be punished. If the world wouldn't do it for him, then he would have to do it himself.[19]

The reasoning is curious, since the world would have likely done it for him had he turned himself in. But such is the logic of the fiction and of Hector's life-project. From the aspiring young film-maker, he turns into "Mr Nobody" (which is the title of one of his films). He embarks on a project of self-punishment, exiling himself to a self-created penal colony where he will go on living without being able to pursue his passion. It is a torture of a kind, and for an artist it is torture of the worst kind. It is an aesthetics of erasure and destruction that goes against everything that makes him *him*.

The story takes another cruel turn when, almost in spite of himself, Hector ends up in Spokane, Washington, where Brigid was from, and goes looking for the sports store that is run by her father Red O'Fallon. Running into Brigid's younger sister Nora—a woman like "warm milk"[20] who immediately stirs his desire—, he takes up a job at the store. Nora quickly takes a liking to him. During the speech therapy lessons she offers to give him—this is when he finally loses most of his accent, yet another mark of his changing identity—, the two grow closer and closer together, even though he knows that Nora is off-limits. When ultimately it becomes clear that she is in love with him and wants to marry him, the girl's father poses him an ultimatum. Either he marries her ("takes care of her," as O'Fallon repeats twice), or he gets out of Spokane altogether. The decision is difficult but necessary: Hector leaves town on the same night, and it is this second crime of a kind—for it is hardly noble what he does to Nora—that will bring him to his lowest point so far (he will try to kill himself a day after leaving Spokane).

Until now, Hector's entire project has been to strip himself of what I have called in the previous chapter his *bios*, his individual form of life. He has cut himself off from being a filmmaker, left all of his possessions behind and taken on another identity in response to the horrible crime that he (and Saint John) committed. He has turned himself into an outlaw of a kind, a sacred being by his own creation. The bare life to which Hector has willingly and purposefully reduced himself is most explicitly exposed in the part of his life-story that begins immediately after he leaves Spokane, when he runs into a woman called Sylvia Meers. "Under her guidance," the novel states, "Hector learned that he could go on killing himself without having to finish the job."[21]

Meers is a prostitute who, after Hector has had sex with her, asks him if he can do it again, and again, all within the space of one hour. The second time will be for free; the third will be for free too if he can pull off another ejaculation. If not, he will have to pay. Clearly, something other than just sex is going on here: it turns out that Mann is in fact being interviewed for a job. When he pulls off the feat, Meers asks him whether he wants to become her partner in a live performance:

> Hector had no idea what she was talking about. She explained it, and when he still didn't understand what she was trying to tell him, she explained it again. There were men, she said, rich men in Chicago, rich men all over the Midwest, who were willing to pay good money to watch people fuck. Oh, Hector said, you mean stag films, blue movies. No, Meers replied, none of that fake stuff. Live performances. Real fucking in front of real people.[22]

Hector agrees to join her, but on the condition that he can take part in it masked. He knows a lot of people in Chicago and he would not want to be recognized.

It is the ultimate and final step in his becoming nobody. With his mask, "he would have no personality, no distinguishing characteristics."[23] In this way, Hector can continue to shape his life through his attempts to destroy it. However, it is not clear during all this time that Hector is really *only* after destruction: "If I want to save my life," he writes in his journal, "then I have to come within an inch to destroying it."[24] Clearly, there is still some curative dimension to this otherwise poisonous project.

It is perhaps no surprise that a star of the silent film business, in which the body is so important, would be a star in the live-fucking business as well.[25] His face may be masked but his body certainly lives up to the expectations. Performing for Archibald Pierson, "a seventy-year-old retired judge who lived alone in a three-story Tudor house in Highland Park,"[26] it becomes clear how "live" the live fucking is expected to be: Hector needs to come three times, the judge explains, each time withdrawing himself from Sylvia just before he is to come in order to ejaculate upon her breasts: "Everything came down to that, the judge said. The spurt was crucial, and the farther it traveled through the air, the happier it was going to make him."[27] "It was," the novel notes, "theater without theatrics, a raw enactment of life itself"[28] that is reminiscent of a Sadean spectacle.

In *Homo Sacer: Sovereign Power and Bare Life*, Giorgio Agamben characterizes the Sadean spectacle as a political "organization of human life founded solely on bare life."[29] In his work, "Sade stages … the *theatrum politicum* as a theater of bare life, in which the very physiological life of bodies appears, through sexuality, as the pure political element."[30] "The growing importance of sadomasochism in modernity"[31] is rooted in this parallel between political theater and the Sadean theatre of bare life. "Not only does Sade consciously evoke the analogy with sovereign power"—represented in Auster's scene by a judge—"but we also find here the symmetry between *homo sacer* and sovereign, in the complicity that ties the masochist to the sadist, the victim to the executioner."[32] The masochist is Hector, who participates in this theater only because he wants to punish himself. The sadist is the judge. Meers—the woman—is merely the vehicle around which Agamben's story, which explicitly inscribes itself in Foucault's work on biopolitics, is played out.[33]

Reading these pages in Auster's novel through the lens of Agamben's remarks on sadism, a connection between the novel and sadism is arguably laid bare. In the previous chapters, I have begun to explore the novel's relation to biopolitics, laying out a brief history of biopolitics in Chapter One, and linking it to Ian Watt's discussion of the novel in *The Rise of the Novel*. I showed there that the logic of governmentality and biopolitics is uncannily close to the logic of novel-writing. The novel can thus be read, I argued, as the literary expression of the political imagination of governmentality. In Chapter Two, I extended this analysis by exploring Kazuo Ishiguro's suggestion that the novel is like a camp, and character-life like bare life. Uncovering the single reference to the camps in Watt's theory of the novel, I suggested that Defoe's concentration on the particular lives of individuals can very much by tied to what Agamben calls the logic of the concentration camps, which he argues to be characteristic of political modernity. Watt famously describes the novel as the characteristic genre of modernity. Although the novel and the camp are clearly not the same, this begs the question of their relation.

My discussion of the scene of live-fucking in Auster's novel enables one to see, as a continuation of this argument, the importance of sadism in this context. Indeed, sadism is arguably linked to both the history of political modernity (the French Revolution) and the camps (think, for example, of Liliana Cavani's film *The Night Porter*). It does not take too much imagination to think of the novel and the power-play that is operative there—deciding on the life and death, the health and reproduction, of ordinary people—as a *sadistic play*.[34] The novel becomes, in this sense, a theater of bare life that is also a political theater.[35]

I will explore the ways in which *The Book of Illusions* addresses this problematic in a meta-fictional way in the next section of this chapter. I already want to note, however, that Auster has explored this problematic—the connection between the novel, biopolitics, the camp, and sadism—in a short little book titled *Travels in the Scriptorium*. In this book, an old man referred to as Mr. Blank is locked in a room where he is visited by characters (referred to in the novel as "operatives") from Paul Auster's novels: Anna Blume, Samuel Farr, John Trause, and so on. Although Blank at first does not remember these characters, slowly but surely information about some of them begins to return to him, and he remembers that he is responsible for sending them out on a mission sometimes ten, sometimes twenty years ago. By the early twenty-first century, when the novel is set, these characters have grown older, and some have returned to question Blank about their existence. Echoing Susan Barton's pleas to the author Daniel Foe in J. M. Coetzee's meta-fictional novel *Foe*, some feel that their "whole life depends"[36] on Blank. Clearly, Blank—who refers to these characters as "My victims. All the people I've made suffer over the years"[37]—is a stand-in for the author, who is being held captive by his own characters (locked rooms are a recurrent theme in Auster's fiction). There is a strange, camp-like feeling of imprisonment to *Travels in the Scriptorium*: one that provides a unique insight, I would argue, not just into Auster's fiction but into the biopolitics of the novel as a genre.

Several accounts of sadism and literature already exist, but as far as I know none establishes these connections. Distinguishing the work of the Marquis de Sade from that of Alain Robbe-Grillet (to whom I will turn in the next chapter), literary critic Susan Suleiman notes in an early article from 1977 that

> the Sadean text, despite its militant espousal of transgression, excess, antinaturalism, remains paradoxically within the formal boundaries of the realist novel: Sade's "scenes," however unimaginable as lived events, are narrated "as if" they had really happened. Even Justine, that consummate storyteller, ostensibly tells not "stories" but *the* story of her *life*.[38]

From this, she concludes that "Sade's text must be called realist: the fictions they enact are never designated as fictions; the text never explicitly calls attention to itself as invention, as *text*; its origin, like its destination, is ostensibly the world of flesh and blood."[39] This means something in relation to Paul Rayment's musing, in *Slow Man*, that his entire life might be no more than a novelist's "biologico-literary experiment"; it means something in view of Ishiguro's suggestion, in *Never Let Me Go*, that characters are like clones, or clones like characters. If Sade, unlike Robbe-Grillet, presents the theater of bare life as a realist theater, a "theater without theatrics," as Auster writes, he may have been doing so for a good reason: in order to show, one could venture, that the text is a biologico-literary experiment, that to *write* about *fucking* has something to do with the *politics* of *sex* (this is, as I have discussed in the previous chapter, the point that Foucault makes in *The History of Sexuality*). He was drawing out, in other words, the connection between writing and biopolitics, between the desire to create a literary work of flesh and blood and the emergent logic of biopolitical governmentality. That is, of course, not the only way to do it: Robbe-Grillet, Suleiman notes, went the other way, constantly drawing attention to the constructedness of the text (that is why his work is foundational for Tom McCarthy's project, which I discuss in Chapter Four).[40]

In her book *The Bonds of Love*, Jessica Benjamin has drawn attention to the relation between sadism and Hegel's master–slave dialectic. If so many critics have argued that Coetzee's novels are meta-fictional allegories in which a Hegelian master–slave dialectic is being played out between author and character, one cannot but take into account the Sadean resonances of his dialectic as well.

Doing so leads one to reconsider the meta-fictional allegory from a feminist perspective,[41] and to ask whether it matters, in this investigation of care and biopolitics, that in most of the cases I have considered so far, I have encountered *men* writing the lives of *women*: Coetzee (or Foe, within the novel) writing the life of Susan Barton in *Foe* and of Elizabeth Costello in *Slow Man* (he makes up for it by turning the woman he is writing into an author herself—it might be a response to his feminist critics, who have taken him to task for writing in the voice of a woman); Ishiguro writing the life of Kathy, in all its intimate details. Auster's book is perhaps the most explicit, as we will see in the next section of this chapter, because it reflects very openly upon the dynamic of a man writing the life of a woman, writing the life of a companion, who responds to his every whim and want. At stake here is, as Benjamin points out,

> a dialectic of control: If I completely control the other, then the other ceases to exist, and if the other completely controls me, then I cease to exist. A condition of our own independent existence is recognizing the other. True independence means sustaining the essential tension of these contradictory impulses; that is, both asserting the self and recognizing the other. Domination is the consequence of refusing this condition.[42]

This is the dialectic—Hegel's master–slave dialectic—that we are confronting in the genre of the novel as well, but with a Sadean, biopolitical emphasis added to it, one that becomes particularly resonant today in the biotechnological age in which all of human life appears to have become "writable." Auster is struggling with these issues throughout his *oeuvre*, and *The Book of Illusions* is no different in this respect.

One other story that could be considered in this context, and that continues the historical references that I have laid out in the previous chapters, is Nathaniel Hawthorne's story "The Birthmark," dating from 1843, shortly after the publication of Shelley's *Frankenstein* (we have moved from the first English-language novel *Robinson Crusoe*, to British romanticism, to American romanticism; Sade's *Justine* is published some time in between *Robinson Crusoe* and *Frankenstein*, in 1791).[43] As in Shelley's *Frankenstein*, a scientist takes up a central place in the story. Aylmer wants to remove the birthmark from his wife Georgiana's face. However, the mark turns out to be intimately tied to her being. It is a mark of mortality that makes her being cohere: if one removes it, one removes her life. And indeed, she dies as a result of the process. "In those days when the comparatively recent discovery of electricity and other kindred mysteries of Nature seemed to open paths into the region of the miracle," Hawthorne writes,

> it was not unusual for the love of science to rival the love of woman in its depth and absorbing energy. The higher intellect, the imagination,

> the spirit, and even the heart might all find their congenial alignment in pursuits which, as some of their ardent votaries believed, would ascend from one step of powerful intelligence to another, until the philosopher should lay his hand on the secret of creative force and perhaps make new worlds for himself.[44]

One recognizes in this passage science's, and ultimately philosophy's, life-making desire. Hawthorne must have been aware that when he was writing this, he was also reflecting on his own practice as a writer. It is *he* who called the woman with the birthmark into being; it is *he* who will make her die. Within this dialectic, one should note, it is ultimately the scientist's slave—Ayler's servant Aminadab—who knows best: "If she were my wife," "he muttered to himself," "I'd never part with that birthmark."[45]

Auster includes a reference to this story in his book because of Alma Grund, the daughter of Hector's cameraman. She has a birthmark on the left side of her face, just like Aylmer's wife, and knows Hawthorne's story by heart (she calls it "my story").[46] But the story also resonates, at a deeper level, with Auster's project, and with all attempts to bring life into art, to make art life-like, or to mix the orders of reality and fiction. Science is ultimately implicated in this, because it continuously tries to make human imagination real. Politics, of course, is implicated in it as well. Like science, it is world-making. Literature has a close relation to both, but importantly that relation is also one of difference, and literature's importance in the science/politics/literature constellation may very well come from this difference. It is in this sense, I would argue, that romanticism's defining characteristic of failure, its defining trait of an aspiration that fails, needs to be read: not as actual failure, but as literature realizing its place next to science and politics, and linking science and politics to the potential of that failure as well. It is in this domain that science and politics have something to learn from the humanities. The novel can never offer live fucking, but in its attempt to do so we understand something about our scientific and political desires, and this understanding can inform whatever scientific and political realities we create. Literature, importantly, holds back. It practices a critical restraint through the otherwise transgressing faculty of the imagination.

When it becomes clear one day that Meers has recognized Mann, and begins to exploit him on the basis of her knowledge, Mann realizes he must leave again. This is how he finally ends up in Sandusky, Ohio, where (in the profile Zimmer digs up earlier on in the novel) he pretended he was from. It is there that his life will begin to develop into yet another direction. Considering suicide once again, he becomes involved in a bank robbery and saves the life of a young, rich girl called Frieda Spelling by catching a bullet that was meant for her. After he has recuperated, the girl (who has seen his films and had recognized him at the bank) proposes marriage to him. He accepts, and they move out to New Mexico to start a new life as Hector and Frieda Spelling. The relationship blossoms and the couple has a son. However, their happiness abruptly ends when the son dies of a bee sting at a very early age. It is through Frieda's insistence that Hector ultimately returns to film-making, taking it up again as a work of mourning that might help him to get over the loss of his son. In order to remain faithful to the event that constituted his subjectivity, namely Brigid's death and his decision not to make films ever again, he can do so only on two conditions: that no one will ever see his work, and that it will be destroyed after he dies.

Zimmer's book comes out towards the very end of Mann's life, in 1988, and after reading the book Mann invites him to the ranch in order to watch the films. *The Book of Illusions* describes not only those films by Hector Mann that are accessible through various film archives. It also describes one of the films that Hector made after his disappearance in 1929. It is to that film, which is central to Auster's novel and mobilizes the novel's deeper thematic about life's relation to art, that I now turn.

The Inner Life of Martin Frost

While Zimmer is at the ranch, he has time to see only one of Hector's films: *The Inner Life of Martin Frost*. It turns out to be a high realist film that pays "scrupulous attention to the particulars of everyday life."[47] The story is about a writer, Martin Frost, who gets to holiday at his friends' country house after finishing a novel. The friends are called Hector and Frieda and the entire film is filmed at their house. As soon as he is there, however, he is visited by a story, and not just by a story: a woman also shows up in his bed, and he has no idea how she got there. She, too, appears to be confused. It turns out that both of them were given a key by Frost's friends.

The woman is called Claire Martin, she says, and she is Hector and Frieda's niece. Martin is irritated at first because he intended to be alone, and work on the story. However, the girl is preparing for a philosophy exam, and she will need her time alone as well, so it seems that they will be able to work something out ("as long as they are stuck with each other, they might as well act like civilized people,"[48] as Martin puts it – in this context, his remark echoes my discussion of "The Politics of Companionship" in Coetzee's *Slow Man*).

The two quickly fall in love. When Hector checks in with Martin a few days into his stay to warn him about a cold front that is on its way to the ranch, it turns out he has never heard about Claire. So who is Claire?

"Don't you get it, Martin?,"[49] she asks him. *You are a week into your story. Have you not figured it out by now?* It never becomes entirely clear who or what Claire is. Little by little, however, it becomes clear that there is a relation between Claire's life and Martin's writing. When the story is more than half done, Claire comes down with a fever and it is immediately evident that she is in bad shape. She dies just as Martin is finishing up the story. Realizing that Claire is somehow related to his story—in other words, that her life and more specifically her death somehow depend on his writing—, he begins to throw the pages of the story, of which there is only one copy, into the fire, thus destroying his work in order to win back her love. "It's the best bargain I have ever made," he says, "[t]hirty-seven pages for your life."[50] Martin turns into a Faustian character who closes a deal with those governing the realms of fiction. Claire—who is revived by this burning—points out in panic that this is against the rules. Martin, however, is changing the rules: by burning his story, he is able to bring Claire back to life.[51]

So once again: who is Claire? From Zimmer's description of Mann's film, one gathers she might be a character in the story, a character whose life Frost is writing. When the story finishes, her life is finished as well and she dies. To undo the story means to bring her back to life. The logic is not watertight, given that she only came into being with the story in the first place; therefore, she would also need to disappear with the first page of the story. But that is what we are presented with in the film. By tying Martin's writing so closely to Claire's life, and by linking the progress of a text to the progress of a life, going from birth to death, Auster is playing with the old theme of linking narrative to life—the theme of a life-narrative. Several authors have played with its reversal, and given the irrevocability of death, one understands the power of such fictions. This motif is entirely part of the problematic of *Narrative Care* and the biopolitical tendency in fiction that I am uncovering.

Interestingly, Auster also turned *The Inner Life of Martin Frost* into an actual film.[52] The first part of the film sticks very closely to Auster's narrative, repeating it almost to the letter. But whereas in the book, the film ends with Claire's revival, the actual film adds a whole new part to the story. In the film, Martin (David Thewlis) and Claire (Irène Jacob) are forced to confront the consequences of Martin's actions: what are they going to do now that Claire has somehow been torn from the world to which she belongs, and been brought into the real world? At first, things do not go well. Claire is called back (literally—she gets a telephone call while Martin is off to replace a tire on their car) by an off-scene presence referred to as "they," and Martin is alone again. In this miserable state, however, during which he is torn between the real world and the world of his dreams in which Claire visits him, he gets the company of a memorable character, the plumber and reader/

writer James "Jim" Fortunato (Michael Imperioli). Fortunato ultimately sets Martin up with his niece, Anna (played by Auster's daughter, Sophie). Like Claire, Anna turns out to be a muse who is sent to writers, painters, and sculptors when they are working on a project. This girl, however, ended up with Jim by mistake (he is not a good writer). And so Martin takes her in, and takes care of her.

Anna is somehow related to Claire, however, and so she can bring Claire back into Martin's life. It turns out that Martin's move has caused much chaos amongst "them." As a result, "they" are confused, and Anna ended up with Jim. In response to Martin and Claire's situation, and out of thanks that Martin is putting up with Anna and has offered to turn her into a real person (although she can act and sing, she is lacking in social skills and needs an education), "they" have offered that after one year, Claire will be allowed to stay with Martin. During that year, however, he cannot look at her. He can touch her, kiss her, et cetera but he cannot look at her: that is the deal. The second condition is that they cannot have sex. And so he touches her blindfolded, and they do not have sex. Thus, Martin is able to found a little family with this two muses, Claire and Anna. At the end of the film, it is revealed that seeing each other in the mirror is fine. Clearly, the film is also a rewriting of the "Orpheus and Eurydice" myth that was famously linked to the problematic of literature and the author's relation to her/his characters by Maurice Blanchot.[53]

It therefore seems that in Auster's film, Claire is a muse, and not a character. Whatever the case may be, the film engages with art's potential to call forth life from another realm, and with art's desire to make this life real. How can we care so much about fictional life, about the life of characters, or muses? Why are we so attached to them if they are not even real? Why do we love them so much, sometimes even more than the real people around us? These are some questions that underlie Auster's story and film, and that I encountered in my discussion of Coetzee and Ishiguro as well.

In this context, I am particularly interested in Zimmer's characterization of Hector's late work as highly realist, "paying scrupulous attention to the details of everyday life." As I discussed in the previous chapters, this is exactly the way in which Watt describes the logic of the novel. Since Hector "was out of the commercial loop," Alma explains, "that meant he could work without constraints."[54] She continues:

> Hector used his freedom to explore things other filmmakers weren't allowed to touch, especially in the forties and fifties. Naked bodies. Down-to-earth sex. Childbirth. Urination, defecation. Those scenes are a bit shocking at first, but the shock wears off rather quickly. They're a

> natural part of life, after all, but we're not used to seeing them presented on film, so we sit up for a couple of seconds and take notice.[55]

Live fucking, once again—but it seems different here. It seems as if the grotesque, Sadean performance of bare life with Sylvia Meers has turned into something else—something that is not necessarily less dangerous. Alma Grund's mother, Faye Morrison, is the star in this film, and her presence on the screen confuses Zimmer because he recognizes Alma in her mother. One major difference is that the mother does not have a birthmark. The film thus seems to make real the fiction of Hawthorne's story "The Birthmark."

My interest, of course, lies in the film's proximity to life.[56] One should remember that Hector used to make silent films (*The Inner Life of Martin Frost* is the only talkie that Zimmer gets to see). In silent films, as Zimmer's descriptions of Hector films make clear, life—specifically the body—is always a major component.[57] Indeed, they are perhaps more physical, more material, than any other kind of film. In this sense, they could perhaps be read as a theater of bare life. This may be part of why Charlie Chaplin's *The Great Dictator*—a talkie from 1940, but essentially still a silent film, as Susan Sontag has noted[58]—is such a successful film: because the philosophical problematic of Nazism relates so very well to the philosophical problematic of silent film. It might explain why Chaplin's *Modern Times*—which he started preparing as a talkie in 1934 but which quickly turned into a silent film—is such a perfect work of art as well: because of the appropriateness of Chaplin's bodily antics within the biopolitical set-up of the factory. Through its realism, Hector's film appears to reflect on these issues.

One should note as well that the issue of naturalism was central to the production of silent films in the early twentieth century. One finds it, for example, in debates about the work of G. W. Pabst, a German filmmaker whose most famous work dates from around the same time when Mann was making films. Pabst's most famous star was Louise Brooks, an American actress who has attracted some critical descriptions that become highly interesting in this context. Critics admire her liveliness, her naturalness, and for this reason she was the perfect girl for Pabst's films. I rehearse some quotations included in Kenneth Tynan's extraordinary text on Brooks, "The Girl in the Black Helmet" (reproduced in the booklet that accompanies the DVD of Pabst's classic *Pandora's Box*):

> Louise is the perfect apparition, the dream woman, the being without whom the cinema would be a poor thing. She is much more than a myth; she is a magical presence, a real phantom, the magnetism of the cinema.[59]

All of this could apply to Faye in *The Inner Life of Martin Frost* as well. Consider the following quote:

> As soon as [Brooks] takes the screen [another critic writes] fiction disappears along with art, and one has the impression of being present at a documentary. … Complete naturalness and complete simplicity. Her art is so pure that it becomes invisible.[60]

The critical fascination with Brooks speaks to the cinema's fantasy, in the wake of the rise of the novel, to bring real life to the screen.

I do not want to suggest, of course, that this article was part of Auster's references when he was writing his book. I am simply saying that some of the concerns of silent filmmakers at the time, concerns that are central in the critical debates about silent films, appear to resonate with Auster's concerns as a contemporary novelist. In addition, I am reframing those concerns here within the history of governmentality and biopolitics.

It is interesting to note, however, that when Tynan in "The Girl in the Black Helmet" describes his meeting with Louise Brooks, he writes: "She was seventy-one years old, and until a few months earlier I had thought she was dead."[61] "Everyone thought he was dead," Auster's novel begins. "When my book about his films was published in 1988, Hector Mann had not been heard from in almost sixty years."[62] Tynan's encounter with Brooks takes place in Rochester, NY, which is also the place where Zimmer begins his research on Mann's work. At that point, in 1979, Brooks "has not left her apartment since 1960, except for a few trips to the dentist and one to the doctor."[63] "You're doing a terrible thing to me," she said as she ushered me in. "I've been killing myself off for twenty years, and you're going to bring me back to life."[64] Those words could just as well have been spoken by Mann, when Zimmer visits him at his bedside in his ranch in New Mexico. Auster's description of the end of the visit is memorable:

> As I stood up from the chair, he [Hector] reached out and grabbed my arm. That I do remember. I remember the cold, clawlike feel of his hand, and I remember thinking to myself: this is happening. Hector Mann is alive, and his hand is touching me now. Then I remember telling myself to remember what that hand felt like. If he didn't live until morning, it would be the only proof that I had seen him alive.[65]

When Tynan meets Brooks, "she nodded and beckoned me in. I greeted her with a respectful embrace. This was my first physical contact with Louise Brooks."[66] In both cases, physical contact appears to matter a lot, as if our narrators are trying to convince themselves of the fact that Hector and Brooks are real. "I am rather a doubting Thomas," as Elizabeth Costello states when she meets Paul Rayment. "I mean, wanting to explore for myself what kind of being you are. Wanting to be sure … that our two bodies would not just pass through each other. Naïve, of course. We are not ghosts, either of us."[67]

This reflection about life's relation to art continues in Brooks' discussion of the talkies. After Brooks' discussion of anger fits by Martha Graham and Buster Keaton, both of whom she admires, she states the following:

> People tell you that the reason a lot of actors left Hollywood when sound came in was that their voices were wrong for talkies. That's the official story. The truth is that the coming of sound meant the end of the all-night parties. With talkies, you couldn't stay out till sunrise anymore. You had to rush back from the studios and start learning your lines, ready for the next day's shooting, at 8:00am. That was when the studio machine really took over. It controlled you, mind and body, from the moment you were yanked out of bed at dawn until the publicity department put you back to bed at night.[68]

It is not exactly the biopolitics I am talking about in reference to Brooks' appearance in Pabst's films, but it certainly is a description of the biopolitics of modern life.

One of the most influential critics to have reflected on the issues that I am raising with respect to modern cinema's relation to life is Walter Benjamin.[69] Although his essay "The Work of Art in the Age of Mechanical Reproduction" (literally, "The Work of Art in the Age of Technical Reproducibility"), is clearly infused by a certain enthusiasm for photography and film, one also senses Benjamin's skepticism and concern about what these developments will do to the originality, uniqueness, or what he calls the "aura"[70] of the work of art. Reading this text next to his essay "The Storyteller," where the novel (and the new form of writerly production called the newspaper) are aligned with the modern era and contrasted with storytelling,[71] one understands how both the novel and the cinema are caught up, in Benjamin's perspective, in the same problem. This problem is, importantly, the problem of life. Whereas good stories are still able to communicate experiences, the novel lacks this capacity, which is altogether absent in newspapers. The latter merely pass on plausible information. Whereas life, according to Benjamin, can still be associated with the story, the novel and the newspaper—and, judging from his essay on mechanical reproduction, photography and the cinema—paradoxically lose life in their attempts to capture it.

That is Benjamin's perceptive analysis of the biopolitical moment of modern, mechanical reproduction. It is *life* that glimmers as the aura of the work of art, and it is *life* that is lost once the work of art becomes reproducible, or clonable (one could also say, recalling my discussion of Ishiguro).

Benjamin thus offers a critique of modern biopolitics, one that revolves around the alternative practice of storytelling. It is no coincidence, from this perspective, that Agamben borrows the notion of bare life from Benjamin's essay "Critique of Violence."[72] Indeed, I have demonstrated elsewhere the connections between this essay and the essay "The Storyteller."[73] Although thinkers like Foucault might suggest that in the modern era, life finally became entirely saturated with power, Benjamin would argue that what power truly lost at that moment was life. Foucault might not disagree, but Benjamin puts a different spin on his arguments.

In light of this skepticism towards modern cinema and towards the modern novel, it is perhaps no coincidence that Mann achieves his naturalist work only on the double condition of it never being seen and of it being destroyed after his death. Mann was able to make hyper-realist work, but he did so only on these conditions. It is possible to understand such destruction not only as a private decision going back to Mann's burial of Brigid, but also as a destruction that resonates at the level of aesthetics and aesthetics' connection to biopolitics. By calling for the work's destruction, Mann was working against the way in which his films captured life. Such a practice of unworking, which has been part and parcel of aesthetic theory and practice,[74] begins to make even more sense if one considers the connections between Hector's life and world-history. With the exception of a single reference to Germany's invasion of Poland in 1939, the events of the Second World War and the Holocaust are entirely absent from Auster's novel. But it is difficult, given the burning that occurs at the end of the book, to leave this history out of consideration. Indeed, it is only by considering this history, and Hector's ultimate decision to have Alma write his biography as well as to have Zimmer watch his films, that we can move from the "nuclear criticism" that Hector adopts after burying Brigid to a "pharmacological criticism" that he comes to embrace at a later age.[75]

History's Remains

In order to confront the way in which the history of the Second World War is written into Auster's novel, I need to rehearse again, very briefly, the most important facts about Hector's life. One morning in 1929, Mann walks out of his rented house in Los Angeles and is never heard from again. Everybody thinks he is dead. In June 1988, three months after the publication of his book on Mann's films, Zimmer receives a letter—signed "Frieda Spelling (Mrs. Hector Mann)"[76]—saying Mann has read his book and would like to meet him at his ranch in New Mexico. At that time, Zimmer, whose wife and two sons were killed in a plane crash three years earlier, is already working on a translation of Chateaubriand. He replies with just a few sentences: "Of course I would like to meet Hector Mann. But how can I be sure he's alive?"[77] Nine days later, Zimmer hears from Spelling again: "If I told you that [Hector] wrote and directed a number of feature films after leaving Hollywood in 1929—and that he is willing to screen them for you here at the ranch—perhaps that will entice you to come."[78] There is some urgency to the matter, since Mann "is almost ninety years old and in failing health" and has instructed his wife "to destroy the films and the negatives of those films within twenty-four hours of his death."[79] Again, Zimmer does not allow himself "to get carried away."[80] He replies that in order for him to go "all the way to New Mexico" (from Vermont, where he is living at the time), he needs "to know that your statements are credible and that Hector Mann is indeed alive."[81] Considering the fact that by then, he has already travelled to "major film archives around the world" to study Mann's films, Zimmer's resistance to a trip to New Mexico is strange, to say the least.

Two weeks later (time is ticking), Alma Grund shows up at Zimmer's house. She is living at the ranch, she says, working as Hector's biographer, and she has come to take Zimmer with her, back to New Mexico. Once again, Zimmer stubbornly resists. Only after being held at gunpoint and almost shooting himself in the head does he decide to join Alma. They fly to New Mexico. Mann dies a few hours after Zimmer arrives. Frieda leaves Zimmer time to watch only the shortest of the fourteen unreleased films, *The Inner Life of Martin Frost*. At last, Zimmer realises that he "should have come here a month ago."[82] When at the end of the novel both Frieda and Alma tragically die, it becomes clear that if Zimmer had indeed gone to New Mexico a month ago, he would have been the only witness to Mann's unreleased work. As that witness, however, he fails dramatically: his passion is eclipsed by his professional scepticism. As a consequence of that darkening, history loses not only Mann's films but also every single other document that is related to their production. Under the spell of Mann's last request, Frieda decides to burn "every piece of evidence that could prove those movies ever existed"[83]—including Alma's manuscript of Hector's biography.

To a certain extent, *The Book of Illusions* makes up for this. It discusses a number of Hector's released films and also recreates the one unreleased film that Zimmer saw at the ranch. It also contains (spread out over Chapters Five and Six) excerpts from Hector's biography: things that Alma told Zimmer during the flight to New Mexico and "that bore on Hector's destiny as a hidden man, the years he had spent in the desert writing and directing films."[84] The book closes with Zimmer hoping that Alma made copies of

Mann's late films, and suggests the films have not been lost but are only "missing": "sooner or later a person will come along who accidentally opens the door of the room [note that *Zimmer* is the German word for "room"] where Alma hid them, and the story will start all over again."[85]

Auster may be suggesting that by opening the door of *The Book of Illusions*—Zimmer's story—, the movies will be recovered and the story will start all over again. However, the book does not only defend the recovery of its remembrance. *It also presents itself as an* imitatio *of Mann's annihilating project.* "Following Chateaubriand's model," Zimmer writes in the novel's closing pages,

> I will make no attempt to publish what I have written now. I have left a letter of instruction for my lawyer, and he will know where to find the manuscript and what to do with it after I am gone. If and when this book is published, dear reader, you can be certain that the man who wrote it is long dead.[86]

Hector's request to have all of his work destroyed echoes, as Alma notes, Kafka's last request to Max Brod: Kafka asked for everything that was left behind in his office to be burned *entirely* and *unread.* Brod did the exact opposite. He published everything: diaries, manuscripts, sketches, and letters. The initial ethical outrage directed toward Brod soon wore off. As John Zilcosky notes in his 2002 text "Kafka's Remains," "it has now become a critical commonplace to thank [Brod] for this indiscretion."[87] Did Kafka really want his work to be burned? Did Hector want his films to be destroyed? After the death of Alma's mother, it is Hector who asks Alma to stay on the ranch and to start working on his biography: "He said he was ready to talk, and he needed someone to help him."[88] Zimmer interprets this as a loss of courage, but Alma points out that he is wrong: "Hector changed his mind because of me. He told me I had a right to know the truth, and if I was willing to stay there and listen to him, he promised to tell me the whole story."[89] "But how", Zimmer asks, "does a private confession turn into a book? […] [A]s soon as he tells his story to the world, [Mann's] life becomes meaningless."[90] "Only if he's still alive when it's published," Alma counters. "But he won't be. I've promised not to show it to anyone until after he's dead."[91]

It is unclear whether Hector is "acting out of fear, out of vanity, [or] out of some last-minute surge of regret."[92] What *is* certain, however, is that he wants Alma to write the story of his life, and invites Zimmer to come see the films he made after 1940. Both of these requests contradict his "last" request (a request that actually *precedes* the two other requests). Of Kafka's last request, "Brod claimed that Kafka's real, tacit intention differed from his explicit one: if Kafka had *really* wanted his work to be burned, he would have done so himself or asked someone other than the adoring Brod to do it."[93] As Zilcosky observes, Walter Benjamin took Brod's position one step further by suggesting that Kafka manipulated Brod: "because Kafka wanted to retain his principled belief that his unpublished work was incomplete, imperfect, and private, he transferred his own ambivalence toward publication onto Brod, thereby freeing himself of this impossible decision."[94] According to Alma, Hector's nihilism exceeds Kafka's. However, Kafka did *not* order a biography, he did *not* invite a critic to his house to read all of his work before it was thrown into the fire (or perhaps that was what his request to Brod was about?). Also, Kafka's request had little to do with Mann's longing for self-punishment. Zilcosky argues that Brod's decision to publish divested Kafka "of what Maurice Blanchot termed, in 1949, Kafka's 'right to death.'"[95] In a letter from 1922 that Zilcosky is quoting from, Kafka "sees his impending death as tragic, first because he has never 'really' lived and, second, because he fears that part of him will carry on past the point of death."[96] "His 'real self' (*mein wirkliches Ich*) will die, while his writerly self will carry on as an immortal supplement."[97] "The only way to prevent his 'terrible' scenario of writerly intranscience, as Kafka claims later in the same letter, is to arrange for the 'real' and scriptive selves to die simultaneously."[98] "At the moment when his body is approaching death, Kafka claims, he wants simultaneously to 'renounce' all of his writing."[99]

Kafka's request originates in the relation he observes to exist between his real and his scriptive selves. A similar relation between the realms of the text and of the real world, albeit one of an entirely different nature, is represented in the film that Zimmer sees at the ranch, *The Inner Life of Martin Frost*. Now, the fact that Hector asked Alma to write his biography and that he invited Zimmer to the ranch for a screening of his movies, may indicate that Hector was changing his mind about his decision to destroy the movies he made after 1940. Stubbornly refusing to recognize Mann's possible change of mind, Zimmer repeatedly and admiringly emphasizes the consistency of Hector's nihilism. But where would be the shame, one might ask, in Hector changing his mind after sixty years—where would be the shame in Hector's inconsistency? Hector made his promise in 1929. He invites Zimmer to the ranch in 1988. Much has happened in between, if not in Hector's life, then in history. Why would one expect Hector's 1929 decision to stop making films and his 1940 decision to start making films again to remain unaffected by the events of the twentieth century? In the final pages of the novel, Zimmer writes: "Circumstances changed, and once they changed, I changed my mind as well."[100] He keeps projecting Hector, however, as someone immune to historical change. What is the place of history in *The Book of Illusions*? How do Hector's life and work light up in it?

After hearing from Frieda for the second time, Zimmer puts a moratorium on his translation of Chateaubriand's memoirs and pulls out his old research files on Hector Mann. Intrigued by Frieda's suggestion that Mann is still alive, he begins to comb through the information he collected when he was writing his study of Mann's films. As I have discussed, Zimmer notes that most of it is unreliable: "articles from the tabloid press, junk from fan magazines, bits of movie reportage rife with hyperbole, erroneous suppositions, and out-and-out falsehoods."[101] Urging the reader not to believe what he or she reads, he goes on to summarize four profiles of Hector that were written between August 1927 and October 1928. Each profile contains a different version of Hector's past. According to Brigid's article, Hector's parents were born in Germany. They left that country when Hector was still a baby to begin a new life in Argentina. The fourth profile suggests that Hector's parents were from the city of Stanislav on the eastern edge of the Austro-Hungarian Empire; Hector's first language is Polish, not German. And so on.

Some of this information is confirmed later in the novel—for example, Hector did indeed speak with a heavy Spanish accent at the time when the profiles were written—but most of it turns out to be deceptive. "[A]fter sifting through this jumble of fraudulent memories and spurious anecdotes,"[102] Zimmer does feel that he has discovered one minor fact. According to him, Hector's mentioning of the city of Stanislav betrays a momentary lapse of attention. With Hector doing everything to downplay his foreignness, it seems to be an odd admission to name that city as his birthplace ("Poland is a remote country to Americans, far more remote than Germany"[103]). The oddity leads Zimmer to conclude that Mann was indeed born in Stanislav, a city that "had once been part of Austro-Hungary" but that "after the breakup of the empire at the end of the war [...] had been handed over to Poland."[104] "If that was the terrain of Hector's childhood," Zimmer continues, "then there was every reason to suppose that Hector was born a Jew"[105]:

> The fact that the area was thick with Jewish settlements was not enough to persuade me, but combine the Jewish population with the fact that his family left the area, and the argument becomes quite convincing. The Jews were the ones that left that part of the world, and beginning with the Russians pogroms in the 1880s, hundreds of thousands of Yiddish-speaking immigrants fanned out across Western Europe and the United States. Many of them went to South America as well.[106]

Although Zimmer attributes several pages to Hector's Jewishness, the biographical "fact"—a "little discovery" of which Zimmer is quite "proud"[107]—does not affect his reading of Hector's life and work. Taking into account that Zimmer's discovery is preceded by an invitation to read against the grain, I suggest we approach Zimmer's book through the lens of Hector's supposed Jewishness.

Zimmer's first representation of Hector is a description of a two-minute sequence taken from the film *The Teller's Tale*. Set in a bank, it shows the cosmopolitan Hector in the role of a hardworking assistant clerk, counting out money. Although it seems that nothing can distract Hector from his task (he is working with "furious efficiency," "lightning speed," and "manic concentration"[108]), the comedy of the clip depends on his repeatedly losing track of the count and having to start all over again—upstairs, repairmen are installing planks in the floor and sawdust is falling on Hector's jacket, and there is a pretty secretary across the room Hector wants to make eye contact with. What does it mean that "Hector the Jew" is represented as "counting money"?[109] What does it mean that Hector's counting is *upset*—that although he does nothing but count, the only thing he does not get to do is count? What does it mean that "to count" also means "to tell" (as the title of the film suggests), that there is a story to all this counting, a counting to all this telling, a complicity of counting and telling?[110]

In the fifth chapter of the book, after Alma has already told Zimmer that in 1932, Frieda and Hector moved to the ranch in New Mexico and that in 1940, Hector started making movies again, she—without any reason at all—refers to the year 1939 (the year in which Hector asked Alma's father Charlie to join him at the ranch) as "late thirty-nine. November or December, just after the Germans invaded Poland."[111] Alma's mentioning of Poland does not only establish a passage to Zimmer's "little discovery" of Hector's Jewishness early on in the novel, but also puts her entire account in a new perspective. All of what she has already told, the phrase seems to be saying, took place during the rise of fascism in central Europe. The phrase "just after the Germans invaded Poland" establishes a public, historical reference point for the intensely private story that she is telling. She invites us to start listening to the wheels of history that are turning underneath the surface of Zimmer's account. This move is repeated at the very end of the novel, when Zimmer notes—"with a certain grim satisfaction"[112]—that as he is coming to the end of his story (an intensely private story as well), "we are also closing in on the last weeks of the century—Hector's century, the century that began eighteen days before he was born and which no one in his right mind will be sorry to see end."[113]

In 1933, Adolf Hitler came to power. In 1939, Germany invaded Poland, which led to the beginning of the Second World War. Hector's act of "breath-taking nihilism" begins in the very same year in which the Third Empire decides to realize what it considered to be the final solution: the complete destruction of the Jewish race.

1940 was also the year in which Walter Benjamin committed suicide. Four years earlier, Benjamin had written his famous essay "The Work of Art in the Age of Mechanical Reproduction". Mann's work seems to take Benjamin's thought as a point of reference. One could argue that Mann's project goes against the reproducibility that Benjamin in his essay is describing. Mann takes the work of art out of the hands of the masses. Benjamin analyzes film as a public work of art. Hector turns it into a private work of art. In a way, Mann's project restores the authenticity of the original that (according to Benjamin) was lost in the age of mechanical reproduction. Mann pushes this restoration to its extreme: he restores originality with the sole intention of destroying it. The authority of the work of art is restored, its aura is restored, its unique existence is reaffirmed *against* the contemporary plurality of art, but all of this takes place within the temporality of a soon-to-be-realized promise of destruction. For Benjamin, there is a connection between transitoriness and reproducibility and between uniqueness and permanence. In Hector's project, however, uniqueness is (perversely) connected to transitoriness. Hector turns Benjamin's thesis upside down. The work of art is not designed for reproducibility. It is designed for destruction.

Benjamin's essay closes with the observation that fascism says *Fiat ars—pereat mundus*: "[Mankind's] self-alienation has reached such a degree that it can experience its own destruction as an aesthetic pleasure of the first order."[114] It seems that the connection fascism establishes between the being of art and the not-being of the world is reflected by Hector's project: the being of Hector's art would divest Hector's life of all meaning. Importantly, however, Hector does not experience the destruction of his art as an aesthetic pleasure: for him, it is a *practical* and an *ethical* necessity.[115] The impulse of his work is thus different from the proto-fascism of the avant-garde movements that were thriving in Europe before the First World War and during the Interwar Period.

Hector's tragedy is mirrored by Zimmer's own story. For Zimmer, the writing of a study of Mann's twelve released films is an ethical and practical necessity. After the death of his wife and two sons, he *must* start "working at something"[116] in order to save himself from complete self-destruction—work is his pharmakon, his medicine. But what about this second book, written in his late life? At the end of *The Book of Illusions*, Zimmer seems to regret that he did not go to the ranch earlier. At the same time, however, he *also* regrets that by going to the ranch, he destroyed Hector's art of destruction. In the first case, "to make up" for what he has done would mean to restore the memory of Hector's life and work (one could argue that *The Book of Illusions* does precisely this: at no point does it claim to achieve the full presence of the past). In the second case, "to make up" would mean for Zimmer *not* to remember, to take his memories with him into the grave. Zimmer's book, impossibly, does both. On the one hand, by keeping its memory a secret until after Zimmer has died, it imitates Mann's act of "breathtaking nihilism." On the other, it recognizes—implicitly—the possibility that by the late 1980s Mann's opinion about his entire project may have changed.

This is the combination of Tommy's anger and Kathy's aesthetics of existence that all of the novels that I discuss in this book are longing for, the very two tendencies that the genre of the novel must follow if it does not want to be blindly complicit with the history of biopolitics, and if it does not want to blindly resist biopolitics either. It can be summed up, I argue, in the notion of pharmacology and the question of a practice that would be partly curative, and partly poisonous. Mann and Zimmer's criticism of the work of art's complicity with biopolitics is thus not a nuclear criticism—a criticism that would blow its object to pieces in order to leave nothing whole. Instead, it is a pharmacological criticism that deals with remains. In an excellent article on Auster's novel, Timothy Bewes sums up the issue as follows—the quotation recalls my discussion of the term "possible" in Ishiguro's *Never Let Me Go*:

> Auster work is engaged, rather, with its own possibility. His fictional works appear to stage the impossibility of the novel and the failure of the literary as such—and yet, I shall argue, it is the idée fixe of postmodernity that has taught us to limit his texts in this way. Auster materializes a struggle with possibility itself: the struggle to produce in a situation where the rules of production are not given.[117]

Bewes does not use the word "biopolitical" here—it does appear at another point in his article—but the "possible" has emerged in recent years as a central category in biopolitical thought.[118]

I borrow the distinction between nuclear and pharmacological criticism from Bernard Stiegler's discussion of Jacques Derrida in *Ce qui fait que la vie vaut la peine d'être vécue: De la pharmacologie*. Stiegler's discussion focuses on "No Apocalypse, Not Now," Derrida's contribution to a 1984 colloquium on "Nuclear Criticism" at Cornell University.[119] Theorizing nuclear criticism as the kind of criticism that might be practiced at the academy, for example in literature departments, Derrida takes the "nuclear" to refer to the explosive nature of such criticism: the fact that it would enable one to think the limit of criticism itself—criticism's auto-destruction. In such a theory of criticism, criticism's very core—its autos, its self—would shatter. But what does it mean, Stiegler asks, to say that this core would shatter? If such shattering is somehow linked to deconstruction, is that what deconstruction is about? Shattering? And if it is, is such a shattering desirable?

In response to these questions, and to Derrida's theory of nuclear criticism, Stiegler develops a pharmacological criticism, what he calls a pharmacology: in this perspective, there is no shattering, no explosion of the autos. One is forced, rather, to take care of oneself, to learn to live pharmacologically, navigate the thin line between cure and poison. It is also a Derridean approach, of course, and one that is mobilized in this particular case against the moment in 1984 when Derrida appears to fail in this navigation, moving instead from deconstruction into destruction. The point applies to Mann and Zimmer's projects as well. What Zimmer achieves, I think, is a kind of deconstruction. Mann was arguably aiming for the same thing. Frieda, however, did not understand this. Under the spell of Mann's project, she turned deconstruction into a holo-caust, an all-burning that resonates with the events of the twentieth century.

Since the 1980s, as a result of the crisis of remembrance in a postmodern culture of amnesia, there has been a renewed interest in memory. The crisis of memory has become particularly urgent in reference to the Holocaust: the survivors of the camps are becoming aged and their memories may die along with them. Even if Hector in 1928 wanted to forget, it may very well be that sixty years later, in a completely different cultural climate, he thought he should remember. Circumstances change, as Zimmer notes, and once circumstances change, people change their minds as well. Cannot (and should not) ethics change with circumstances? It takes courage to be consistent. But to persevere in the ethical also means something else: it means to embrace *interruption*. The ethical is the demand of a crisis that cannot be overcome. Zimmer's description of the twentieth century as "Hector's century" invites us to think of Hector as the body (or the specter) of our time. It invites us to read the story of Hector's life, of his (ethical) struggle with memory and with forgetting (with Lethe and with Mnemosyne) as the struggle of the twentieth century. In order to be able to see this, however, one has to undo Mann's "breathtaking act of nihilism" and read the events of the Second World War in between the lines of Mann's and Zimmer's private works of art.

Notes

1 J. M. Coetzee, *Doubling the Point: Essays and Interviews*, ed. David Attwell (Cambridge, MA: Harvard University Press, 1992), 17.
2 Sophie Calle, *Double Game* (New York: Violette Editions/DAP, 2007), 284.
3 Paul Auster, *Leviathan* (London: Faber and Faber, 1993), 1.
4 Jacqueline Lichtenstein has extended Derrida's argument into an investigation about painting and sculpture: *The Blind Spot: An Essay On*

the Relations Between Painting and Sculpture in the Modern Age (Los Angeles: Getty Research Institute, 2008). I would like to thank Jason Smith for this reference.

5 See Paul Auster, "Black on White: Recent Paintings by David Reed," in Paul Auster, *Ground Work: Selected Poems and Essays 1970–1979* (London: Faber and Faber, 1990), 127–35.

6 The rise of 3D-technology in the twenty-first century could also be considered within this perspective.

7 See Vandana Shiva, *Biopiracy: The Plunder of Nature and Knowledge* (Boston: South End, 1997).

8 Paul Auster, *The Book of Illusions* (New York: Faber and Faber, 2002), 5.

9 Auster, *Book*, 22.

10 Ibid., 106.

11 Ibid., 208.

12 Ibid., 207.

13 Angela Carter, *The Sadeian Woman and the Ideology of Pornography* (New York: Pantheon, 1978), 12.

14 Auster, *Book*, 1.

15 Ibid., 3.

16 Ibid., 5.

17 Ibid., 81.

18 Ibid., 145.

19 Ibid., 146.

20 Ibid., 153.

21 Ibid., 177.

22 Ibid., 179.

23 Ibid., 180.

24 Ibid., 154.

25 Susan Sontag discusses the connections between silent film and pornography in her essay "The Pornographic Imagination," in Susan Sontag, *Styles of Radical Will* (New York: Delta Books, 1969), esp. 55.

26 Auster, *Book*, 184.

27 Ibid., 186.

28 Ibid.

29 Giorgio Agamben, *Homo Sacer: Sovereign Power and Bare Life*, trans. Daniel Heller-Roazen (Stanford: Stanford University Press, 1998), 135.

30 Agamben, *Homo Sacer*, 134.

31 Ibid.

32 Ibid., 134–5.

33 It is worth noting the significance of the fact that Hector is masked. As such, the scene recalls the photographs of hooded Abu Ghraib prisoners. The relation of these photographs to pornography and sadism has received some critical discussion. W. J. T. Mitchell considers it through a biopolitical lens, with reference to Agamben's work. See W. J. T. Mitchell,

Cloning Terror: The War of Images, 9/11 to the Present (Chicago: University of Chicago Press, 2011).

34 In *Sadeian Woman*, Angela Carter has remarked that "pornographic writing retains this in common with all literature—that it turns flesh into word" (Carter, *Sadeian*, 13). It is, indeed, this relation between flesh and word that I am interested in. As Carter notes, for Sade this is a political relation: "he treats all sexuality as a political reality" (ibid., 27).

35 One finds resonances of sadism in both *Slow Man* and *Foe*, in the relations between Foe and Susan Barton and Paul and Elizabeth Costello (i.e. between authors and characters).

36 Paul Auster, *Travels in the Scriptorium* (New York: Picador, 2006).

37 Auster, *Travels*, 90.

38 Susan Rubin Suleiman, *Subversive Intent: Gender, Politics, and the Avant-Garde*. (Cambridge, MA: Harvard University Press, 1990), 70.

39 Suleiman, *Subversive*, 70.

40 Ibid.

41 I return to this point in my conclusion, where I consider Pedro Almodóvar's film *Talk to Her* as a film about narrative care.

42 Jessica Benjamin, *The Bonds of Love* (New York: Random House, 1988), 52.

43 The connection between Hawthorne's work and Auster's has been made, but it usually involves other texts. See, for example, Richard Swope, "Approaching the Threshold(s) in Postmodern Detective Fiction: Hawthorne's 'Wakefield' and Other Missing Persons," in *Critique* 39: 3 (1998): 207–27.

44 Nathaniel Hawthorne, "The Birthmark," in *The American Tradition in Literature*, ed. George Perkins and Barbara Perkins (New York: McGraw-Hill, 1994), 767.

45 Hawthorne, "Birthmark," 771.

46 Auster, *Book*, 120.

47 Ibid., 242.

48 Ibid., 251.

49 Ibid., 257.

50 Ibid., 268.

51 See also Jim Peacock's discussion of these issues in "Carrying the Burden of Representation: Paul Auster's *The Book of Illusions*," in *Journal of American Studies* 40: 1 (2006): 53–69.

52 See Paul Auster, *The Inner Life of Martin Frost* (Paris: Alfama, 2007).

53 Paul Auster is one of Maurice Blanchot's English translators.

54 Auster, *Book*, 209.

55 Ibid.

56 As Timothy Bewes has noted, Auster's work is infused by a longing for something that writing ultimately cannot attain: "presence, immediacy, sensation, the simultaneity of past, present and future" ("Against the

Ontology of the Present: Paul Auster's Cinematographic Fictions," in *Twentieth Century Literature* 53: 3 (2007): 285). "Auster's works, it seems, are defined by a wish that the novel might achieve the 'immediacy' that other, supposedly more sensuous forms enjoy so effortlessly" (ibid.): cinema is, of course, such a form. "Auster's *The Book of Illusions*, at least the beginning, looks longingly toward cinema as a symbol of everything that writing is unable to achieve" (ibid., 291)—but things are of course, not that simple, as the rest of the novel shows. Bewes already made this point about Auster's fiction in his earlier "The Novel as an Absence: Lukács and the Event of Postmodern Fiction," in *Novel* 38: 1 (2004): 5–20.

57 See Auster, *Book*, 15. There are, of course, numerous articles on the role of the body in silent film. For one that discusses Chaplin and takes literature into account, see, for example, Kenneth S. Calhoon, "Blind Gestures: Chaplin, Diderot, Lessing," in *MLN* 115: 3 (2000): 381–402. Robert Spadoni considers the question of the body in relation to the transition from silent film to sound film in "The Uncanny Body of Early Sound Film," in *The Velvet Light Trap* 51 (2003): 4–16.

58 See Susan Sontag, *Against Interpretation* (New York: Delta, 1966), 149.

59 Kenneth Tynan, "The Girl in the Black Helmet," 23. Tynan's text is included in the DVD booklet added to Georg Wilhelm Pabst, *Pandora's Box* (New York: Criterion, 2006).

60 Tynan, "Girl," 23.

61 Ibid., 53.

62 Auster, *Book*, 1.

63 Tynan, "Girl," 54.

64 Ibid.

65 Auster, *Book*, 226.

66 Tynan, "Girl," 53.

67 J. M. Coetzee, *Slow Man* (New York: Viking, 2005), 81.

68 Coetzee, *Slow*, 63.

69 Another critic that must be mentioned is Georg Lukács. Timothy Bewes has discussed Lukács' *Theory of the Novel* (London: Merlin, 1978), as well as his remarks on cinema, in relation to Auster's novel. In "Against the Ontology of the Present," Bewes uses the word "biopolitical" in his discussion, adopting it from Walter Benn Michaels.

70 Walter Benjamin, "The Work of Art in the Age of Mechanical Reproduction," in Walter Benjamin, *Illuminations: Essays and Reflections*, ed. Hannah Arendt, trans. Harry Zohn (New York: Schocken, 1985), 221.

71 Benjamin, *Illuminations*, 83–109.

72 Writing about Georg Lukács, Susan Sontag has noted that Benjamin "thought the movies embodied the abolition of tradition and historical consciousness, and therefore—once again!—fascism" (Sontag, *Interpretation*, 91).

73 See Arne De Boever, "Politics and Poetics of Divine Violence: On a

Figure in Giorgio Agamben and Walter Benjamin," in *The Work of Giorgio Agamben: Law, Life, Literature*, ed. Justin Clemens, Nick Heron, and Alex Murray (Edinburgh: Edinburgh University Press, 2008), 82–96.

74 One can think here of the notion of *désoeuvrement* or worklessness and the ways in which it has been theorized by Georges Bataille, Maurice Blanchot, Jean-Luc Nancy, and Giorgio Agamben—all of them working after G. W. F. Hegel, whose dialectic of creation and destruction is central to *The Book of Illusions*. In terms of aesthetic practice, I refer first and foremost to Jean-Luc Godard's use of the jump-cut aesthetic; the history of the *nouvelle vague* is worth considering within the biopolitical framework that I have set up here. Note as well that Godard made a tribute to Louise Brooks in *Vivre sa Vie* (Tynan, "Girl," 60). Finally, photographer Jeff Wall—whose work is deeply influenced by Walter Benjamin's writings—notes growing tired with the jump-cut aesthetic and trying to achieve its interruption in another way. See Arielle Pelenc, "Interview: Arielle Pelenc in Correspondence with Jeff Wall," in Thierry de Duve, Arielle Pelenc, Boris Groys et al. *Jeff Wall* (London: Phaidon, 2003), 11. It is this latter development that is closest to Auster's novel, as will become clear in the closing section of this chapter.

75 I discuss the difference between these two kinds of criticism in more detail below.

76 Auster, *Book*, 4.

77 Ibid., 5.

78 Ibid., 78.

79 Ibid.

80 Ibid.

81 Ibid.

82 Ibid., 239.

83 Ibid., 302.

84 Ibid., 127.

85 Ibid., 321.

86 Ibid., 318.

87 John Zilcosky, "Kafka's Remains," in *Lost in the Archives*, ed. Rebecca Comay and Ian Balfour (New York: Distributed Art Publishers, 2002), 632.

88 Auster, *Book*, 216.

89 Ibid., 217.

90 Ibid.

91 Ibid.

92 Ibid.

93 Zilcosky, "Kafka," 632.

94 Ibid.

95 Ibid.

96 Ibid., 635.

97 Ibid.

98 Ibid., 636.
99 Ibid.
100 Auster, *Book*, 318.
101 Ibid., 76.
102 Ibid., 84.
103 Ibid., 84.
104 Ibid.
105 Ibid., 85.
106 Ibid.
107 Ibid., 86.
108 Ibid., 10.
109 Compare, for example, the way in which Auster's book confirms and upsets another stereotype: in Brigid O'Fallon's profile, Hector—an Argentinian immigrant—is represented to be speaking with a heavy Spanish accent. Her renderings of Hector's speech—"Ees very simple," "when I was a leetle baby" (Auster, *Book*, 80–1)—are painfully stereotypical. The third profile undercuts the stereotype: it states that Hector's English is "flawless." Later in the novel, however, this third profile turns out to be fraudulent. Alma confirms that O'Fallon's descriptions were correct: "that was essentially how Hector spoke at the time" (ibid., 128). This seeming confirmation of the stereotype is once again undercut, however, by Zimmer's long descriptions of the "speech therapy" (ibid., 156) that Hector takes with Brigid's sister Nora. After nine months of practical exercises, Hector "had advanced to a point where it was becoming increasingly difficult to tell where he had been born. He didn't sound like an American, perhaps, but neither did he sound like a raw, uneducated immigrant" (ibid., 157). What does it mean that the stereotype of Hector's heavily accented English is first undercut, then reconfirmed, only to be undercut once more (this time for real)?
110 For another, related book that mobilizes these associations, see W. G. Sebald, *The Emigrants*, trans. Michael Hülse (London: Harvill, 1993). Various references to "counting" can be found in the book: Henry Selwyn, in Sebald's first story, is "counting blades of grass" (Sebald, *Emigrants*, 5); Sebald informs us that Paul Bereyter, the central figure in the second story, is "only three quarters an Aryan" (ibid., 50); the book closes with the description of a picture by (and of) the accountant Genewein, a book-keeper and financial expert, who "recorded the exemplary organization within the [Litzmannstadt] ghetto" in pictures and "who is himself in one of the pictures, counting money at his bureau" (ibid., 236). To think the association between "counting" and "telling" means to think the association between the novel and the camp. Benjamin's remarks on the difference between the novel and storytelling, to which I have referred earlier in this chapter, complicate this association and need to be considered in this context.

111 Auster, *Book*, 212.
112 Ibid., 318.
113 Ibid.
114 Benjamin, "Work of Art," 242.
115 After the death of his son, he has to start making movies again to save himself from a nervous breakdown. But there is also Brigid's death and the promise he made in 1928 never to make movies again… Hector is saved by his work. He is saved by the work that ultimately will have to be destroyed in order for Hector to be saved once more, for the last time.
116 Auster, *Book*, 212.
117 Bewes, "Against the Ontology of the Present," 278–9.
118 See, for example, the work of Giorgio Agamben. I have commented on the importance of the pair "possible/actual" in Foucault's work in: "The Allegory of the Cage: Foucault, Agamben, and the Enlightenment," in *Foucault Studies* 10 (2010): 7–22: http://rauli.cbs.dk/index.php/foucault-studies/article/viewFile/3124/3288
119 See Bernard Stiegler, *Ce qui fait que le vie vaut la peine d'être vécue: De la pharmacologie* (Paris: Flammarion, 2010), esp. 67–96.

4

"Just Being": On Tom McCarthy's *Remainder*

... however much we may long to repair the disorders in the natural harmony of man created by consciousness, this is not to be accomplished by the surrender of consciousness. There is no return, no going back to innocence. We have no choice but to go to the end of thought, there (perhaps), in total self-consciousness, to recover grace and innocence.[1]

—Susan Sontag, *Styles of Radical Will*

The Irreparable is that things are just as they are, in this or that mode, consigned without remedy to their way of being. States of things are irreparable, whatever they may be: sad or happy, atrocious or blessed. How you are, how the world is—this is the Irreparable.[2]

—Giorgio Agamben, *The Coming Community*

Very Little, Almost Nothing

The narrator of Tom McCarthy's *Remainder* has suffered an accident about which he is not allowed to speak—and which he does not appear to remember. "It involved something falling from the sky," the opening paragraph of the novel states. "Technology. Parts, bits. That's it, really: all I can divulge. Not much, I know."[3] He is not allowed to speak about it because of an £8.5 million settlement he has received as compensation. The settlement came through on the condition that "you can't discuss the accident in any public arena or in any recordable format."[4] Since he does not remember anything about the accident, however, this does not really pose a problem.

Although the settlement is large by any standard, it appears to be warranted. The novel's second chapter recounts how after the accident, the narrator had to relearn how to move again. This involves a process that is referred to in the novel as the "rerouting" of the brain: "finding a new route through the brain for commands to run along."[5] For example, if you need to relearn how to pick up a pen, your physiotherapist will ask you to *imagine* picking up the pen first: to think, several times over, each and every movement that you would need to make to pick up the pen—as if the entire movement would be broken down into an Eadweard Muybridge series of photographs. In this way, circuits are cut through the brain "that will eventually allow you to perform the act itself. That's the idea."[6] In order to learn how to move again, the narrator thus needs to remake his brain. "The brain is a work," as Catherine Malabou writes in *What Should We Do With Our Brain?*, "and we do not know it."[7] McCarthy's narrator learns this lesson first-hand. Although the therapy is successful—the narrator does learn to move again—the particular procedure, which relies heavily on understanding in order to achieve doing, prevents him from feeling natural. Since every single one of his actions is shot through with consciousness, he feels he has lost touch with the real, and cannot "just be." Instead, all of his actions feel unnatural, "second-hand."[8]

In order to get rid of this feeling, the narrator embarks on a mad series of "re-enactments" that lead from the relatively innocent reconstruction of a building that he thinks he remembers to the re-enactment of a fake bank heist that ends in death and destruction. These projects are funded by the settlement he has received, in particular his sky-rocketing stocks. Going against his financial advisor, the narrator puts all his money in technology and telecommunications without diversifying or top-slicing. It makes for huge gains but also risks tremendous losses. The re-enactment projects propel the narrator into such a high degree of exposure that he will ultimately get some tingling sense of the real: they enable him to jump in the volcano, enter into the heart of the event, and somehow come out alive. But this experience also arrives at the cost of other people's lives and indeed, given the novel's ending, possibly at the cost of the narrator's own life (which might, of course, be worth it). Throughout this pursuit, the re-enactments begin to function as addictive drugs that are curative but also—and perhaps even more so—poisonous, ultimately risking the death of the narrator and those who surround him. As I show in this chapter, *Remainder* thus raises important questions about art's pharmacological relation to "life," which circulates in the novel under different but related names: authenticity, naturalness, the real. Ultimately, the novel seems to suggest that life can only enter into the work of art as death. The work of art can only begin to include life in its destruction.

Thus, the narrator learns an important lesson about his authenticity fetish, namely that the authenticity he desires—that of the actor Robert De Niro in *Mean Streets*—is the authenticity of a scripted life, of a life that coincides entirely with the law of its writing. If such a life seems natural to him, it is because there is no separation between this life and the script that has been written for it. Since he is not an actor, however, and since there is no script for his life, to be authentic in his case would mean to coincide with nothing other than his life. Thus, the narrator completes his path towards "just being," a phrase that resonates throughout the book as the form-of-life that would dismantle the novel's complicity with biopolitics. How to write a novel in which the characters can "just be"? And how to read a novel in such a way that the characters can "just be"? These are the questions that I confront in this chapter.

The Pharmacology of Re-enactment

The narrator's authenticity problem is drawn out most explicitly when, shortly after getting out of the hospital, he goes to see Martin Scorcese's film *Mean Streets* at the Ritzy theatre in Brixton, London. What strikes him, as he is watching the film, is

> how perfect De Niro was. Every move he made, each gesture was perfect, seamless. Whether it was lighting up a cigarette or opening a fridge door or just walking down the street: he seemed to execute the action perfectly, to live it, to merge with it until he was it and it was him and there was nothing in between.[9]

"He's natural when he does this," the narrator concludes. "Not artificial, like me. He's flaccid. I'm plastic."[10] Rehearsing the understanding of plasticity that, in Chapter Two, I also uncovered in Malabou's book—namely as being linked to rigidity and transformation[11]—, the narrator paradoxically associates De Niro, an actor in a film, with being natural. De Niro becomes the narrator's authenticity fetish, the figure that represents everything that he is not.

When his friend Greg points out that he just means De Niro is "cool"[12]—"[a]ll film stars are cool"[13]—, the narrator replies that this is not what it is about. "It's about just being," he continues, "De Niro was just being; I can never do that now."[14] Further down on that same page, it suddenly hits him that "[e]ven before the accident" he had "always been inauthentic": "if I'd been walking down the street just like De Niro, smoking a cigarette like him, and even if it had lit first try, I'd still be thinking: *Here I am, walking down the street, smoking a cigarette, like someone in a film*."[15] The problem of the book, then, is that the narrator's accident and specifically the care he received in its aftermath, intensified this feeling of inauthenticity to the point where it has become unbearable. It is through his accident and the therapy that follows it that the narrator learns something about his life that was already true before the accident.

Shortly after he has received the money of the settlement, the narrator embarks on another therapeutic project through which he intends to recover this real that he thinks he has lost or never had. It is a mad project that attempts to reconstruct, starting from a crack in the bathroom wall in the house of one of his friends, the entire world that is born from it. The project's foundational scene takes place at a party on Plato Road—the reference to Plato, whose theory of ideas is crucial to McCarthy's own philosophy is not accidental (I will return to this later). "I was standing by the sink looking at this crack in the plaster when I had a sudden sense of déjà vu":

> I'd been in a space like this before, a place just like this, looking at the crack, a crack that had jutted and meandered in the same way as the one beside the mirror. There'd been that same crack, and a bathtub also, and a window directly above the taps just like there was in this room—only the window had been slightly bigger and the taps older, different.[16]

A little further down on the page, the déjà vu is described as a memory: "I remembered it all," the narrator says, "but I couldn't remember where I'd been in this place, this flat, this bathroom."[17] What he does realize as his memory of this crack is expanding—he remembers the building in addition to the bathroom and the flat, the people in the building, and even the buildings surrounding that building—is that everything he remembers had been "real." "I'd been real—been without first understanding how to try to be: cut out the detour. I remembered this with all the force of an epiphany, a revelation."[18] "Right then, I knew exactly what I wanted to do with my money. I wanted to reconstruct that space and enter into it so that I could feel real again."[19]

Whether it is an actual building that is being remembered here, or whether the crack in the bathroom wall merely triggers a desire to return to the womb ("You been giving birth in there?,"[20] someone asks when the narrator finally gets out of the bathroom; when the crack is reconstructed later in the novel, we find out that it needs to have the color of flesh[21]), remains unresolved in the novel. Instead, the rest of the novel revolves around the narrator's obsessive reconstruction of this space as well as of other spaces catching his interest: a tire shop, a murder scene, a bank.

To facilitate the reconstruction, the narrator engages Nazrul Ram Vyas, a man who is working for a company called Time Control. Here is how the narrator explains his project to Naz:

> I want to buy a building, a particular type of building, and decorate and furnish it in a particular way. I have precise requirements, right down to the smallest detail. I want to hire people to live in it, and perform tasks that I will designate. They need to perform these exactly as I say, and when I ask them to. I shall most probably require the building opposite

> as well, and most probably need it to be modified. Certain actions must take place at that location too, exactly as and when I shall require them to take place. I need the project to be set up, staffed and coordinated, and I'd like to start as soon as possible.[22]

Ultimately, this is exactly what Naz will help the narrator to set up. But the "politics" of the project, if that is a word that can be used in this context, appear problematic. From "I want to" to "I shall" to "exactly as and when I shall," one senses the intensification of control in the narrator's description. Indeed, now that he has received a large amount of money through the settlement, it appears that he intends to exercise a fantasy of total control that will involve not simply buildings, but also people, and even the sun.[23]

Whereas some might ultimately not care about the buildings and the animals involved in the project (he has cats walk across the roof of the building opposite to his, and he cares very little about the fact that several of them crash to their deaths), it is ultimately around the involvement of people that some questions are raised. Clearly, the narrator's project will have a tremendous influence on his employees' lives. Referring to them first as performers, he will later insist that they are not: "All the ... performers," he goes—"no, not performers: that's not the right word… the participants… staff…."[24] Ultimately, he calls them "re-enactors."[25] The important thing, however, is that they "must be… I mean, we'll need complete… jurisdiction over all the space."[26] His use of the term "jurisdiction" is telling: within the building, it is the narrator's word that is law. He will rule his building as a sovereign and micro-manage the lives of the re-enactors he engages. Meanwhile, "I shall move throughout the space as I see fit"—the tone of grandeur is unmistakable.[27] Naz executes this totalitarian fantasy without skipping a beat. In her article on *Remainder*, novelist and literary critic Zadie Smith reads Naz in relation to the novel's obsession with authenticity. But one might just as well add an "i" to his name, and consider his relation to such figures as Adolf Eichmann who, because of his organizational talents, became responsible for the mass deportation of Jews during the Second World War.

Re-enactors can live in the building, the narrator explains, but "[t]hey'll have to get used to being in two modes": "*on* and *off*."[28] Like robots, he imagines them to operate according to a switch over which he has full control. Given these statements, it seems that what Naz is facilitating is not so much time control but life control: total control over the lives of those who are hired as re-enactors. This becomes perhaps most clear in the novel when the narrator orders "a model of the building"[29], "a scale model" that has "little figures in it" representing the different characters in the building: "the motorbike enthusiast next to his bike, the pianist with his bald pate, the liver lady [a woman who is cooking liver all day] with her headscarf and her snake strands of hair, the concierge with her stubby arms and white mask [she wears a mask because the narrator cannot remember her face]."[30] Executing his fantasy of total control, the narrator will move around these figures in the model of his building like pawns on a chess board. Of course, the people will be expected to follow his movements, as if he were moving the actual people around. If things were not already explicit enough, McCarthy also has his narrator marking the model with blood later on.[31] Importantly, however, it is his own blood and not that of the re-enactors. So the suggestion seems to be that he is not simply controlling the re-enactors from the outside, but that his own biological life is very much involved in this project as well. If this is indeed a project of life-control, as I have suggested, it is worth asking whose life is being controlled: the lives of the characters? Or the narrator's life? Perhaps both? By whom? Who is writing whom in this meta-fictional allegory?[32]

To a certain extent, the question of the narrator's control over the re-enactors' lives is relevant for those who are involved in fixing up the building as well. Because of certain oversights within the reconstruction planning—oversights that may or may not have been made deliberately[33]—workers are sometimes made to undo jobs they had already completed. Motivation, however, was not lacking: "the people we'd hired were being paid vast amounts of money."[34] The cynical assumption appears to be that as long as you pay people enough money, you can make them do anything. "What was lacking, if anything, was comprehension: making them understand exactly what it was that was required of them."[35] The directive is very specific:

> And making them understand at the same time how little they needed to understand. I didn't need to make them share my vision, and I didn't want them to. Why should they? It was my vision, and I was the one with the money. They just had to know what to do.[36]

Ask no critical questions. An order is an order.

The narrator notes, however, that "this wasn't easy."[37] One major crisis is caused by the pianist, one of the characters that were part of the narrator's original vision of the building. A doctoral student in music, this man is required to run through Rachmaninov all day while making mistakes, retaking passages, and so on and so forth. It needs to sound as if he were *practicing* Rachmaninov. Lying on the floor of the staircase one day, "studying the way the light fell from the large windows onto the patterned floor"[38] "while the piano music looped and repeated in the background,"[39] he suddenly sees the pianist walk up the stairs. "This, of course, was physically impossible: I was listening to him practicing his Rachmaninov two floors above."[40] The explanation is simple: what the narrator is hearing is a recording, the mechanical reproduction of the pianist practicing Rachmaninov. Although the pianist argues that "it's the same thing, more or less," the narrator shouts that "it is not! It is just absolutely not the same thing!"[41] What makes his project successful, clearly, is that *real* people are involved in it. He is exercising his control not over characters, but over *real* people. It is as if the novel's biopolitical fantasy has become real. Indeed, McCarthy's own novel is arguably complicit with the narrator's project. Its logic of conception arguably resembles that of the narrator's reconstructions.

For now, I want to focus on the fact that the reconstructions function as a kind of therapy for the narrator. He engages in them as a practice of care, in the hope that they will restore to him a sense of being real, first-hand, natural, authentic. As such, they appear to be successful. Checking out a building—the one that will eventually become his building—early on in the novel, the narrator "felt a tingling start up in my right side."[42] Thinking about how the entire scene of his déjà vu would fit in the building, "[t]he tingling became very intense."[43] Experiences like this return again and again throughout the book and appear to be related to his project of experiencing the real. Perhaps because of this reason, the experiences are addictive. If he has them once during a particular re-enactment, he wants to do that re-enactment again, so as to have them again. He also tries to change the re-enactment—to slow it down, for example—so as to try to extend the feeling (one can think, for example, of a slowed-down scene in *Mean Streets* in which De Niro cruises through a bar in Little Italy, New York, with one girl on each arm and wearing no trousers). It is as if the narrator wants to disappear into these moments entirely and thus finally achieve the authenticity he desires.

That is what happens later in the novel when, looking at the diagrams of a murder scene that he will want to re-enact, he goes into a trance.

> The longer I stared at these pictures, the more intense the tingling in my upper body grew. It had moved into my brain, like when you eat too much monosodium glutamate in a Chinese restaurant. My whole head was tingling. The diagrams seemed to take on more and more significance.[44]

And so he "drifted off"[45] into the world that he was seeing. One and a half hours later, he wakes up looking into the concerned faces of Naz and a doctor. The doctor suggests that these trances, which will recur and intensify in the book, are linked to trauma. As such, they are pharmacological:

> He's manifesting ... the autonomous symptoms of trauma ... [R]esponse to trauma is often mediated by endogenous opioids, That is to say, the body administers its own painkillers—hefty ones. The problem is, these can be rather pleasant—so pleasant, in fact, that the system goes looking for more of them. The stronger the trauma, the stronger the dose, and hence the stronger the compulsion to trigger new releases. Reasonably intelligent laboratory animals will return again and again to the source of their trauma, the electrified button or whatever it is, although they know they'll get the shock again. They do it just for that fix: the buzzing, the serenity...[46]

The suggestion appears to be, as Naz notes, that the narrator is doing the same thing.

This reveals something rather disturbing about the narrator's therapy. Whereas he thought it was therapeutic, it might actually have been poisonous, no more than an elaborate way to return to the trauma from which he suffered (but which he does not remember and cannot talk about publicly) and to the opioids that his body released at that time. It is through this experience—through the tingling he appears to experience in this condition—that he thinks he is approaching the real. It might very well be that his trauma—the event that reconfigured his existence—operates for him as the real to which he does not have access. Not remembering it, and not being allowed to talk about it publicly, our narrator's existence is ultimately scripted by a foundational event that is inaccessible to him. It was a moment of near-dying that functioned as a kind of re-birth—but one that exposed to him the inauthenticity of his life. In response, the narrator is trying to get back to that originary moment (remember, in this context, how the crack in the bathroom wall is associated with birth) in order to access the real. But the process, although it takes place under the guise of therapy, is clearly pharmacological. Like a laboratory rat, the narrator is running against the inaccessible source of his trauma over and over again, only to experience that tingling feeling that he associates with the real.

It is worth noting then, at the very least at the level of my criticism, that the novel's concern with trauma thus becomes linked to its concern with biopolitics. I am proposing, in part, that we rewrite the concern with trauma as it is developed in *Remainder* as a biopolitical concern—as the obsessive search for life and for an apparatus that would be able to capture it, as *authentically living*. In this sense, and in particular in terms of the limits that it poses to representation, trauma turns out to be closely aligned with life. It is, indeed, through his trauma that the narrator is able to enter into life, to be authentic. Trauma provides the contact with life, the authentic, the real that the narrator desires. The question then becomes how he can reproduce this experience in his own life. It is to this question that the re-enactments provide a tingling, addictive answer.

Dismissing the advice of the doctor, and pursuing the tingling even more obsessively than before, the narrator inevitably rushes on towards the moment of his destruction which arrives with the final re-enactment: a bank heist.

"Strategy of the Real"

There is a memorable section in Jean Baudrillard's text "Simulacra and Simulations," where Baudrillard asks a fascinating question: "For example", he writes,

> it would be interesting to see whether the repressive apparatus would not react more violently to a simulated hold up than to a real one? For a real hold up only upsets the order of things, the right of property, whereas a simulated hold up interferes with the very principle of reality. Transgression and violence are less serious, for they only contest the *distribution* of the real. Simulation is infinitely more dangerous since it always suggests, over and above its object, that *law and order themselves might really be nothing more than a simulation.*[47]

And so Baudrillard advises his readers to

> Go and organize a fake hold up. Be sure to check that your weapons are harmless, and take the most trustworthy hostage, so that no life is in danger (otherwise you risk committing an offence). Demand ransom, and arrange it so that the operation creates the greatest commotion possible. In brief, stay close to the "truth," so as to test the reaction of the apparatus to a perfect simulation. But you won't succeed: the web of artificial signs will be inextricably mixed up with real elements (a police officer will really shoot on sight; a bank customer will faint and die of a heart attack; they will really turn the phoney ransom over to you). In brief, you will unwittingly find yourself immediately in the real, one of whose functions is precisely to devour every attempt at simulation, to reduce everything to some reality: that's exactly how the established order is, well before institutions and justice come into play.[48]

As at least one critic has noted, Baudrillard mobilizes in these passages some concerns that are central to McCarthy's novel. The final chapters of the book can arguably be read—as Bernadette Buckley in a footnote on Baudrillard and *Remainder* has suggested[49]—as a literary version of Baudrillard's fake hold up.[50]

Although the narrator at first wants to re-enact a hold up in a warehouse that he has rented for the re-enactment, he ultimately decides that he wants the fake hold up to happen at an actual bank. This should happen, however, without any of the people at the bank being aware that it is a fake hold up, and without any of the re-enactors being aware that the people at the bank do not know that the hold up is fake. The re-enactment is meticulously prepared. Even before this decision is taken, Naz and the narrator meet with a famous bank robber called Edward Samuels to collect information. Slowly but surely, they decide on the particular "choreography"[51] for the re-enactment. This choreography is then practiced over and over again until everyone knows by heart what is expected from them. During one of these practice rounds, one of the re-enactors "tripped on a wrinkle in the carpet and fell over."[52] Whereas "[e]veryone laughed," the narrator surprisingly tells the re-enactor to "[d]o that each time."[53] Here is his rationale: "I calculated that if he slightly tripped on purpose, this would prevent his tripping by mistake—forestall that event, as it were."[54] But this is not what happens: in the material world, a negative does not cancel out a negative.

The result is a genuine work of art, a literary version of Pieter Breugel the Elder's *The Blind Leading the Blind*. When the re-enactor during the actual re-enactment pretends to stumble, the wrinkle in the carpet is not there. And so he trips over, hitting another re-enactor who also falls, and whose gun accidentally goes off during the fall. The bullet hits another re-enactor in the chest and the man dies during the re-enactment. It is at this point that the re-enactors realize their guns were loaded with actual bullets; and that the people at the bank do not know they are involved in a re-enactment.

This leads the narrator to conclude that "thanks to the ghost kink,"[55] the re-enactment became real as it was going on. He can actually feel the realization of the re-enactors rise to the surface. Like a doubting Thomas, he "poked my finger into the wound in his chest"[56] and feels that it is real. It is as if the entire realm of fiction has suddenly been zapped into the real, and vice versa—as if fiction and reality are being turned inside out. As if we are in one of M. C. Escher's drawings, and the narrator has been walking on a Moebius strip all this time. Appearance and truth collapse, and although the re-enactment obviously went horribly wrong, the narrator also describes the event as "a very happy day."[57]

Oblivious to the lives that are lost in the process—indeed, he himself also kills one of the other re-enactors after he and Naz have rejoined at the airport for their great escape—, the narrator thus remains entirely focused on his pursuit of the real. Within this pursuit, he has learned an important lesson: "Matter … played a blinder,"[58] as he puts it. He thought he could outwit it and have his fantasy coincide perfectly with the real—dance with the real up until the real and the fantasy became indistinguishable—but this is not what happened. However, what he learns from this is that it is precisely in the collapse of this coincision that the real is obtained. It is only with the undoing (the unworking or *désoeuvrement*) of his project by matter, in other words at the moment when matter—and a peculiar kind of matter in this case: a ghost kink in the carpet—makes his project fall apart, that he is able to touch the real. Whereas this entire time he has been trying to be real like De Niro and to "merge with actions and with objects until there was nothing separating us,"[59] this merger ultimately comes about *not* through the perfect execution of one of his mad projects *but* through their destruction, in the moment when matter interferes with his elaborately constructed choreography. It seems that the real can only be encountered within the collapse, through matter's undoing of a maddening project that attempts to become the real.

Contrary to Bernadette Buckley, one could thus argue that *Remainder*'s fake hold up operates as an odd *reversal* of Baudrillard. Baudrillard's fake hold up fails because the real swallows up the simulation, thus *preventing* one from experiencing simulation (which is Baudrillard's central concern). McCarthy's fake hold up is interrupted by the real, and becomes successful because of this. However, the novel leaves it unclear whether the hold up is successful *because the narrator experiences the real*, or *because the narrator experiences the simulation*. The point is that in this final scene, the one passes into the other, and one is thus capable of experiencing both—something that without such a passing remains impossible.

As such, the scene recalls the passing of reality and fiction that J. M. Coetzee evokes at the end of his Nobel Lecture "He and His Man." It also recalls the scene at the end of Hector Mann's *The Inner Life of Martin Frost*, where Frost throws his story into the fire in order to save the life of Claire. It captures powerfully the space and time in which Ishiguro's *Never Let Me Go* takes place: "England, late 1990s," a fictional space-time that comes uncannily close to the real because it is our recent past. *This has already happened to you*, Ishiguro's novel appears to be saying. Fiction thus creeps up on reality, enabling the reader to touch something—to see the passing between fiction and the real—that would otherwise remain untouched.

In a fascinating review of *Remainder* and of Joseph O'Neill's novel *Netherland*, Zadie Smith ties these concerns to a reading she witnessed in New York in which Tom McCarthy was involved. The reading was organized by the International Necronautical Society and involved McCarthy as well as philosopher Simon Critchley, whose book *Very Little, Almost Nothing* is alluded to in *Remainder*'s opening sentences. Being read was the society's manifesto. I quote here from Smith's review. "We begin," the manifesto goes, "with the experience of failed transcendence … Being is not full transcendence … but an ellipsis, an absence, an incomprehensibly vast lack scattered with … debris and detritus."[60] In the history of philosophy, this debris and detritus—this matter—is generally considered to be a corruption of perfect form (think, for example, of Plato, who is closely related to the birth of the narrator's re-enactment project, on Plato Road). But necronauts, as Smith points out, "feel differently":

> They are "modern lovers of debris" and what is most real for them is not form or God but the brute materiality of the external world … In short, against idealism in philosophy and idealist or transcendent conceptions of art, of art as pure and perfect form, we set a doctrine of … materialism.[61]

Considered in this way, the bank heist is about how the pure and perfect form of its design—practiced over and over again, to the point of including a rehearsed tripping that would anticipate and undo a tripping in reality—collapses into materialism, into the reality of a matter that is not even there (of a ghost kink in the carpet).

This is the answer, I would argue, that McCarthy gives to projects such as the one that Naz executes for the narrator. While they try to capture life and make contact with the real, this contact can only become possible in their collapse, when *life* enters upon the scene of their attempts as *death*. It is a powerful lesson for all the megalomaniac projects that crowd the history of literature; and for all the megalomaniac projects that crowd political history.

There is another re-enactment that is described in the book that captures the philosophical tension between form and matter that is central to the novel. Smith discusses it in her article as well. When the narrator is getting a punctured car tire replaced one day, he asks for the windscreen washer reservoir to be refilled. After the boy working at the shop has poured a liter of the washer liquid into the reservoir, the narrator pushes "the spurter button to make sure it worked."[62] However, nothing comes out. "It's all gone!" he concludes—and he feels wonderful about it. "'Two litres!', I said, 'Where has it all gone?' They'd vaporized, evaporated."[63] As far as he can tell, the liquid has "transubstantiated," and he considers it to be a "miracle."[64] However, when the narrator turns on his car to drive off, the liquid comes gushing out of the dashboard, and he is covered by it. It turns out that there has not been a miracle after all. He will try to enact one when he starts re-enacting this scene in a 24-hour loop. He asks his collaborators to design a system that would have the blue liquid evaporated. However, since one can never get the upper hand on matter, this is not the fiction with which *Remainder* will conclude. In the bank heist re-enaction, matter wins out over form: it is in matter that form collapses, releasing an experience of the real.

The Re-enactment of the Novel (Re-enactment and Politics)

I want to return, however, to a point Jean Baudrillard makes in the first passage from "Simulacra and Simulations" that I have quoted, namely that simulation is more dangerous than transgression and violence. Whereas the latter merely changes the distribution of the real, the former "always suggests, over and above its object, that *law and order themselves might really be nothing more than a simulation*." If McCarthy's novel invites one to reverse Baudrillard's second point, about wanting to find oneself in a simulation that is ultimately always swallowed up by the real, it also invites one to reverse this first proposition, in order to consider how a simulation—and specifically, the simulation of the novel—is really law and order.

Indeed, there is an intimate connection between creative writing and law-making—the subfield of law and literature is devoted entirely to the study of this connection. The consideration is particularly appropriate with respect to McCarthy's novel, in which the narrator moves like a sovereign through his building and lays down the law of his subjects' lives. However, given that the sovereign moment of this subjection—the killings that occur in the novel's closing pages, which include the suggestion that everyone related to the bank heist project will be vaporized—only occurs at the very end of the book, and that much of what happens before is not so much about killing subjects but about keeping them alive, almost until the point of death (for the life they lead can hardly be called a life), it seems that the novel is considering in particular sovereignty's connection to biopolitics. Giorgio Agamben has done this as well, thus in part distancing himself from Michel Foucault who associates biopolitics with governmentality. This seems to me to be the political question about the present that McCarthy's novel puts forward, one that far exceeds the ethical concerns with memory that Joyce Carol Oates has singled out in the novel.

In a review of *Remainder* and a number of other contemporary texts about amnesia, Oates notes the connections between McCarthy's novel and the "documentary trend"[65] of re-enactment in contemporary art. Oates mentions artist Jeremy Deller, who "reprised a bloody battle between striking coal miners and police that took place in 1984 in South Yorkshire."[66]

To anyone who has seen the work, it will be clear that the issue here is ultimately not that of amnesia but the question of politics.

Distinguishing between popular re-enactments—which she defines as "a historically correct re-creation of a socially relevant event"[67]—and artistic re-enactments, curator and critic Inke Arns characterizes the latter as focused on "*the relevance of what happened in the past for the here and now*."[68] "Thus one can say that artistic re-enactments are not an affirmative confirmation of the past; rather, they are *questionings of the present* through reaching back to historical events that have etched themselves indelibly into the collective memory."[69] *Remainder* arguably plays this out at the level of its narrator's private history: thus, it would be *questioning the present by going back to the trauma that the narrator does not remember*. Needless to say, this trauma remains inaccessible—and it might indeed be that the historical events that the artistic re-enactments return to, remain so as well. But what is the present that *Remainder* draws into question? Which present does it challenge?

Distinguishing between the historical re-enactments as discussed by Vannessa Agnew in her article "What is Reenactment?" and artistic re-enactments as discussed by Jonathan Kahana in "What Now? Presenting Reenactment?", Arns propels us into a consideration that is closer to Paige Sarlin's treatment of politics in "New Left-Wing Melancholy: Mark Tribe's 'The Port Huron Project' and the Politics of Reenactment."[70] That is, I argue, where *Remainder* is pushing us to go—hence the appropriateness of Arns' reference to *Remainder* in the opening paragraph of her essay. However, to all of this, one would need to add a literary critical turn of the screw (we are dealing with a novel, after all): I argue that McCarthy mobilizes these concerns within the context of a *novel*, in order to reflect on the practice of *novel-writing* and the history of the novel *as a genre*. Although the philosophical concerns he addresses—the tension between form and matter, the relation between a simulation and the real—return in articles on re-enactment (for example, in Amelia Jones' "'The Artist is Present': Artistic Re-enactments and the Impossibility of Presence"[71]), none of these articles mobilize these concerns with reference to the novel. For this, we need to return to Zadie Smith.

When Smith reviews the book, she situates it somewhat awkwardly in the post-9/11 era, reviewing it next to O'Neill's 9/11 novel *Netherland*. I think that as a political novel, *Remainder* engages with the biopolitical, hyper-sovereign moment post-9/11 that established a shift in the relations between disciplinary, sovereign, and governmental power, bringing sovereignty to the foreground of attention again. But the novel's politics are also aesthetic, as Smith points out, and in a way its challenge is for us to see the relation between both. Smith focuses on a crucial scene early on in the book when the novel is having what she describes as a "nervous breakdown."[72] When the narrator is drinking a cappuccino one day in "one of those Seattle-theme coffee shops"[73] where he has a loyalty card—because he is obsessed with the loyalty card filling up, he will be having more than one cup—, he notices the people outside of the coffee place, specifically how they are looking "just like me: completely second-hand"[74]: they "acted out the roles" of characters in advertising.[75]

After his sixth cappuccino, however, he "noticed a group of homeless people" and in this case his experience is entirely different: "After a while I started thinking that these people, finally, were genuine."[76] Like De Niro, the homeless are thus turned into an authenticity fetish. And so the narrator "decided that I would make contact with them."[77] Asking one of them to join him for dinner, they end up at a Greek restaurant—possibly a reference to Greek philosophy and the tension between form and matter that it contributed to the history of Western philosophy in which the narrator is caught up—, where they are met by a waitress, "an old woman with big glasses."[78] The narrator "ordered a bottle of white wine" and when the waitress comes back with the wine, "[m]y homeless person [note the possessive mine] watched her breasts as she leant over the table to pour it. I watched them too. Her shirt was unbuttoned at the top and she had nice, round breasts. She must have been about his age, eighteen, nineteen."[79] At this point, one might still gather that they have changed waitresses. But when, a little further along, the narrator spills red wine over the white tablecloth and "the waiter"[80] comes back over, the novel appears to be just as confused as the reader: "He was… she was young, with large dark glasses, an Italian woman. Large breasts. Small."[81] Clearly, the narrative is collapsing. And indeed, on the next page, the narrator informs the reader that "[t]here wasn't any table. The truth is, I've been making all this up—the stuff about the homeless person. He existed all right, sitting camouflaged against the shop fronts and the dustbins—but I didn't go across to him."[82]

In other words: everything we have just been reading was invented. What we witnessed, in the chapter, was a moment of novelistic invention, during which several characters were called into being—the homeless person (who really existed, but did not participate in the events that were described), the waitress. Significantly, given my discussion of sadism in the previous chapter, the descriptions of the waitress are infused with sexual desire, thus playing into the scene's ultimate conclusion that all of this is the narrator's fantasy. Indeed, the tingling that the descriptions of the waitress might produce in some readers might be related to the power-trip that the narrator is also having: *do you want a sexy waitress, the narrator seems to be asking? I'll give you a sexy waitress: I'll transform the old woman into a young one, enlarge her breasts, unbutton her shirt, and if you want her to go down on you while you are sipping your wine, I can arrange that as well.* It is an experience of the narrator's power, of the power over life that the narrator appears to have. And yet, after this demonstration, the narrator takes it all back again. None of this was real, it was all invented. But that does not mean the narrative cannot go on: indeed, this is only the end of the third chapter. There is a lot more to come.[83]

As I have already said, Smith reads this moment as a "nervous breakdown," a moment when the narrative collapses. She ties the scene—and I think she is correct to do so—to the novel's long-standing relation to realism and the "credos upon which [it] is built: the transcendent importance of form, the incantatory power of language to reveal truth, the essential fullness and continuity of the self."[84] *Remainder* is clearly critical of these credos and the scene I have just described arguably features realism's collapse. For Smith, this is ultimately an aesthetic issue, one that she also relates to the question of authenticity and identity in McCarthy's novel. That is about as political as the article gets. Perhaps because she is reluctant to read the novel after 9/11, Smith does not consider the biopolitical implications of realism's aesthetic collapse. However, something happens to the novel's power over life when a novelist acknowledges—explicitly—the power he wields and the impossibility of the life-writing project he has adopted.

The contrast that Smith develops here between *Remainder* and O'Neill's novel *Netherland* is illuminating. As Urszula Terentowicz-Fotyga has noted in her article "Unreal City to City of Referents," Smith argues that whereas *Netherland* is perfectly written and executes the credos of realism impeccably, the novel is nevertheless highly anxious about this perfection. Constantly referring to the clichés that characterize its language, it reveals itself to be a master of realism, but one troubled by anxiety. Smith points out that *Remainder* takes an entirely different track. The novel's "minimalist narrative and withdrawal from linguistic bravado remind her [Smith] of Beckett, Joyce, and Kafka, writers who transgress the neat categorizations of realism and anti-narrative, modernism and postmodernism."[85] Samuel Beckett is mentioned early on in the novel, during a scene in which the narrator is looking for re-enactors. One of the actors who has come to audition has "prepared a passage to perform for us: some piece of modern theatre by Samuel Beckett."[86] "We don't want to hear that,"[87] the narrator says. He is explicitly not interested in acting, but in re-enacting. The irony is, of course, that what the re-enactors get involved in is ultimately very close to a Beckett play.

Smith turns to Alain Robbe-Grillet and his experiments with realism. Given that McCarthy has written the introduction for Robbe-Grillet's *Jealousy*, one assumes that this is no coincidence. In the introduction, which was also published in *Artforum*, McCarthy starts with the issue of realism. Critics have noted, he writes, that Robbe-Grillet's work "forswore any attempt to be 'believable' or to engage with the world in a 'realistic' way."[88] By doing so, however, they "displayed an intellectual shortcoming typical of Anglo-American empiricism."[89] He explains:

> [F]irst, in their failure to understand that literary "realism" is itself a construct as laden with artifice as any other; and second, in missing the glaring fact that Robbe-Grillet's novels are actually ultrarealist, shot through at every level with the sheer quiddity of environments to which they attend so faithfully. What we see happening in them, again and again, is space and matter inscribing themselves on consciousness, whose task, reciprocally, is to accommodate space and matter. As Robbe-Grillet was himself fond of declaring: "No art without world."[90]

It is, indeed, the unbearable weight of the realization that realism is a construct that triggers the anxiety of O'Neill's novel and the nervous breakdown in *Remainder*. What McCarthy adds to this, however, is that a narrative practice that responds to this can be read as "ultrarealist." In other words, as a practice that does not break with realism, but continues it in the ulterior regions where the first insight forces it to go.

It is a novel theory of a kind: one that works particularly well with the novels I have discussed in this book, and with the pharmacological theory of the novel that I have developed (the distinction between nuclear and pharmacological criticism becomes particularly useful to describe Robbe-Grillet's narrative practice as McCarthy sees it). In addition, it links up remarkably well with the theory of literature that McCarthy has developed in his book *Tintin and the Secret of Literature*. In this book, McCarthy asks whether the Belgian artist and writer Hergé's comic book series *Tintin* can be considered literature. The book operates from the assumption that it can, and lays bare—through creative close-readings of Hergé's life and work—the ways in which the comic books can be shown to operate "like" literature. Indeed, McCarthy goes so far as to develop a theory of literature on the basis of his discussion of Tintin.

As the title of his book reveals, that theory revolves around the notion of the secret.[91] Literature presents us with a world, McCarthy notes, but a world that must ultimately remain secret. We cannot take a DNA test of a character, he writes. Ultimately, the life of a character is not known to us: not to the reader and not to the writer either. Thus, character-life ultimately remains "eternally unreadable, absolutely indecipherable, even refusing itself to any promise of deciphering or hermeneutic."[92] "The text creates the secret," McCarthy goes on, "making it readable through its own unreadability."[93]

Here too, McCarthy presents a powerful critique of the novel's relation to biopolitics and a theory of the novel as a camp. Although something of the logic of biopolitics and of the camp might inform the project of novel-writing, the novel ultimately resists these complicities and writes a life of the secret. In this case as well, the category of the possible that I discussed towards the end of my chapter on Ishiguro's *Never Let Me Go* takes on supreme significance. Literature is a secret "whose possibility assures the possibility of literature." In literature, "the secret 'remains infinitely private through and through', stays hidden even as it is spread on the surface of the page."[94] If bare life marks the saturation of private life with public life, the absolute coincision of the private and the public (as Giorgio Agamben has noted), the secret of literature resists precisely this identification—*but not through a withdrawal into silence*. Importantly, the secret assures literature's possibility. It guarantees that it can be written. Thus, although a theory of literature's secret presents a critique of narrative, it also guarantees its future.

Indeed, Smith presents *Remainder* as one of two future paths she sees for the novel. Either we can go the way of *Remainder*, and openly critique narrative while continuing to practice it. Or we can go the way of *Netherland*, that perfect novel which is nevertheless so anxious about its own perfection. *Netherland* is indeed that perfectly composed, controlled narration that one associates with *Never Let Me Go*. *Remainder*, on the other hand, rages like Tommy and Hector Mann, like Paul Rayment when he confronts Elizabeth Costello. I argue that the fate of these two novels is also the fate of their complicity with biopolitics and the camp. It is clear that we cannot go on as before. But how to go on, then, as Beckett already asked? Will we keep writing novels that are models of biopolitical perfection, so perfect in fact that they—in their acknowledgement of this perfection—risk to burn up in the light of their own brilliance? Or will we keep writing novels that challenge this model, that might not have much to say or might not say it very beautifully—novels of debris and detritus—but that distance themselves from the dubious politics with which the rise of the novel as a genre is aligned? Paradoxically, *Remainder* achieves this distantiation by its representation of a narrator who creates camps. McCarthy's novel, clearly, can be read as such a camp. And yet, it is the narrative's nervous breakdown that makes such a reading impossible. As such, *Remainder* appears to be much closer to the camp than *Netherland*. But ultimately, it is *Netherland* that, in its relative silence, risks to be all the more complicit.

Synecdoche, New York

Although there does not appear to be any direct relation between the novel and the film, Charlie Kaufman's directorial debut *Synecdoche, New York* can easily be read as a cinematic adaptation of McCarthy's novel. Indeed, if this had been a book about film's relation to biopolitics, Kaufman would have had to take up a central place in it. As the writer of contemporary film classics such as *Being John Malkovich*, a story about a puppeteer who discovers a gateway into the actor John Malkovich's mind and ultimately manages to control him like a puppet, as well as *Eternal Sunshine of the Spotless Mind*, which deals—like *Remainder*—with the problem of amnesia or more precisely memory erasure, Kaufman has shown himself to be obsessed with art's relation to life, leading critic Edward Lawrenson to speak of "the Kaufmanesque blurring of life and art."[95]

Synecdoche is about theater director Caden Cotard (Philip Seymour Hoffman), a character who is named, as one other reviewer of the film remarks, after Jules Cotard, "a nineteenth-century French neurologist who gave his name to a syndrome in which a very depressed patient believes that his organs are rotting and eventually insists that he is dead."[96] Caden does indeed appear to be depressed. He mentions, in the film's opening scenes, that there may have been blood in his stool—proof of his rotting organs? His wife, Adele Lack (Catherine Keener), paints miniature canvases and appears to be entertaining a romantic relationship with Maria (Jennifer Jason Leigh). She will ultimately leave Caden in order to pursue her artistic career—and her love for Maria—in Berlin. Taking their daughter Olive with her, she leaves Caden exposed to his depression and his rotting organs.

But things are about to change for Caden as well. Against all expectations, he receives a MacArthur Fellowship—the so-called genius grant—which famously comes with a lot of money, and no strings attached. Caden will use the funds to stage, in a gigantic warehouse in New York, an elaborate re-enactment of his life: both of scenes that actually happened to him, and of scenes that could have happened to him, that were communicated to him, as he puts it at one point in the film, by his own personal god. The statement recalls Elizabeth Costello's remark in *Slow Man* that she is not entirely in control over the stories she tells. Instead, Paul Rayment's story came to her, and now she is stuck with him and he with her. But as Baudrillard notes in "Simulacra and Simulations," to work at the border of simulation and reality is dangerous business—for the simulation perpetually risks to be swallowed up by the real. Kaufman reverses the situation, and shows us a life that is swallowed up by the simulation.

Caden presumably embarks on his mad project because he wanted to find himself. The play accomplishes, however, the most radical erasure of self. By the time we have reached its end, Caden is no longer Caden but a character who executes, without thinking, the commands that are spoken into his ear by Ellen, a re-enactor who has taken Caden's place as director. Caden takes up her role, and becomes her. He dreams her dreams, wipes his butt the way a woman would, and ultimately dies her death. As was perhaps to be expected, the blurring of life and art also effects Kaufman's own film. Slowly but surely, it becomes clear that from the beginning of the film, we may have been watching a document that is part of Caden's elaborate re-enactment of his life—of all of his possible lives—thus turning Kaufman into Caden, or into the person managing the camera that is recording this madness. Indeed, Kaufman's entire work—most explicitly, the film *Adaptation*—is said to be autobiographical, and to thrive on the writer's personal, real-life obsessions. As such, *Synecdoche* is no different.

The film is clearly a story of a life that becomes entirely appropriated by art, and is kept alive through art until the closing moment of its destruction. By the time Kaufman turns off the camera at the end, one has the feeling that one is witnessing a bare kind of life that is entirely artificial, or perhaps purely natural within the limits of the artifice—a character-life that was born from the ways in which art stripped Caden's life from his way of life. The Caden we witness at the end of the film is thus cinema's (or theatre's) creation, a Frankensteinian figure whose life is thoroughly saturated with art. Caden's life is no longer Caden's. It has become entirely scripted, it fully coincides with the law. There is no longer any Caden left. Instead, Caden has become Ellen and Ellen has taken the director's place. One could read this, perhaps, as a re-enactor's revenge on the director. But it remains a sorry story all the same. What we are witnessing at the end of the film feels like a kind of murder: the murder of a being that cinema is wholly responsible for. The only thing that makes the murder acceptable, perhaps, is that it can be read as a form of euthanasia, as a form of shutting off the life-support technology. Caden, whose life has at this point begun to resemble the life of a neomort or overcomatose patient, should no longer be kept alive. He should be let go. His life is no longer a life that is worth living. Given Caden's depression, and the illness from which he is likely suffering—believing that his organs are rotting and eventually insisting he is dead—this may have been the fate that was laid out for him from the beginning. All this time, he has believed that his insides were rotting away, and now that this process is finally completed, he is convinced that he is dead.

The story is, like all of the others I have discussed in this book, a meta-fictional allegory that reflects on the author's relation to her or his characters. In this film, Kaufman arguably explores character-life: what it means to be a character in a film. Although one might ultimately think of this as a silly concern—the type of thing that mad people are interested in, and that may as such be worthy of study—, I have tried to show in this chapter as well as the previous chapters that there is ultimately more going on here. As a reflection on art in the modern era, and on art's relation to political developments in modern times, specifically the rise of biopolitics and the history of the camps, Kaufman's film arguably presents itself as a kind of camp in which its characters are caught up. Indeed, the huge warehouse in which the re-enactment of Kaufman's life takes place—and which will never see an audience, it should be noted—comes to resemble a ghetto or a kind of prison work camp, in which hundreds of people are laboring—for what? They labor as the re-enactors of one author's life, an author who moves his characters—real-life people—around like pawns in a game of chess. No wonder that Sammy Barnathan, one of the re-enactors who play Caden, commits suicide in the film. Although this is also due to a love-complication—he falls in love with the woman that Caden is in love with—, the moment is also one of escape, where one of the re-enactors tries to leave Caden's mad project behind. Caden's response recalls the insensitivity of McCarthy's *Remainder*: *I never did this*, he yells at Sammy; *and since I never did this, you can't do this either*. It amounts to saying that Sammy has no life of his own, that everyone who is participating in Caden's project ultimately becomes Caden's life. A life that is stretched to such an extent that it turns inside out, like the fiction of *Remainder*'s fake bank heist, thus turning Caden into a fiction of his characters' lives (rather than the other way round). It is Caden who ultimately loses his life to the benefit of his characters. The only way they can liberate themselves from his maddening play is by killing their author.

Notes

1 Susan Sontag, *Styles of Radical Will* (New York: Delta, 1969), 80.
2 Giorgio Agamben, *The Coming Community*, trans. Michael Hardt (Minneapolis: University of Minnesota Press, 2003), 90.
3 Tom McCarthy, *Remainder* (New York: Vintage, 2005), 3.
4 McCarthy, *Remainder*, 7.
5 Ibid., 19.
6 Ibid., 20.
7 Ibid., 1.
8 Ibid., 54.

9 Ibid., 23.
10 Ibid.
11 In this, plasticity is crucially different from flexibility, which is eternally transformable and does not explode.
12 Ibid., 24.
13 Ibid.
14 Ibid.
15 Ibid.
16 Ibid., 65.
17 Ibid.
18 Ibid., 67.
19 Ibid.
20 Ibid., 68.
21 Ibid., 128.
22 Ibid., 83.
23 Ibid., 228.
24 Ibid., 88.
25 Ibid., 90.
26 Ibid., 88.
27 Ibid., 89.
28 Ibid., 86.
29 Ibid., 162.
30 Ibid., 163.
31 See ibid., 199.
32 These questions have been central in the previous chapters as well. It is not surprising that they would come up in novels about care, since they are part and parcel of care as a philosophico-political issue: who gives care, who takes it? Who is the agent of care, who is the receiver? Who is taken care of in a relation of care: the one who gives, or the one who receives? The brilliance of the novels I have looked at lies in the fact that they tie these questions about care to questions about literary and artistic production.
33 See ibid., 112.
34 Ibid., 113.
35 Ibid.
36 Ibid.
37 Ibid.
38 Ibid., 156.
39 Ibid., 157.
40 Ibid.
41 Ibid., 158.
42 Ibid., 106.
43 Ibid., 108.
44 Ibid., 192.
45 Ibid., 192.

46 Ibid., 220.
47 Jean Baudrillard, "Simulacra and Simulations," trans. Paul Foss, Paul Patton, and Philip Beitchman, in Jean Baudrillard, *Selected Writings*, ed. Mark Poster (Stanford: Stanford University Press, 1998), 177.
48 Baudrillard, "Simulacra," 178.
49 See Bernadette Buckley, "The Workshop of Filthy Creation: Or Do Not Be Alarmed, This is Only a Test," in *Review of International Studies* 35: 4 (2009): 855n. 98.
50 Steven Soderbergh's *Ocean's Eleven* (Burbank: Warner, 2002) or Spike Lee's *Inside Man* (Universal City: Universal Studios, 2006), whose plots revolve around fake hold ups, could also productively be read through the lens of Baudrillard's text.
51 McCarthy, *Remainder*, 250.
52 Ibid., 257.
53 Ibid.
54 Ibid.
55 Ibid., 296.
56 Ibid., 194.
57 Ibid., 282.
58 Ibid.
59 Ibid., 240.
60 Zadie Smith, "Two Paths for the Novel," in *New York Review of Books* 55: 18 (2008): http://www.nybooks.com/articles/archives/2008/nov/20/two-paths-for-the-novel/
61 Smith, "Two."
62 McCarthy, *Remainder*, 170.
63 Ibid., 171.
64 Ibid., 174.
65 Joyce Carol Oates, "Lest We Forget," in *New York Review of Books* 54: 12 (2007): http://www.nybooks.com/articles/archives/2007/jul/19/lest-we-forget/?pagination=false
66 Ibid.
67 Inke Arns, "History Will Repeat Itself: Strategies of Re-enactment in Contemporary (Media) Art and Performance": http://www.agora8.org/reader/Arns_History_Will_Repeat.html
68 Arns, "History," 2.
69 Ibid.
70 See Vanessa Agnew, "What is Reenactment?", in *Criticism* 46: 3 (2004): 327–39; Jonathan Kahana, "Introduction: What Now? Presenting Reenactment," in *Framework* 50: 1/2 (2009): 46–60; Page Sarlin, "New Left-Wing Melancholy: Mark Tribe's 'The Port Huron Project' and the Politics of Reenactment," in *Framework* 50: 1/2 (2009): 139–57.
71 See Amelia Jones, "'The Artist is Present': Artistic Re-enactments and the Impossibility of Presence," in *The Dramatic Review* 55: 1 (2011): 16–45.

72 Smith, "Two," 3.
73 McCarthy, *Remainder*, 52.
74 Ibid., 54.
75 Ibid., 53. Interestingly, the clones in Ishiguro's *Never Let Me Go* are described in the same way. As was to be expected in a novel whose protagonists are clones, there is an emphatic concern with authenticity that runs throughout Ishiguro's novel.
76 Ibid., 56.
77 Ibid.
78 Ibid., 57.
79 Ibid., 58.
80 Ibid., 59.
81 Ibid.
82 Ibid., 60.
83 Of course, one might argue that what we are confronting here is merely a "game" that the author is playing, to recall the title of Peter Hutchinson's book *Games Authors Play* (New York: Methuen Young Books, 1983); and indeed, within the limits of postmodernism, we could probably leave it at that. But my argument throughout this book has been that there is a biopolitical significance to the novel's play: what the novel is enacting through its aesthetic production, I argue, is a play that mimics—through its relation to life—the biopolitical mode of production that rises to prominence at the same time as the genre of the novel. Thus, although to govern life in a novel is of course not quite the same as governing life in the real world, the latter assumes an imaginary that is unmistakably active in the former. To see this connection means to raise the political stakes in one's discussion of the rise of the novel as a genre.
84 Smith, "Two," 1.
85 Urszula Terentowicz-Fotyga, "Unreal City to City of Referents: Urban Space in Contemporary London Novels," in *Journal of Narrative Theory* 39: 3 (2009): 312.
86 McCarthy, *Remainder*, 117.
87 Ibid.
88 Tom McCarthy, "The Geometry of the Pressant," in *Artforum* 46: 10 (2008): 392.
89 McCarthy, "Geometry," 392.
90 Ibid.
91 I have addressed this problematic in Chapter Three of Arne De Boever, *States of Exception in the Contemporary Novel: Martel, Eugenides, Coetzee, Sebald* (New York: Continuum, 2012).
92 Derrida quoted in Tom McCarthy, *Tintin and the Secret of Literature* (Berkeley: Counterpoint, 2008), 146.
93 McCarthy, *Tintin*, 146. It is worth noting, in the context of this book, that

Hergé referred to Tintin as "his child" (ibid., 159) and was a great fan of Buster Keaton and Charlie Chaplin (ibid., 165).

94 Ibid.,146.

95 Edward Lawrenson, "Gone in 60 Years," in *Sight and Sound* 19: 6 (2009): 26.

96 Alan A. Stone, "The Mind's Eye," in *Boston Review* 34: 1 (2009): 53.

Conclusion: Pedro Almodóvar's *Talk to Her* as a Narrative of Care

"Comas are rare phenomena," Linus told me once. "They're a byproduct of modern living, with almost no known coma patients existing prior to World War Two. People simply died. Comas are as modern as polyester, jet travel, and microchips."[1]

—Douglas Coupland, *Girlfriend in a Coma*

Narrative Coma

In the final section of his book *Homo Sacer: Sovereign Power and Bare Life*, Giorgio Agamben invites his readers to "enter the hospital room where the body of Karen Quinlan or the overcomatose person is lying, or where the neomort is waiting for his organs to be transplanted."[2] "Here", he writes:

> biological life—which the machines are keeping functional by artificial respiration, pumping blood into the arteries, and regulating the blood temperature—has entirely been separated from the form of life that bore the name Karen Quinlan: here life becomes (or at least seems to become) pure *zoe*. … Karen Quinlan's body is really only anatomy in motion, a set of functions whose purpose is no longer the life of an organism. Her life is maintained only by means of life-support technology and by virtue of a legal decision. It is no longer life, but rather death in motion.[3]

Quinlan's case is the last in an "extreme, if not arbitrary"[4] series of examples of bare life that Agamben is giving. It includes, in addition to Quinlan, the Flamen Diale (the Roman priest that I discussed in Chapter Two), "the person of the Führer in the Third Reich,"[5] the "figure of the concentration camp inhabitant,"[6] and "the case of Wilson, the biochemist who decided to make his own body and life into a research and experimentation laboratory upon discovering that he suffered from leukemia."[7] Not everyone will agree that these figures belong to the same set. Leaving these objections aside, I want to focus on Karen Quinlan as a figure of bare life.

In Chapter Two as well as at the end of Chapter Four, I suggested that in a biopolitical theory of the novel as a camp, character-life can be aligned with the life of the overcomatose person or the neomort, as a life that is being kept alive by the life-support technology of the novel. Susan Barton in J. M. Coetzee's *Foe* explicitly casts her life in these terms. In the case of Ishiguro's *Never Let Me Go*, which establishes a connection between clones and characters, this comparison becomes particularly appropriate as well. Indeed, the Quinlan case is thought to have inspired at least one other contemporary novelist: Douglas Coupland's *Girlfriend in a Coma* revolves around a woman called Karen and includes references to the 1970s, the period when Quinlan's story was in the news. Interestingly, the story's crucial dates—Quinlan collapses in 1975, is taken off life-support in 1976, and goes on living until 1985—coincide with the period when Michel Foucault is working on biopolitics, from 1975 (when he first mentions the notion in the final lecture of his 1975–6 course *"Society Must Be Defended"*) until 1984, the year of his death.

Quinlan has a contemporary counterpart whose case has become of interest to scholars working in Foucault's tracks: Terri Schiavo. Like Quinlan, Schiavo collapsed one day while she was on an intense diet, going into a coma that doctors would soon diagnose as a Persistent Vegetative State. Consistent with his wife's desire not to be kept on life-support technology, Michael Schiavo requested for her feeding tube to be removed. Terri's parents, however, thought otherwise. The case turned public when various advocacy groups (the pro-life movement, most notably) got involved. In a biopolitical turn of events, Jeb Bush, the Republican governor of Florida (Terri's home state), passed a state law called "Terri's law," which enabled him to order that Terri's feeding tube be put back in. When the decision went to the Supreme Court, the judge there ruled that such a law was unconstitutional because it encroached too much upen a person's private life. Anticipating that ruling, Bush had already taken the case to the federal level, attracting the attention of his brother, President George W. Bush, who returned from a holiday to vote on the case. Ultimately, Terri was disconnected from her life-support technology and she peacefully died of dehydration afterwards.

Without going into all of the case's complicated details, it is worth noting that it has attracted the attention of critical theorists. John Protevi has dedicated a chapter to Schiavo in his book *Political Affect*.[8] Around the time when his book *On Creaturely Life* was published, Eric Santner published a short text on the University of Chicago Press website, in which he read the Schiavo case next to the other story that dominated the news at the time, the Abu Ghraib prison photographs. Both cases present, Santner argues, stories in which "human life is positioned with respect to law and political power."[9] However, if Abu Ghraib—or also, a place like Guantánamo Bay—"represent sites where life, lacking all legal status and protection, stands in maximal exposure to political power," Schiavo's case "offers us a strange reversal": here, we get "an intrusive excess of legal 'protection' that effectively serves to suspend the law … and take direct hold of human life."[10] At this point, Santner notes, "Schiavo's life assumes a 'biopolitical' dimension in which life and politics can no longer be fully distinguished."[11] Summarizing the contrast between the two cases a little later in the article, Santner writes: "In one case we have human life stripped of the cover of a symbolic status/value, in the other the intrusive imposition [of] a symbolic value/status in the absence of sentient life."[12] The point is important, because it shows that bare life does not only come about when *zoe* is stripped from *bios*; it also comes about when *bios* is forced onto *zoe*. In Santner's article, this ultimately leads into a discussion of soul murder, and he goes on to consider the theological dimensions of the Schiavo case.

Santner's book on creaturely life—which his text on the University of Chicago Press website is supposed to advertise—is emphatically a book on literature, but it does not establish the connections between character-life and bare life that I have laid out in this study. As I have shown, this connection is central to contemporary fiction and to the genre of the novel at large, and the novel's long history can arguably be read as an extended struggle with a biopolitical understanding of the novel as a camp. Of course, such an insight—which depends, to a large extent, on one's understanding of the novel as a typically modern genre—extends beyond the novel and is arguably related to every form of representation.[13] As such, it is significant that I began the book with a reflection on images, and propose to close it with a reflection on film.

If the photograph, according to some, is removed from narrative—Susan Sontag famously argued that it needs narrative to be interpreted, and to have a particular political effect; Judith Butler has challenged her on this, arguing that a frame always already constitutes interpretation, and that the photograph is thus always already infused with politics[14]—it is certainly worthwhile considering how each of the four novels I have discussed *also* revolves around a removal from narrative, as if the novels are trying to distance themselves from the practice with which they are complicit. J. M. Coetzee's *Slow Man* challenges the authority of the novelist Elizabeth Costello, and depicts Paul Rayment's struggle against Costello's narrative cruelty and/or narrative care. Kazuo Ishiguro's *Never Let Me Go* exposes the ideological nature not only of Kathy's caring practice, but also of her narrative: neatly composed, it reflects an eerie, inhuman calm that few readers are able to sympathize with. Paul Auster's *The Book of Illusions* pushes this critique to the extreme in its representation of a filmmaker, Hector Mann, who makes films on the condition that no one will see them and that they will be destroyed after his death. As the novel informs us, not even the surrealists agreed to such a holo-caust or all-burning when Luis Buñuel proposed it to them. Finally, Tom McCarthy's *Remainder* includes a scene that Zadie Smith has described as a nervous breakdown within the structure of the novel: the novel's narrative is interrupted, and exposed as false. And yet, it is *also* allowed to continue.

That is, indeed, the key feature of all of these texts: these are novels that continue narrating *through* and *beyond* their critique. It is for this reason that I have characterized them as pharmacological texts. Investigating the complicity of the novel as a genre with what I have called biopolitics—a politics *over* life—, they also seize the possibilities *of* life-narrative as a technique of emancipation and liberation (one could call this a biopolitics *from below*—a politics *of* life).[15] The novels recognize, in other words, both the curative and the poisoning dimensions of their practice and it is for this reason that they are particularly interesting for an investigation of the novel's relation to care, life, and politics in the twenty-first century. From the modern era in which it was born, that is, from its originary complicity with biopolitics, the novel has transformed into a twenty-first century genre that is no longer central to literary culture, but whose legacy continues nevertheless—and a political legacy at that.

What about the novel in a time of crises, emergencies, and exceptions? What about the novel in a time when life is exposed as extremely vulnerable? In a time of neoliberalism, when life has become saturated with power to such an extent that it has come to live by default, within the regulations of a government that ultimately comes to coincide with life? If what is needed in a time of profound disorientation is a therapeutics or practice of care, then how might the novel participate in this? Indeed, how might other forms of narration, or perhaps even simply of representation, become newly relevant today? These are the questions that have informed *Narrative Care*.

Although these questions are presented in this book through an analysis of contemporary novels and of the rise of the novel as a modern genre, the particular history I have laid out includes other modern cultural developments such as the rise of photography and film (of silent film and sound film). Film took up an important role in my third and fourth chapters, on Auster's *The Book of Illusions* and McCarthy's *Remainder*, and it would be interesting to pursue a study of the relation between film and narrative care. I am interested in this in particular because film, as a visual medium that presents its materials in an entirely different way than the novel, appears to be very much attuned to the critique of narrative. Many of the twentieth-century developments in the history of the novel—think of the development of the *nouveau roman* that I have mentioned at various points in this book—were closely related to film and in fact cannot be separated from it. Since film as a visual medium *can* and even *demands* to be read differently from the novel, this might lead one to theorize a politics of reading that would need to be practiced in the face of any representation's power over life.[16] When I theorize the novel as a camp, it is important to remember that this is ultimately not a statement about the novel as such. Instead, it is a statement that applies to a practice: the practice of novel-writing/reading. It is within this practice of writing and also of reading, that the novel *can* emerge as camp. *But there is no reason why this should be so*. Indeed, film might invite one to move away from a practice of writing/reading in which each and every detail of a character's life must become meaningful.

As Sontag in an article from 1964 already wrote, "interpretation … is *the* modern way of understanding something."[17] As such, it relates to the novel, *the* characteristically modern literary genre (Ian Watt) and the camp, *the* paradigm of political modernity (Agamben). Inspired by the *nouveau roman*, and by the films that influenced these developments in literature, Sontag argues against a criticism in which everything ultimately comes to stand for something else—in which everything ultimately comes to mean something else—and defends instead what she calls "an erotics of art."[18] Although for many, that phrase might not exactly solve much either—Jonathan Franzen notes that "[n]ot even the French poststructuralists, with their philosophically unassailable celebration of the 'pleasure of the text'"[19] can help him out when it comes to theorizing reading—it nevertheless puts one on the track of another kind of engagement with the text, beyond the logic of the camp.

Care and Gender

Sontag's critique of interpretation may be old news, but it applies very well to the work of Pedro Almodóvar, who has become famous for his sensuous, erotic style of filmmaking.[20] His recent work includes a so-called "brain-dead trilogy"[21] that revolves around narratives of care. Indeed, several other films have reflected on this problematic, and on the related question of assisted dying. Euthanasia is, of course, closely related to the question of biopolitics.[22]

As Gwynne Edwards has noted, Almodóvar is not a political filmmaker,[23] and with the exception of his film *Live Flesh*, which opens with a dictionary definition of the so-called "state of exception" and explores the continuation of sexuality's excepted position in individual and collective life after Franco's emergency regime has ended, his work has steered clear from political questions.[24] The film I propose to consider, *Talk to Her*, is not a political film either. However, it is through the reflection on care it develops that it becomes political. One of its central characters—a care-taker—will end up going to jail because he cares too much, or cares in the wrong way. Thus, the film explores the pharmacological dimension of care—its curative and its empoisoning dimension—, and it is because of this that I am interested in it here.

The film furthers questions about sex, gender, and sexuality that I raised in my third chapter, and that are already included in the work I discussed at the very beginning of this book, Sophie Calle's *Take Care of Yourself*. As I have explained, Calle's work revolves around a break-up letter she receives from her boyfriend. In it, he states that he cannot stick to his promise of not being with a number of other women. Closing his letter with the formula "Take care of yourself," he makes Calle wonder about what that sentence might mean. And so she writes to over one hundred women to ask them to interpret the sentence according to their professional activities. Thus, Calle appears to reconfirm women's age-old relation to care. Indeed, care-oriented feminism—*à la* Carol Gilligan—embraces this relation as part of the feminist struggle.

However, Calle also changes something in this relation and the association of women with the private sphere that it often assumes. With the exception of a few odd cases (a parrot; a minor) most of the women that Calle writes to are women who work and have a professional career. As such, this changes these women's association with care, because it liberates the association from the private sphere—without, however, undoing it. Women do not have to sacrifice their career in order to be able to care. It might even be that it is *by virtue of* their career, and *through* their professions, that they are able to advise Calle how to take care of herself. As will be clear, this does not necessarily suggest that working men would be equally capable of giving advice. By preserving women's association to care *and* by contacting working women, Calle is able to have it both ways—to establish women's unique relation to care, but not at the cost of their domestication.

Within the context of these questions, one must also consider sexuality, and the heteronormative understanding of care that recurs throughout this book. In the overwhelming majority of situations I have considered, care occurs in relations between men and women: Marijanna and Rayment, Costello and Rayment, Kathy and Tommy, David and Alma. Of course, there is also the relation between Kathy and Ruth, and between David and Hector—but these are not explored outside of heteronormativity. To a certain extent, this heteronormativity is due to my choice of novels.[25] However, the question of this exclusion clearly also speaks to the problematic of care at large, and to issues like gay marriage, gay-partner visitation in hospitals, and so on. Almodóvar puts the question of gender and sexuality on the map within the debates about care.

Indeed, the film's title, *Talk to Her*, immediately mobilizes some of these concerns: clearly, "she" is the one that needs to be talked to. But who will be doing the talking? A man? Or a woman? Women do talk a lot, as the cliché goes; capricious as they are (another cliché—*la donna è mobile*), they also tend to need a "talking to." "Talk to her" also calls up other associations: tell her what you are really thinking. Tell her how you feel. Tell her that you love her. Or also: "Talk to her"—she may have misunderstood. She may be angry, but it is due to a misunderstanding; you should talk to her to clear things up. Or: you have done something wrong and she wants you to go talk to her. Your mother is not happy with how you have treated her—you will need to go talk to her. And so on and so forth. If the talking that the title refers to is part of a psychoanalytic talking cure, the relations would be shifting once again. In this case, it would be the person talking who would be in need of a cure. The "she" who is listening would be the analyst.

This is not a random series of imaginary situations. All of them recur in one form or another in the film. The protagonist of *Talk to Her* is a male nurse, Benigno—literally, the benign, harmless one—who is taking care of a comatose young woman, Alicia. From what we see in the film, Benigno appears to be an excellent carer and a great colleague, sometimes taking over a shift from another nurse who is having family issues. Although the film, by presenting us with a male nurse, reverses the gender politics of care, it also confirms a cliché by suggesting that Benigno is gay.[26] However, this is never fully established in the film. Although some aspects of Benigno's appearance may strike one as gay, he does not appear to have come out yet. For a while, the viewer thinks that he may be attracted to the film's other male lead, Marco. Such a reading is complicated, however, when Alicia turns out to be pregnant—from Benigno.

The revulsion one might feel as the result of this rape is attenuated—not unproblematically so—by Benigno's caring administrations for Alicia (compare this situation, for example, to the scene at the beginning of Quentin Tarantino's *Kill Bill*, where a male nurse is renting out the comatose body of the character known as "the bride" to truckers interested in a quick fuck). However, all the care in the world cannot hide the fact that Benigno takes his job a little too far. Talking to Alicia as if she were his girlfriend, and discussing with Marco his plan of asking her to marry him, he takes care—as a nurse would—of every single part of her body, intimate and non-intimate places. After seeing a silent film one day about a shrunken lover who disappears into the vagina of his sleeping wife to give her sexual pleasure (presumably dying in the act), Benigno is thrown off when he exposes

Alicia's breasts to take care of her. The film then cuts to the organic motions of a lava lamp, suggesting that sex and even conception have occurred.[27]

As I have already said, Benigno will go to jail for his rape. However, the film also informs us that although his child was stillborn, giving birth also made Alicia wake up from her coma. Marco rushes to jail to let Benigno know, but he arrives too late: Benigno has taken his own life. And so we are moved—at least I was—to see the rapist dead. The film includes a number of suggestions as to why Benigno's sexuality is "abnormal." Until a very late age, he took care of his mother—working, basically, as her private nurse. From the balcony of her house, he would observe Alicia taking dancing lessons in a studio across the street (the studio is managed by Katerina Bilova, played by Geraldine Chaplin, Chaplin's daughter). Noticing Alicia's wallet slip out of her bag one day, he catches up with her to return it, and ultimately accompanies her home. Trying to see her again, he sets up an appointment with her father, a psychoanalyst. That is when Benigno's relation to his mother, as well as his presumed homosexuality, are discussed. The scene appears to have been included in the film more as a joke than as anything else. It does not really reveal anything about Benigno other than the clichés that the film already plays into (of course, this male nurse who lived with his mother for such a long time must be gay!—we do not need psychoanalysis to tell us that). Benigno is, crucially, in between straight and gay, woman and man. It is in part because of his peculiar upbringing that he cannot be categorized.

Rebellions of Care

The film plays with categorizations in some of its other stories as well. Speaking of Geraldine Chaplin, it is worth noting that Almodóvar includes a silent film in this story about care. It is a tribute to the silent film era that, for reasons I have discussed in Chapter Three, is closely related to the problematic I have addressed in this book. In line with my discussion of silent film in that chapter, and with the remarks I included there (in relation to my reading of Nathaniel Hawthorne's "The Birthmark" about literature, politics, and science), it is interesting to note that the film—which is titled *The Shrinking Lover*—involves a scientist and is vaguely pornographic. Almodóvar plays with gender politics in this film within the film. The scientist turns out to be a woman, who is working on a new invention. Her husband generously offers to be the guinea pig for the brew she has concocted. She refuses at first, but—perhaps in order to prove his manhood to his career wife—he ultimately drinks her recipe to the bottom. Although all is well at first, he soon begins to shrink, and ultimately moves back to his mother's house out of shame and humiliation. His wife goes to fetch him there, however, and of course they end up in bed together—the tiny husband next to the gigantic wife. While his wife is asleep, the husband starts mounting her body. Climbing the hills of her breasts, and descending into the valley of her private parts, he ends up between her legs, in front of the lips of her vagina. After taking off all his clothes, he disappears inside of it, giving her (that is, at least, what his wife's facial expression appears to reveal) sexual pleasure. One assumes that he dies in the act—a little death, quite literally so in our man's case.

It is the eros–thanatos connection once again but it becomes inscribed here—because of the similarities, as critics have noted, between this story and the story of Benigno and Alicia—into a story of care, with eros taking up a destabilizing position in the semantic field of love. As in Coetzee's novel *Slow Man*, the relations between eros and care are unclear. Although eros might according to some include care, it is much less certain that care would include eros. It risks slipping into eros, as Paul Rayment's relation to Marijana and Benigno's relation to Alicia show, but at that point the caring relation becomes disturbed.[28] Although the two are closely related, there is nevertheless a border between eros and care that must be maintained.

Also part of this semantic field is *philia*, friendship. The film prominently features the homosocial friendship between Benigno and Marco, a story that ends with Marco crying his heart out when he hears about Benigno's death. What is the exact nature of Benigno's relation to Marco, and of Marco's relation to Benigno? Can it be determined/is it necessary to determine it (not just in one's reading of the film, but also in life)? Must these relations of love—whether it is care, or eros, or *philia*—be determined, named, and spoken? Or could one simply dwell in their indeterminacies, floating along in a sea of affections that may allow for a more exciting—but potentially more complicated—existence?

One should also consider in this context Marco's girlfriend, Lydia. A woman bullfighter who is terrified of snakes (as the stereotypical woman would be!), she regularly hoists herself into her toreador's outfit to confront a raging bull. One day, the bull gets the better of her, and she ends up in a coma. It is during this already difficult period that Marco finds out that on the day she was attacked by the bull, she was going to break up with him: she is still in love with her ex-partner, a toreador. Her death may have been a consequence of her reluctance to speak of her love—to stay silent, while Marco (the man!—not like the stereotype at all…) is chatting away.

The contrast between Benigno's relation to Alicia and Marco's relation to Lydia is stark. Unlike Benigno, who talks to Alicia as if she were alive, Marco cannot talk to Lydia in this way—perhaps because he already knew her, and knew her well, from before her accident. Marco cannot care for the comatose. He appears to care only for the living. Benigno does care for the comatose—and cares too much, as *Talk to Her* shows. Ultimately, both Benigno and Lydia will die. In the closing scenes of the film, it is suggested that Marco and Alicia will get together.

Thus, the heteronormative ultimately triumphs in this tale of care, which is one of Almodóvar's most heterosexual films. However, this triumph can only come about through the mediation of the in-between figures of Benigno and Lydia. They function in the film as vanishing mediators. In terms of their status as rebellious figures within the framework of care that I have set up, one thus cannot but wonder about the status of their rebellion. Are we dealing here, as Judith Butler in her reading of the memoirs of the hermaphrodite Herculine Barbin has suggested, with rebellions of which the law can ultimately guarantee that they "will—out of fidelity—defeat themselves—defeat themselves and those subjects who, utterly subjected, have no choice but to reiterate the law of their genesis"[29]? If Benigno and Lydia's tragedy is in a way born from heterosexual normativity, from the rules and regulations that (biopolitically) govern sexuality, do they ultimately reiterate, through their deaths that make the relation between Marco and Alicia possible, the heteronormative law from which their tragedy has sprung? Is that the final word of Almodóvar's film?

The film ends, indeed, with Marco and Alicia (who is in the company of her dance teacher) attending a performance of a dance piece by Pina Bausch.[30] Marco (a man!—once again, he defies the stereotype) is moved to tears by the piece, and Alicia notices his emotions. This little play returns the reader to the opening scene of the film, where Marco and Benigno—at that point still strangers to each other—are also watching a Pina Bausch performance. In this scene as well, Marco is crying—and Benigno notices it (he is not crying, even though one might have expected him to, given the stereotype of gay, effeminate men). The parallel aligns Alicia with Benigno, and suggests that in Alicia, Benigno lives on. And indeed he does, given that it was ultimately he who brought her back to life. It also suggests that through Alicia's interest in Marco, Benigno's interest in Marco is living on. Finally, the suggestion may also be that in Marco's love for Alicia, his friendship/love for Benigno is living on. Ultimately, the relation between Marco and Alicia may thus be less heteronormative than one thinks. For in each of these characters, different love interests live on. In their relation, different loves circulate.

One wonders, finally, to what extent it matters that this complicated scene of love is played out in front of a dance performance. Almodóvar has insisted that discovering the Pina Bausch piece made him realize how he should begin and end the film. In the context of this book, one is tempted to ask, of course, about how dance relates to the problematic of care and its relation to biopolitics. For with the entry of dance upon our scene, we have moved from the novel to photography, and from silent film to sound film, in order to arrive at what is perhaps—even more so than film and theater, which I discussed in Chapter Four—the most emphatically physical form of art, dance. If dance arguably makes the power-relation between character and author (or, in this case, between choreographer and dancer) even more real, then what might be dance's relation to biopolitics? Of course, the question far precedes the modern age—dance is likely one of the oldest art forms. It is interesting to note, in this context, that in his discourse on inequality, Jean-Jacques Rousseau suggests that the first step towards inequality began with dance. "The one who sang or danced the best," he writes, "the handsomest and the strongest, the most adroit or the most eloquent became the most highly regarded."[31] "And this was the first step toward inequality and, at the same time, toward vice."[32] I do not know whether Rousseau is correct in this assessment—most likely, he is not. But it does cast an interesting light on the politics of modern dance, as we see it played out in Almodóvar's film.[33]

Here, it is not a question of "[t]he one who sang or danced the best" or "the handsomest and the strongest, the most adroit or the most eloquent." Indeed, Bausch is known for playing with these conventions and for inserting a sense of humor, clumsiness, and awkwardness into modern dance. In *Café Müller*, the piece that Benigno and Marco are watching at the beginning of *Talk to Her*, dancers are stumbling across the stage bumping into chairs and tables. Could one not read this as a commentary on the politics of dance as Rousseau lays it out, through which dance is transformed from something one tries to do best, and which therefore stands at the origin of inequality, into something one can only do stumbling, and which therefore pulls us back into equality?

It may indeed be in front of *such* a scene that the caring relation between Marco and Alicia, as well as the caring relations I have discussed throughout this book, become most meaningful: as *both* critiques of care's relation to biopolitics *and* creative continuations of care beyond these dark complicities.

Notes

1 Douglas Coupland, *Girlfriend in a Coma* (New York: HarperCollins, 2008).
2 Giorgio Agamben, *Homo Sacer: Sovereign Power and Bare Life*, trans. Daniel Heller-Roazen (Stanford: Stanford University Press, 1998), 186.

3 Agamben, *Homo Sacer*, 186.
4 Ibid.
5 Ibid., 184.
6 Ibid.
7 Ibid., 185.
8 See John Protevi, *Political Affect: Connecting the Social and the Somatic* (Minneapolis: University of Minnesota Press, 2009).
9 Eric Santner, "Terri Schiavo and the State of Exception": http://www.press.uchicago.edu/Misc/Chicago/05april_santner.html
10 Santner, "Schiavo."
11 Ibid.
12 Ibid.
13 W. J. T. Mitchell has explored the consequences of this statement in *Cloning Terror: The War of Images, 9/11 to the Present* (Chicago: University of Chicago Press, 2011).
14 See Susan Sontag, *On Photography* (New York: Farrar, Strauss, and Giroux, 1977); Judith Butler, *Frames of War: When is Life Grievable?* (New York: Verso, 2009).
15 I am using terminology developed by David Kishik in *The Power of Life: Giorgio Agamben and the Coming Politics* (Stanford: Stanford University Press, 2012).
16 I am preparing a book titled *Plastic Sovereignties: Giorgio Agamben and the Politics of Aesthetics* in which I will theorize such a politics of reading.
17 Susan Sontag, *Against Interpretation* (New York: Delta Books, 1966), 8–9.
18 Sontag, *Against*, 14.
19 Jonathan Franzen, *How to Be Alone* (New York: Farrar, Strauss, and Giroux, 2002), 74.
20 About the image of a swimmer in the film, Almodóvar has suggested that it has no other place in the narrative than the fact that with it, "he wanted to convey the feeling of summer": Kevin Ohi, "Voyeurism and Annunciation in Almodóvar's *Talk to Her*," in *Criticism* 51: 4 (2010): 538.
21 Marsha Kinder, "Reinventing the Motherland: Almodóvar's Brain-Dead Trilogy," in *Film Quarterly* 58: 2 (2004): 9–25.
22 Another film that has been discussed in this context is Alejandro Amenábar's *The Sea Inside* (United States: New Line, 2005).
23 Gwynne Edwards, *Almodóvar: Labyrinths of Passion* (London: Peter Owen, 2001), 166; Edwards' claim is nuanced in Kathleen M. Vernon and Barbara Morris, *Post-Franco, Postmodern: The Films of Pedro Almodóvar* (Westport: Greenwood Press, 1995).
24 For the relation between sex/sexuality/gender and the state of exception, see Arne De Boever, *States of Exception in the Contemporary Novel: Martel, Eugenides, Coetzee, Sebald* (New York: Continuum, 2012), esp. Chapter Two.
25 I could also have chosen novels that revolved around a homosexual

relation of care; I am thinking of Allan Hollinghurst's *The Line of Beauty* (New York: Bloomsbury, 2005), for example.

26 Several critics have noted in this context the relation of Almodóvar's film to the fairy tale *Sleeping Beauty*. In the fairy tale, it is of course a straight man who attends to the sleeping woman; Almodóvar reverses this paradigm by having a potentially gay man attend to Alicia. See Kinder, "Reinventing." Adriana Novoa draws from Hélène Cixous' analysis of *Sleeping Beauty* in her discussion of Almodóvar's film: "Whose Talk Is It? Almodóvar and the Fairy Tale in Talk to Her," in *Marvels and Tales* 19: 2 (2005): 224–48.

27 Kevin Ohi has challenged such a reading in his article "Voyeurism and Annunciation." Recalling the film's title, he notes that we never see such a rape occur. "What we are shown is his talking to her" (ibid., 523). Ohi very interestingly reads this as a scene of annunciation, which repeats Mary's impregnation through the word of god, because god spoke to her. As Ohi notes, "Talking thereby derives an extraordinary power that we ought not to underestimate" (ibid.). Ohi's reading becomes particularly meaningful in the context of this project, because it suggests language has the power to bring to life.

28 Almodóvar has read Coetzee, and recommends his fiction. See Paul Julian Smith, "Only Connect," *Sight and Sound* 12: 7 (2002): 2.

29 Judith Butler, *Gender Trouble: Feminism and the Subversion of Identity* (New York: Routledge, 1999), 135.

30 Anette Guse has discussed Almodóvar's film and Pina Bausch's work together, focusing on the importance of gender relations in both. See Anette Guse, "Talk to Her! Look at Her! Pina Bausch in Pedro Almodóvar's *Hable con ella*," in *Seminar* 43: 4 (2007): 427–40.

31 Jean-Jacques Rousseau, "Discourse on the Origins of Inequality," in Jean-Jacques Rousseau, *The Basic Political Writings*, trans. Donald A. Cress (Indianapolis: Hackett, 1987), 64.

32 Rousseau, "Discourse," 64.

33 See David Kishik's brilliant excursus on this issue in *Power of Life*, 27–32.

Bibliography

Agamben, Giorgio. *Homo Sacer: Sovereign Power and Bare Life*. Trans. by Daniel Heller-Roazen. Stanford: Stanford University Press, 1998.

—*The Coming Community*. Trans. by Michael Hardt. Minneapolis: University of Minnesota Press, 2003.

—*The Time that Remains: A Commentary on the* Letter to the Romans. Trans. by Patricia Dailey. Stanford: Stanford University Press, 2005.

—*What is an Apparatus? And Other Essays*. Trans. by David Kishik and Stefan Pedatella. Stanford: Stanford University Press, 2009.

—*The Kingdom and the Glory: For a Theological Genealogy of Economy and Government*. Trans. by Lorenzo Chiesa with Matteo Mandarini. Stanford: Stanford University Press, 2011.

Agnew, Vanessa. "What is Reenactment?" *Criticism* 46: 3, 2004: 327–39.

Amenábar, Alejandro, dir. *The Sea Inside*. United States: New Line, 2005.

Armstrong, Nancy. *How Novels Think: The Limits of Individualism from 1719–1900*. New York: Columbia University Press, 2005.

Arns, Inke. "History Will Repeat Itself: Strategies of Re-enactment in Contemporary (Media) Art and Performance": http://www.agora8.org/reader/Arns_History_Will_Repeat.html [accessed 14 November 2012].

Attridge, Derek. "A Writer's Life." *The Virginia Quarterly Review* 80: 4, 2004: 254–65.

Auster, Paul. "Black on White: Recent Paintings by David Reed." In Auster, Paul. *Ground Work: Selected Poems and Essays 1970–1979*. London: Faber and Faber, 1990. 127–35.

—*Leviathan*. London: Faber and Faber, 1993.

—*The Book of Illusions*. New York: Faber and Faber, 2002.

—*Travels in the Scriptorium*. New York: Picador, 2006.

—dir. *The Inner Life of Martin Frost*. Paris: Alfama, 2007.

—*Invisible*. New York: Picador, 2010.

Badiou, Alain. *Saint Paul: The Foundation of Universalism*. Trans. by Ray Brassier. Stanford: Stanford University Press, 2003.

Baudrillard, Jean. "Simulacra and Simulations." In Baudrillard, Jean. *Selected Writings*, ed. by Mark Poster. Trans. by Paul Foss, Paul Patton, and Philip Beitchman. Stanford: Stanford University Press, 1998. 166–84.

—*The Agony of Power*. Trans. by Ames Hodges. Los Angeles: Semiotext(e), 2010.

Benarayo, Lazare, Céline Lefève, Jean-Christophe Mino, et al. (eds). *La philosophie du soin: Éthique, médecine, et société*. Paris: PUF, 2010.

Benjamin, Jessica. *The Bonds of Love*. New York: Random House, 1988.

Benjamin, Walter. "The Work of Art in the Age of Mechanical Reproduction." In Benjamin, Walter. *Illuminations: Essays and Reflections*, ed. by Hannah Arendt. Trans. by Harry Zohn. New York: Schocken, 1985. 217–51.

Bewes, Timothy. "The Novel as an Absence: Lukács and the Event of Postmodern Fiction." *Novel* 38: 1, 2004: 5–20.

—"Against the Ontology of the Present: Paul Auster's Cinematographic Fictions." *Twentieth Century Literature* 53: 3, 2007: 273–97.

Black, Shameem. "Ishiguro's Inhuman Aesthetics." *Modern Fiction Studies* 55: 4, 2009: 785–807.

Boever, Arne De. "Politics and Poetics of Divine Violence: On a Figure in Giorgio Agamben and Walter Benjamin." In *The Work of Giorgio Agamben: Law, Life, Literature*, ed. by Justin Clemens, Nick Heron, and Alex Murray (Edinburgh: Edinburgh University Press, 2008), 82–96.

—"Biopolitics in Deconstruction": http://derridaseminars.org/workshops [accessed 14 November 2012].

—"Derrida's Theory of the Novel": http://derridaseminars.org/workshops [accessed 14 November 2012].

—"Bio-Paulitics," *Journal for Cultural and Religious Theory* 11.1, 2010: http://www.jcrt.org/archives/11.1/boever.pdf [accessed 14 November 2012].

—"The Allegory of the Cage," *Foucault Studies* 10, 2010: 7–22: http://rauli.cbs.dk/index.php/foucault-studies/article/viewFile/3124/3288 [accessed 14 November 2012].

—"Agamben et Simondon: Ontologie, technologie, et politique." Trans. by Jean-Hugues Barthélémy. *Cahiers Simondon* 2, 2010: 117–28.

—"The Philosophy of (Aesthetic) Education." In *Everything is in Everything: Jacques Rancière Between Intellectual Emancipation and Aesthetic Education*, ed. by Jason Smith and Annette Weissman. Zürich: Art Center Graduate Press/ JRP Ringier, 2011. 34–48.

—*States of Exception in the Contemporary Novel: Martel, Eugenides, Coetzee, Sebald*. New York: Continuum, 2012.

Brown, Wendy. *States of Injury: Power and Freedom in Late Modernity*. Princeton: Princeton University Press, 1995.

Buckley, Bernadette. "The Workshop of Filthy Creation: Or Do Not Be Alarmed, This is Only a Test." *Review of International Studies* 35: 4, 2009: 835–57.

Butler, Judith. *Gender Trouble: Feminism and the Subversion of Identity*. New York: Routledge, 1999.

—*Precarious Life: The Powers of Mourning and Violence*. New York: Verso, 2004.

—"Indefinite Detention." In Butler, Judith. *Precarious Life: The Powers of Mourning and Violence*. New York: Verso, 2004. 50–100.

—*Frames of War: When is Life Grievable?* New York: Verso, 2009.

—"Torture and the Ethics of Photography: Thinking with Sontag." In Butler, Judith. *Frames of War: When is Life Grievable?* New York: Verso, 2009, 63–100.

Calhoon, Kenneth S. "Blind Gestures: Chaplin, Diderot, Lessing." *MLN* 115: 3, 2000: 381–402.

Calle, Sophie. *Double Game*. New York: Violette Editions/DAP, 2007.
—*Take Care of Yourself*. Trans. by Charles Penwarden et al. Arles: Actes Sud, 2007.
Carter, Angela. *The Sadeian Woman and the Ideology of Pornography*. New York: Pantheon, 1978.
Chesney, Duncan McColl. "Toward an Ethics of Silence: Michael K." *Criticism* 49: 3, 2007: 307–25.
Clarke, Andy. *Natural-Born Cyborgs: Minds, Technologies, and the Future of Human Intelligence*. Oxford: Oxford University Press, 2003.
Clowes, Edith W. "The Robinson Myth Reread in Postcolonial and Postcommunist Modes." *Critique* 36, 1995: 145–59.
Coetzee, J. M. *Life and Times of Michael K*. New York: Penguin, 1985.
—*Foe*. New York: Penguin, 1986.
—*Doubling the Point: Essays and Interviews*, ed. by David Attwell. Cambridge, MA: Harvard University Press, 1992.
—*Disgrace*. New York: Vintage, 1999.
—*Waiting for the Barbarians*. New York: Vintage, 2000.
—*Elizabeth Costello*. New York: Viking, 2003.
—*Slow Man*. New York: Viking, 2005.
—"He and His Man": http://nobelprize.org/nobel_prizes/literature/laureates/2003/coetzee-lecture-e.html [accessed 14 November 2012].
—Rev. of Defoe, Daniel. *An Essay on the History and Reality of Apparitions*. *Common Knowledge* 15: 1, 2009: 92–3.
Cohn, Dorrit. "Optics and Power and the Novel." *New Literary History* 26: 1, 1995: 3–20.
Cooper, Melinda. *Life as Surplus: Biotechnology and Capitalism in the Neoliberal Era*. Seattle: University of Washington Press, 2008.
Cornwell, Gareth. " 'He and His Man': Allegory and Catachresis in J. M. Coetzee's Nobel Lecture." *English in Africa* 33: 2, 2006: 97–114.
Coupland, Douglas. *Girlfriend in a Coma*. New York: HarperCollins, 2008.
Davis, Todd F. and Kenneth Womack (eds). *Mapping the Ethical Turn: A Reader in Ethics, Culture, and Literary Theory*. Charlottesville: University Press of Virginia, 2001.
Defoe, Daniel. *Robinson Crusoe*. New York: Random House, 2001.
Deleuze, Gilles. *Essays Critical and Clinical*. Trans. by Daniel W. Smith and Michael A. Greco. Minneapolis: University of Minnesota Press, 1997.
Derrida, Jacques. *Dissemination*. Trans. by Barbara Johnson. Chicago: University of Chicago Press, 1981.
—*Rogues: Two Essays on Reason*. Trans. by Pascale-Anne Brault and Michael Naas. Stanford: Stanford University Press, 2005.
—*The Beast and the Sovereign*, Vol. I. Trans. by Geoffrey Bennington. Chicago: University of Chicago Press, 2008.
Dick, Kirby, dir. *Private Practices: The Story of a Sex Surrogate*. New York: Zeitgeist, 1986.

Dougherty, Stephen. "The Biopolitics of the Killer Virus Novel." *Cultural Critique* 48, 2001: 1–29.

During, Simon. *Foucault and Literature*. London: Routledge, 1992.

Edwards, Gwynnne. *Almodóvar: Labyrinths of Passion*. London: Peter Owen, 2001.

Engel, John D. Joseph Zarconi, Lura L. Penthel, et al. *Narrative in Health Care*. Oxford: Radcliffe, 2008.

Fluet, Lisa. "Immaterial Labors: Ishiguro, Class, and Affect." *Novel* 40: 3, 2007: 265–88.

Foucault, Michel. *The Order of Things: An Archeology of the Human Sciences*. Trans. by [not listed]. New York: Vintage, 1973.

—"Introduction." *Herculine Barbin, Being the Recently Discovered Memoirs of a Nineteenth-Century French Hermaphrodite*. Trans. by Richard McDougall. New York: Pantheon Books, 1980. vii–xvii.

—*The Care of the Self: The History of Sexuality*, Vol. 3. Trans. by Robert Hurley. New York: Vintage, 1988.

—"The Minimalist Self." In *Politics, Philosophy, Culture: Interviews and Other Writings, 1977–1984*, ed. by Lawrence D. Kritzman. New York: Routledge, 1990, 3–16.

—*The History of Sexuality: An Introduction*, Vol. I. Trans. by Robert Hurley. New York: Vintage, 1990.

—*"Society Must Be Defended": Lectures at the Collège de France 1975–1976*, ed. by Arnold I. Davidson. Trans. by David Macey. New York: Picador, 2001.

—*Security, Territory, Population: Lectures at the Collège de France 1977–1978*, ed. by Arnold I. Davidson. Trans. by Graham Burchell. New York: Picador, 2007.

—*The Politics of Truth*, ed. by Sylvère Lotringer. Trans. by Lysa Hochroth and Catherine Porter. Los Angeles: Semiotext(e): 2007.

—*The Birth of Biopolitics: Lectures at the Collège de France 1978–1979*, ed. by Arnold I. Davidson. Trans. by Graham Burchell. New York: Picador, 2008.

—*Le Gouvernement de soi et des autres: Cours au Collège de France, 1982–1983*. Paris: Gallimard, 2008.

Franzen, Jonathan. *How to Be Alone*. New York: Farrar, Strauss, and Giroux, 2002.

Freundlieb, Dieter. "Foucault and the Study of Literature." *Poetics Today* 16: 2, 1995: 301–44.

Garber, Marjorie, Beatrice Hanssen, and Rebecca L. Walkowitz (eds.). *The Turn to Ethics*. New York: Routledge, 2000.

Gourgouris, Stathis. *Does Literature Think? Literature as Theory for an Antimythical Era*. Stanford: Stanford University Press, 2003.

Guse, Anette. "Talk to Her! Look at Her! Pina Bausch in Pedro Almodóvar's *Hable con ella*." *Seminar* 43: 4, 2007: 427–40.

Guyer, Sarah. "Testimony and Trope in Frankenstein." *Studies in Romanticism* 45: 1, 2006: 77–15.

Hansen, Mark. "'Not thus, after all would life be given': Technesis, Technology and the Parody of Romantic Poetics in Frankenstein." *Studies in Romanticism* 36: 4, 1997: 575–609.
Hawthorne, Nathaniel. "The Birthmark." *The American Tradition in Literature*, ed. by George Perkins and Barbara Perkins. New York: McGraw-Hill, 1994: 767–77.
Hayes, Patrick. "'An Author I have not Read': Coetzee's *Foe*, Dostoevsky's *Crime and Punishment*, and the Problem of the Novel." *Review of English Studies* 57: 230, 2006: 273–90.
Heidegger, Martin. *Being and Time*. Trans. by John MacQuarrie and Edward Robinson. New York: Harper Perennial, 2008.
Herzog, Werner, dir. *Grizzly Man*. Santa Monica: Lions Gate, 2005.
Hollinghurst, Allen. *The Line of Beauty*. New York: Bloomsbury, 2005.
Houen, Alex. "Sovereignty, Biopolitics, and the Use of Literature." *Theory & Event* 9: 1, 2006: 1–33.
Hutchinson, Peter. *Games Authors Play*. New York: Methuen Young Books, 1983.
Ishiguro, Kazuo. *Never Let Me Go*. New York: Knopf, 2005.
Jennings, Bruce. "Biopower and the Liberationist Romance." *The Hastings Center Report* 40: 4, 2010: http://www.thehastingscenter.org/Publications/HCR/Detail.aspx?id=4770 [accessed 14 November 2012].
Jerng, Mark. "Giving Form to Life: Cloning and Narrative Expectations of the Human." *Partial Answers* 6:2, 2008: 369–93.
Jones, Amelia. "'The Artist is Present': Artistic Re-enactments and the Impossibility of Presence." *The Dramatic Review* 55: 1, 2011: 16–45.
Jordan, Nicolle. "Passion as Pharmakon: A Theme in Medicine, Theology, and the Novel." *The Eighteenth Century* 45: 3, 2004: 285–91.
Kahana, Jonathan. "Introduction: What Now? Presenting Reenactment." *Framework* 50: 1/2, 2009: 46–60.
Kant, Immanuel. "What is Enlightenment?" In Foucault, Michel. *The Politics of Truth*, Ed. by Sylvère Lotringer. Trans. by Lysa Hochroth and Catherine Porter. Los Angeles: Semiotext(e), 2007, 29–37.
Kaye, Tony, dir. *American History X*. S.I.: New Line, 1999.
Kenyon, Gary M. *Storying Later Life*. Oxford: Oxford University Press, 2010.
Kinder, Marsha. "Reinventing the Motherland: Almodóvar's Brain-Dead Trilogy." *Film Quarterly* 58: 2, 2004: 9–25.
Kishik, David. *The Power of Life: Giorgio Agamben and the Coming Politics*. Stanford: Stanford University Press, 2012.
Klein, Naomi. *The Shock Doctrine: The Rise of Disaster Capitalism*. New York: Picador, 2007.
Lambert, Gregg. "On the Uses and Abuses of Literature for Life: Gilles Deleuze and the Literary Clinic." *Postmodern Culture* 8: 3, 1998: 1–37.
Lawrenson, Edward. "Gone in 60 Years." *Sight and Sound* 19: 6, 2009: 26–9.
Lecourt, Dominique. *Humain, posthumain: La technique et la vie*. Paris: PUF, 2003.
Lee, Spike, dir. *25th Hour*. United States: Touchstone, 2003.

—*Inside Man*. Universal City: Universal Studios, 2006.
—*When the Levees Broke: A Requiem in Four Acts*. New York: HBO Video, 2006.
Lenta, Patrick. "Discipline in *Disgrace*." *Mosaic* 43: 3, 2010: 1–16.
Lichtenstein, Jacqueline. *The Blind Spot: An Essay On the Relations Between Painting and Sculpture in the Modern Age*. Los Angeles: Getty Research Institute, 2008.
Lukács, Georg. *Theory of the Novel*. London: Merlin, 1978.
MacLeod, Lewis. "'Do We of Necessity Become Puppets in a Story?': or Narrating the World: On Speech, Silence and Discourse in J. M. Coetzee's *Foe*." *Modern Fiction Studies* 52: 1, 2006: 1–18.
Malabou, Catherine. *What Should We Do With Our Brain?* Trans. by Sebastian Rand. New York: Fordham, 2008.
Marks, John. "Michel Foucault: Biopolitics and Biology." In *Foucault in the Age of Terror: Biopolitics and the Defense of Society*, Ed. by Stephen Morton and Stephen Bygrave. New York: Palgrave Macmillan, 2008, 88–105.
Marx, Karl. *The Eighteenth Brumaire of Louis Bonaparte*. Trans. by [not listed]. New York: International Publishers, 1998.
McCarthy, Tom. *Remainder*. New York: Vintage, 2005.
—"The Geometry of the Pressant." *Artforum* 46: 10, 2008: 392–3, 466.
—*Tintin and the Secret of Literature*. Berkeley: Counterpoint, 2008.
McDonald, Keith. "Days of Past Futures: Kazuo Ishiguro's *Never Let Me Go* as 'Speculative Memoir'." *Biography* 30: 1, 2007: 74–83.
McLane, Maureen N. "Literate Species: Populations, 'Humanities', and Frankenstein." *English Literary History* 63: 4, 1996: http://knarf.english.upenn.edu/Articles/mclane.html
Melgosa, Adrián Pérez. "Macedonio Fernández's Narrative Pharmakon: The Shared Project of 'Adriana Buenos Aires' and 'Museo dela Novela de la Eterna'." *Latin American Literary Review* 35: 70, 2007: 5–30.
Meljac, Eric Paul. "The Poetics of Dwelling: A Consideration of Heidegger, Kafka, and Michael K." *Journal of Modern Literature* 32: 1, 2008: 69–76.
Mills, Catherine. "Life Beyond Law: Biopolitics, Law and Futurity in Coetzee's *Life and Times of Michael K*." *Griffith Law Review* 15: 1, 2006: 177–95.
Mitchell, W. J. T. *Cloning Terror: The War of Images, 9/11 to the Present*. Chicago: University of Chicago Press, 2011.
Moraru, Christian. *Rewriting: Postmodern Narrative and Cultural Critique in the Age of Cloning*. Albany: SUNY Press, 2001.
Myer, Eric. "'The Nature of the Text': Ford and Conrad in Plato's Pharmacy." *Modern Fiction Studies* 36: 4, 1990: 499–512.
Novoa, Adriana. "Whose Talk Is It? Almodóvar and the Fairy Tale in *Talk to Her*." *Marvels and Tales* 19: 2, 2005: 224–48.
Oates, Joyce Carol. "Lest We Forget." *New York Review of Books* 54: 12, 2007: http://www.nybooks.com/articles/archives/2007/jul/19/lest-we-forget/?pagination=false [accessed 14 November 2012].

Ohi, Kevin. "Voyeurism and Annunciation in Almodóvar's *Talk to Her*." *Criticism* 51: 4, 2010: 521–57.

Peacock, Jim. "Carrying the Burden of Representation: Paul Auster's *The Book of Illusions*." *Journal of American Studies* 40: 1, 2006: 53–69.

Pelenc, Arielle. "Interview: Arielle Pelenc in Correspondence with Jeff Wall." In Duve, Thierry de, Arielle Pelenc, Boris Groys, et al. *Jeff Wall*. London: Phaidon, 2003: 8–22.

Plato, *Republic*. Trans. by G. M. A. Grube. Indianapolis: Hackett, 1992.

Probyn, Fiona. "J. M. Coetzee: Writing with/out Authority." *Jouvert: a Journal of Postcolonial Studies* 6.3, 2002: english.chass.ncsu.edu/jouvert/v7is1/probyn.htm [accessed 14 November 2012].

Protevi, John. *Political Affect: Connecting the Social and the Somatic*. Minneapolis: University of Minnesota Press, 2009.

Puchner, Martin. "When We Were Clones," *Raritan* 27:4, 2008: 34–49.

Robbins, Bruce. "Cruelty is Bad: Banality and Proximity in *Never Let Me Go*." *Novel* 40:3, 2007: 289–302.

—*Upward Mobility and the Common Good*. Princeton: Princeton University Press, 2008.

Rose, Nikolas. *The Politics of Life Itself: Biomedicine, Power, and Subjectivity in the Twenty-First Century*. Princeton: Princeton University Press, 2007.

Rousseau, Jean-Jacques. "Discourse on the Origins of Inequality." In Rousseau, Jean-Jacques. *The Basic Political Writings*. Trans. by Donald A. Cress. Indianapolis: Hackett, 1987, 24–109.

Said, Edward. *Culture and Imperialism*. New York: Knopf, 1993.

—*On Late Style: Music and Literature Against the Grain*. New York: Pantheon, 2006.

Sanders, Mark. Rev. of Derek Attridge's *J. M. Coetzee and the Ethics of Reading*. *Modern Fiction Studies* 53: 3, 2007: 641–5.

Santner, Eric. *On Creaturely Life: Rilke, Benjamin, Sebald*. Chicago: University of Chicago Press, 2005.

—"Terri Schiavo and the State of Exception": http://www.press.uchicago.edu/Misc/Chicago/05april_santner.html [accessed 14 November 2012].

—*The Royal Remains: The People's Two Bodies and the Endgames of Sovereignty*. Chicago: University of Chicago Press, 2012.

Sarlin, Page. "New Left-Wing Melancholy: Mark Tribe's 'The Port Huron Project' and the Politics of Reenactment." *Framework* 50: 1/2, 2009: 139–57.

Sarvan, Charles. "'Disgrace': A Path to Grace?" *World Literature Today* 78: 1, 2004: 26–9.

Scott, Joanna. "Voice and Trajectory: An Interview with J. M. Coetzee." *Salmagundi*. 114/115, 1997: 97–8.

Sebald, W.G. *The Emigrants*. Trans. by Michael Hülse. London: Harvill, 1993.

—"Air War and Literature." In Sebald, W. G. *On the Natural History of Destruction*. Trans. by Anthea Bell. New York: Random House, 2003. 1–104.

Shiva, Vandana. *Biopiracy: The Plunder of Nature and Knowledge*. Brooklyn: South End, 1997.
Smith, Paul Julian. "Only Connect." *Sight and Sound* 12: 7, 2002: 24–7.
Smith, Zadie. "Two Paths for the Novel." *New York Review of Books* 55: 18, 2008: http://www.nybooks.com/articles/archives/2008/nov/20/two-paths-for-the-novel/ [accessed 14 November 2012].
Soderbergh, Steven, dir. *Ocean's Eleven*. Burbank: Warner, 2002.
Sontag, Susan. *Against Interpretation*. New York: Delta, 1966.
—*Styles of Radical Will*. New York: Delta, 1969.
—"The Pornographic Imagination." In Susan Sontag. *Styles of Radical Will*. New York: Delta, 1969, 35–73.
—*On Photography*. New York: Farrar, Straus, and Giroux, 1977.
—"Looking at War." *The New Yorker*, 9 December 2002: 82–98.
—*Regarding the Pain of Others*. New York: Farrar, Straus, and Giroux, 2003.
Spadoni, Robert. "The Uncanny Body of Early Sound Film." *The Velvet Light Trap* 51, 2003: 4–16.
Spielberg, Steven. *Artificial Intelligence*. United States: DreamWorks, 2002.
Stengers, Isabelle. *Au temps des catastrophes: Résister à la barbarie qui vient*. Paris: La Découverte, 2009.
Stiegler, Bernard. *Pour une nouvelle critique de l'économie politique*. Paris: Galilée, 2009.
—*Taking Care of Youth and the Generations*. Trans. by Stephen Barker. Stanford: Stanford University Press, 2010.
—*Ce qui fait que le vie vaut la peine d'être vécue: De la pharmacologie*. Paris: Flammarion, 2010.
Stone, Alan A. "The Mind's Eye." *Boston Review* 34: 1, 2009: 53–4.
Storrow, Richard F. "Therapeutic Reproduction and Human Dignity." *Law and Literature* 21:2, 2009: 257–74.
Suleiman, Susan Rubin. *Subversive Intent: Gender, Politics, and the Avant-Garde*. Cambridge, MA: Harvard University Press, 1990.
Swope, Richard. "Approaching the Threshold(s) in Postmodern Detective Fiction: Hawthorne's 'Wakefield' and Other Missing Persons." *Critique* 39: 3, 1998: 207–27.
Szalay, Michael. *New Deal Modernism*. Durham, NC: Duke University Press, 2005.
Terentowicz-Fotyga, Urszula. "Unreal City to City of Referents: Urban Space in Contemporary London Novels." *Journal of Narrative Theory* 39: 3, 2009: 305–29.
Terestchenko, Michel. "Servility and Destructiveness in Kazuo Ishiguro's *The Remains of the Day*." *Partial Answers* 5: 1, 2007: 77–89.
Tynan, Kenneth. "The Girl in the Black Helmet." In Pabst, Georg Wilhelm, dir. *Pandora's Box*. New York: Criterion, 2006. DVD booklet.
Vermeule, Blakey. *Why Do We Care about Literary Characters?* Baltimore: Johns Hopkins University Press, 2009.

Vernon, Kathleen M. and Barbara Morris. *Post-Franco, Postmodern: The Films of Pedro Almodóvar*. Westport: Greenwood Press, 1995.

Veyne, Paul. *Did the Greeks Believe in their Myths? An Essay on the Constitutive Imagination*. Trans. by Paula Wissing. Chicago: University of Chicago Press, 1988.

Walkowitz, Rebecca L. "Unimaginable Largeness: Kazuo Ishiguro, Translation, and the New World Literature." *Novel* 40:3, 2007: 216–39.

Watt, Ian. *The Rise of the Novel: Studies in Defoe, Richardson, and Fielding*. Harmondsworth: Penguin, 1970.

White, Michael and David Epston. *Narrative Means to Therapeutic Ends*. New York: Norton, 1990.

Winnicott, D. W. *Playing and Reality*. New York: Routledge, 2005.

Worms, Frédéric. *Le moment du soin: À quoi tenons-nous?* Paris: PUF, 2010.

Zilcosky, John. "Kafka's Remains." In *Lost in the Archives*, ed. by Comay, Rebecca and Ian Balfour. New York: Distributed Art Publishers, 2002, 632–43.

Žižek, Slavoj. *The Puppet and the Dwarf: The Perverse Core of Christianity*. Cambridge, MA: MIT Press, 2003.

Index

8074357R00107

Printed in Great Britain
by Amazon.co.uk, Ltd.,
Marston Gate.